Really Writing!

Ready-to-use Writing Process Activities for the Elementary Grades

Cherlyn Sunflower

**THE CENTER FOR APPLIED
RESEARCH IN EDUCATION**
West Nyack, New York 10995

10 9 8 7 6 5 4 3

Library of Congress Cataloging-in-Publication Data

Sunflower, Cherlyn
    Really writing : ready-to-use writing process activities for the
elementary grades / by Cherlyn Sunflower.
        p.   cm.
    Includes bibliographical references.
    ISBN 0-87628-113-7
    1. English language—Composition and exercises—Study and
teaching (Elementary)—United States.   I. Title.
LB1576.S893   1994
372.6'23—dc20   93-45005
                                                                      CIP

ISBN 0-87628-113-7

**The Center for Applied
Research in Education**
Business Information & Publishing Division
West Nyack, NY 10995

Simon & Schuster, A Paramount Communications Company

PRINTED IN THE UNITED STATES OF AMERICA

SUNFLOWERING

is
"a process in which a prolific, irreverent plant can grow and
bloom under diverse conditions."
(Bob Stanish, Sunflowering, Good Apple, Carthage, IL 1977.)

Sunflowers care about children and the classroom conditions
that stimulate their minds and help them grow.

DEDICATION

To my mom and dad, Alberta and Robert Henrickson who have been my best teachers throughout my life.

ACKNOWLEDGMENTS

I want to express my thanks to Gene Shepherd who guided my search for teaching excellence, Joyce and Weil for their study of teaching models and how teachers acquire new professional knowledge, Donald Graves who studied the writing process of writers, Gail Tompkins for sharing her knowledge of Language Arts with me, and my 1-6 grade students who taught me how children learn language.

Thanks go to the following teachers who helped develop particular lessons: Mark Boen, a third grade teacher who helped me refine my ideas and co-write several early lessons, Debbie and Bob Grosz, who shared their ideas on campaign speeches, and the hundreds of preservice teachers and classroom teachers who helped me refine the Really Writing lessons.

I am grateful to Moorhead State University for AV support and Jody Bendel in particular for her technical assistance. In addition the following clip art companies have supplied illustrations: Imprint Graphs, Dynamic Graph, Art Master, AAACE's Clip Art, A.A. Archbold Clip Art, Cobb Shinn Art-Pak Illustrations, and Dover Clip Art Series (1983 and 1988).

About the Author

Cherlyn Sunflower (B.A., M.Ed., University of Texas; Ph.D., University of Oklahoma) has been actively involved in elementary education as a teacher and educator for over 20 years. Her experience includes eight years as a 1-6 classroom teacher and resource room teacher in the Austin, Texas, Public Schools, and 10 years as a teacher educator and instructor at Moorhead State University in Minnesota.

Dr. Sunflower has given many presentations on the subject of the language arts at the national, regional, and state levels. She has also authored several other practical teaching/learning resources, including *75 Creative Ways to Publish Students' Writings, URICA—Using Reading in Creative Activities,* and *LATTS—Learning Aids and Teaching Tools.* The first shares ways to call attention to and give value to children's oral and written compositions. The second is designed to help children become more effective readers and the third, to help preservice teachers as they begin their careers.

Cherlyn is presently Associate Professor of Education at Moorhead State University and teaches elementary language arts methods courses.

ABOUT THIS RESOURCE

Students must become effective speakers and writers to be successful communicators in to-day's exceedingly complex world. Equipping them with grammar, usage, spelling, and hand-writing skills is not adequate preparation. Students need to learn the process effective writers use and they need to view writing as an exciting form of communication.

As teachers, we need special skills to help students learn the writing process. Telling students how to do it is not effective. Instead we must guide students through the process of motivation, brainstorming, composing a first draft, self-evaluation, and publishing. To do this, most teachers want more than books of writing ideas; they want to know how to guide a class or individual students through the process. Questions many elementary teachers ask are:

How can I motivate students to write?

What can I do to help students think and organize ideas?

How do I teach the mental steps used by good writers?

What kind of writing do students need to be effective within the social context of home, school, and work?

How do I help students learn various genres?

What can I do to interest students in self-evaluating and improving their first drafts?

How do I teach conventions of the English language in an effective manner?

What are some meaningful purposes and real audiences for students in grades 2-6?

The *Really Writing* lessons will answer these questions and more. *Really Writing* is de-signed for elementary teachers (grades 2-6) who are breaking away from teaching lan-guage arts as isolated skills or want to use a process approach to writing, but who need specific ways to do this. *Really Writing* provides a valuable resource for setting up real communication experiences that teach children not only HOW to write, but also WHEN to write. The *Really Writing* lessons have been used in elementary classrooms by experienced and novice teachers over a nine-year period. All the lessons have repeatedly been proven successful.

The *Really Writing* lessons follow the fundamental steps of the writing process. As you look at each lesson, you will see the following parts: Objectives, Motivators, Brainstorming, Group Composing, Responding to Student Writing, and Publishing. You can follow the steps provided for each lesson as described or you may add to, omit, or change any of the lesson parts to better fit your students' knowledge, skills, and interests and your curriculum. Each of these parts is explained in more detail in the "To the Teacher" section.

The *Really Writing* lessons include instruction in all basic language modes: narrative, descriptive, persuasive, informative ("how to" writings and reports), and expressive (poems and songs.) The resource begins with easy writings to get your students started, followed by sections on each kind of writing. Within each section, lessons are grouped from easiest to most difficult. Each kind of writing can be approached at a word, sentence, paragraph, or multi-paragraph level.

Really Writing is designed to keep you out of the editorial role by providing questioning and responding methods that help students learn to self-evaluate and revise their own compositions. In addition the *Really Writing* lessons provide real audiences and authentic purposes for each lesson. Having a real audience gives students a meaningful reason to revise and improve their compositions.

Specific outcomes have been included under an overall objective because of interest in Mastery Learning and Outcome Based Education. Another reason for specific outcomes is the growing concern about when and how the conventions of the English language should be taught. In the *Really Writing* lessons, instruction for idea and convention outcomes takes place in context at two points: during Brainstorming and during Group Composing *before* students write. When students do not achieve a desired outcome, reteaching is possible during Responding to Student Writing.

Although a wide range of writing abilities exists in most classrooms, you can meet students' varied needs with only slight adjustments. After determining which specific outcomes you want the class as a whole to accomplish, consider the individual differences among students. This is where the "Modifications" sections, found toward the end of each lesson, will help. They suggest simple modifications that allow students of all abilities to participate and succeed. Look for these headings:

Modifications to Encourage Beginning Writers

Modifications to Challenge Advanced Writers

Once you have used some *Really Writing* lessons, you will notice the narrative, descriptive, persuasive, informative, and expressive writing patterns repeated in each lesson. Soon you will be designing your own lessons based on the six basic patterns. Your students' attention will be captured by writing for real audiences for real purposes. You will soon see how to integrate your language arts program into your science, health, social studies, math, and reading curriculum. In addition to teaching writing, you will find that this process approach improves students' speaking, listening, reading, spelling, grammar, and mechanics such as capitalization and punctuation. Parents and administrators will be delighted when your students' writing and other language arts skills blossom from your instruction.

TABLE OF CONTENTS

SECTION 5: PERSUASIVE WRITINGS   255

SECTION 6: INFORMATIVE (REPORT) WRITING   297

SECTION 7: EXPRESSIVE WRITINGS   329

TO THE TEACHER

This section of *Really Writing* provides an orientation to the steps in each lesson and also shares tips and techniques you will find helpful as you introduce young writers to a process that will serve them throughout their lives. Each lesson is designed as a model and follows these steps:

- Objectives
- Motivators
- Brainstorming
- Group Composing
- Responding to Student Writing
- Publishing

Two other important features follow immediately after these steps:

- Modifications: For students with special needs—those who need extra encouragement as well as those who need a challenge.
- Reproducible pages: Valuable time savers.

Now let's take a walk through each of these steps.

Objectives

First, an overall objective such as "Students will write a letter to the President" gives every student a chance for success at some level. The overall objective is followed by specific "idea" and "convention" outcomes that students are expected to meet by the end of the lesson. Two examples of "idea" outcomes are:

- Include three describing words in the "Lost Ad."
- Use at least four details such as size, shape, color, and weight.

Two examples of "convention" outcomes are:

- Insert commas between ideas in a series.
- Put the exact words of a speaker in quotation marks.

Instruction for idea and convention outcomes takes place during Brainstorming and Group Composing. When students do not achieve a desired outcome, reteaching takes place during the step titled "Responding to Student Writing."

After instruction, you can easily assess your students' learning because the outcomes of each lesson have already been identified. There is no need to compare one student's work with another; instead each student's composition can be compared to a preset standard.

One easy way to keep track of student's long term writing growth is to use 5 × 8-inch index cards (with a file box) or a three-ring notebook. Assign one card or page to each student. You may want to organize the file cards or notebook alphabetically. Then once a week or month add to each student's card or page a brief dated note on mastered outcomes. You can do this while conferencing with each student or later before students share their compositions with their intended audience.

Motivators

When learning involved memorization of information, students needed only a good introduction to a lesson. Now students need to learn how to think both creatively and critically. This shift in goals requires teachers to excite students' thought processes and invite them to think. The motivators in this resource are designed to mentally prepare students to think and communicate.

Many kinds of motivators are used. Some take only a few minutes. For example, before writing memories, students might look at photos of themselves of when they were younger; or you might show students political flyers before they write campaign speeches. A short, but effective motivator might be to share a story about a bike accident you had, before students write safety tips. Keep in mind that these aren't the only motivators that you can use, only some possible motivators. The key to creating effective motivators is designing ones that are appropriate for your particular students' interest and grade level.

Each *Really Writing* lesson provides one or more possible motivators at the beginning. Sometimes one possible motivator is given in detail. In other lessons several motivating ideas are provided to get you started. The following list may be helpful in developing your own motivators:

Observe a person, place, animal, or thing.

Read a newspaper, magazine, or piece of literature.

Remember or recall an experience.

Survey a person or a particular group of people.

View movies or videotapes.

Examine pictures, photographs, flyers.

Discuss a topic with a professional.

Interview a person.

Role play, use a puppet, or do oral reading.

Use visual imagery.

Experiment and document observations and/or conclusions.

Draw pictures, paint, or doodle.

Listen to stories, music, or sounds.

Draw upon current events or respond to chance events, such as a new student or a tornado warning, that capture students' natural excitement.

The most powerful and natural motivator is, of course, to have a real reason to communicate. This involves having a real audience and a purpose before writing.

Brainstorming

This section on suggested brainstorming categories incorporates two major methods for capturing a writer's ideas: visual displays and listing of ideas. Effective visual displays for capturing thinking include webbing, mapping, clustering, and outlining. Listing, which includes brainstorming multiple lists, is a more linear way to capture and organize thinking. Multiple listing can be a very powerful technique when guiding and coaching young writers.

Brainstorming typically refers to the process of generating a large number of ideas in a short amount of time. At first 5 to 15 minutes of concentration is enough. The rules are simple:

• Start ideas flowing. Accept every idea as possibly valuable. Save evaluation for later.
• The more ideas the better.
• Involve every student in active participation.

During brainstorming, students see how writers think and then actively participate in that process. To guide students through this process, a teacher needs to use three basic techniques: thought-provoking questions, longer wait time for students to think, and responses to student ideas that support or encourage higher-level thinking.

Often the most difficult part of teaching young people to write is coming up with the categories a writer must brainstorm for a particular type of writing. Effective writers have developed "mental pictures" of what is needed. The rest of us usually have to do a lot of thinking or research to come up with the necessary categories to brainstorm.

For example, if a writer were going to compose a letter to the editor "about environmental waste," he/she might want to brainstorm 1) opinions about waste and 2) reasons to recycle, reuse, and reduce.

If a writer were going to compose travel directions for someone, he/she might brainstorm 1) starting points, 2) ending points, and 3) landmarks alongthe way.

One valuable feature of *Really Writing* is that the brainstorming categories for different writing forms are provided for both you and your students. Eventually students will internalize these and other categories for future compositions.

In addition to the brainstorming categories, you will find examples of key questions that will promote thinking. How questions are worded makes a big difference in students' responses. Compare the following pairs of questions. The second column encourages more thinking than the first column.

Can you tell me who got you interested in your hobby?	Who helped you get interested in your hobby?
Do you have a reason why gum should not be chewed in school?	Why do you think students should be allowed to chew gum in school?
Should you put a question mark at the end of your sentence?	What punctuation is needed at the end of an asking sentence?

Once you are comfortable planning your own key questions for each category, you are off to a wonderful new way of teaching.

During the brainstorming step it is important to have all students actively involved in contributing ideas. Pull quiet students into brainstorming by directly calling on them. Students who cannot or won't contribute creative ideas can be involved when it comes time to "choose" an idea. For example, you might ask, "Out of all our ideas for clues in our mystery story, which clue(s) do you want us to use?"

After asking students questions, it is important to be aware of the time you allow before expecting a response. In the past, a high percentage of the questions teachers would ask were recall questions. Students were expected to show their knowledge by quick, correct responses. When you ask your students thought provoking questions, it is essential to allow more time for thinking. The amount of time will depend on the type of thinking required and the need of each student.

In the beginning you may feel uncomfortable pausing for students to think. It may take a while until you feel comfortable, but the rewards of this method are immense. Students who are used to giving "correct" right/wrong type answers will also need time to adjust.

At first your students will need to be reassured that their growing abilities to think creatively and critically are on the right track. Here are two types of positive responses you can make:

1) While a student shares an idea, model respect by

   - looking at the student,
   - listening intently, and
   - encouraging other students to look at the speaker as he/she is speaking.

2) Accept all ideas no matter how strange; otherwise a student, especially one who has had a history of failure, will not risk sharing. Then reinforce his/her ideas by

- writing the student's actual words on the chalkboard and
- making a general or specific positive oral response.

Compare the following pairs of responses:

Wow! That sounds great.	Wow! Each of your reasons for chewing gum in school is very convincing.
Great Idea!	Your title "Ten Reasons for Putting Off Doing Homework" will certainly catch readers' attention.
Terrific!	You indented all five of your paragraphs. This will really help your readers know when you shift to a new idea. Terrific!

The "quick" general responses (found in column one) are useful in keeping ideas flowing. The specific positive comments (found in column two) are essential when

a) A student who does not usually participate risks sharing.

b) An idea is especially unique. For example, while brainstorming their wishes for a new year, students might wish for *things,* such as a new bike and soccer equipment. Then one student might offer a wish for "no more rainfall in Iowa" (where there has been extensive flooding). This creative response deserves special recognition for two reasons: because it is not a material object and because it is something for others instead of for oneself.

Classroom management suggestions   While many writing experts suggest the acceptance of all ideas that students risk sharing, in practice there are two types of answers that require special responses. First, if a student shares something offensive, it is best to ignore the comment, then give specific praise to the next few students who are "on the right track." If the student continues in an inappropriate manner, a warning followed by removal from the group is usually effective.

The second situation for special management is when a student thinks he/she is on track, but isn't. Here is an example that occurred during a language arts lesson on composing math word problems. While brainstorming "where a problem might take place," a student suggested, in good faith, putting a soccer ball in the problem. The group was brainstorming places, not objects. The most effective response is to acknowledge the student's idea and list it under the necessary equipment column. Then quickly return to brainstorming "where math problems can occur." Another effective action would be to ask where the soccer ball would be used; then write the "playground" response under the place column. Both actions respect students' ideas.

Group composing   Group composing is the second instructional strategy for capturing ideas. During group composing, the teacher both models how writers organize their ideas and guides students through a collaborative effort to compose a particular writing form such as a poem, a thank-you note, an editorial, a recipe, or a complaint letter before releasing students to write alone. The interactive guidance provided in group composing is much more effective than showing students examples of a finished writing assignment. Group composing helps students understand a teacher's expectations, makes the composing step less threatening, and improves students' attitudes toward writing as well as the quality of the final product.

Group Composing is also the time to involve students in applying conventions of the English language, such as capitalization, punctuation, spelling, and correct grammar, and usage such as subjective-verb agreement. As you use the *Really Writing* lessons, you will notice that questions and positive comments are included to involve students in making decisions about how to organize ideas and where to apply conventions.

Another useful technique is to model "Error Recovery." Students of all ages need to see that everyone makes mistakes. They also need to learn how to handle mistakes in a non-threatening way. During group composing, model error recovery by calling attention to any accidental or intentional errors you have made. Think out loud that you really do not want to have to start over. Then state that you know what to do and cross out sentences, draw arrows, leave blanks, add words, or circle words that may be misspelled. Explain to students that during the rough draft the most important thing is getting ideas down on paper; correctness and clean copy will come later. Once students realize these points, they can concentrate on the ideas they want to communicate.

Classroom management suggestions   During the motivator, brainstorming, and group composing segments, it is helpful to have students bring their chairs into a semi-circle or double semi-circle around the chalkboard. Even though moving chairs takes time and makes noise, the "payoff" in management makes it worthwhile. It creates a more intimate atmosphere that involves students. Another advantage is that when one or more students are disruptive, they can be removed from the group and directed to return to their desks until they can listen quietly, keep hands to themselves, or share appropriately. Students with a history of behavior problems may need to be excluded from the group several times before they realize they are missing out on the fun. Don't worry about students missing out on the prewriting activities; they will still be able to hear and learn even though they are at their desks.

Rough draft   After students have participated in group composing, send them to their seats to compose their own rough drafts. Encourage students to write down their ideas without worrying about conventions. As students begin their rough drafts, move through the room, encouraging and coaching them as they get their ideas down on paper.

At this point several modifications can be made for low achievers. Some of your students may be so overwhelmed by the mechanics of writing that they produce very little. Having these students dictate their ideas to a more able student, older student, or an aide can help them to be more productive. As these students become more successful, they will tire of waiting for assistance from others. Still other students can be successful when given structured forms. Here are three examples:

---

1. Cinquain Poems

_____ (noun)

_____, _____ (two describing words)

_____ing, _____ing, _____ing.

_____.

_____ (another name for the noun)

---

2. Tongue Twisters

_____ _____ _____ _____ _____
  (who)   (did what)   (where)   (when)   (why)

3. "Lost" Advertisement

              LOST _____ (what was lost)

It was _____ _____ and _____.
Please return it to _____ at _____.

Students will grow out of using "special forms" when writing activities are geared to their level and as they experience success and gain self-confidence.

Responding to Student Writing

The goal of responding to students' writings is to teach students to self-evaluate rather than to produce "error-free, everything perfect" compositions. Because of a shift in our educational goals, students need to assume the responsibility for rethinking or "reseeing" their compositions instead of depending on teachers and parents to edit them. Current revising approaches are designed to maintain student ownership and promote thinking.

Responding as a teacher can be formal or informal. Informal conferencing is very effective for beginning writers and is less time consuming for teachers. Informal conferencing occurs while writers are drafting their compositions. The teacher circulates around the room holding brief 1- to 3-minute conferences with students who need particular attention. Formal conferencing generally occurs after students' rough drafts are completed. Both methods are valuable tools to use depending on the degree of refinement needed.

Teaching students to self-evaluate requires dropping the traditional correcting and/ or suggestion-giving approach and learning some exciting new instructional techniques. Five basic techniques leave the student writer in control and help build students' self esteem: read aloud, positive comments, question and listen, checklist, and peer feedback.

1. Specific Positive Comment Technique—This technique involves sharing specific aspects of a composition that are effective. This type of response differs from the more general comment type of praise because it focuses on the composition or the audience instead of what the "teacher likes."

2. Question and Listen Technique—This technique involves asking probing, open-ended questions such as who, what, where, why, and how. These questions focus a student's attention on a particular aspect of the composition, yet allow the writer to be the decision-maker. Questions vary in their effectiveness. Some promote thinking; others do not. This technique encourages students to become critical thinkers instead of having the teacher be an editor and grader.

Feedback that Makes the Student Feel Good	**Feedback that Helps a Student Learn and Feel Good**
Outstanding!	"My Dog Toby" is a terrific title because it tells everyone what your story will be about.
You're Incredible.	
On Target!	
Now you have it.	Practicing your piano every day is a fantastic reason you could use as you attempt to persuade your parents to buy a Cabbage Patch Doll.
Beautiful job!	
Super!	
Marvelous!	
You're catching on.	Outstanding! You spelled brontosaurus correctly. What resource did you use?
Remarkable!	
I knew you could do it.	
Way to Go!	In your direction "Turn left at the Donut Shop," you have given a very helpful landmark that everyone will know.
That's correct.	

Students must learn to see their own strengths. They acquire this ability from repeated specific responses of readers. Students with low self-confidence need to be taught to re-enforce themselves through positive self-evaluation.

Poorer Questions	**Better Questions**
Is there a way the dragon can escape?	How do you think the dragon escaped from the castle?
Do you know when to stir in the chocolate chips?	When should the cook stir in the chocolate chips?
Do you need to start a new paragraph here?	How do writers signal they are beginning a new idea?

3. Read Aloud Technique—This technique involves reading a part or all of a composition out loud to a student. Then students can decide whether or not they have communicated what they wish to say. Another variation of this technique: have students' read their own compositions out loud to the teacher or other students to see how it sounds.

4. Checklists—A revising checklist is a useful tool as students begin to evaluate and revise their own work. A checklist gives structure to the revising, but promotes independence at the same time. Checklists can be completed by the student or a peer. Students should be taught to make the revision or correction before marking an item off.

Revising Checklist for Tongue Twisters

1. Does my tongue twister tell who did something? ☐
2. Does my tongue twister tell what they did? ☐
3. Does my tongue twister tell where it was done? ☐
4. Does my tongue twister tell when it was done? ☐
5. Does my tongue twister tell why it was done? ☐
6. Does my tongue twister begin with a capital letter? ☐
7. Does my tongue twister end with a period? ☐

---

5. Peer Feedback—After your students have been actively involved in the first four types of revising techniques, they will gradually acquire skills in asking questions, stating specific positive comments, and making suggestions that can help their peers. Peer feedback is important because it provides an opportunity for students to get reactions from readers and to see how well they have communicated their ideas.

Students can be assigned to revising teams (2 students) or to small cooperative revising groups of 3 to 5 students. Arrange teams or groups with "balance" in mind—pair strong writers with weaker writers and students who have trouble controlling themselves with task-oriented students.

* * *

Over time these five responding techniques will help your students self-evaluate two aspects of their compositions: 1) their ideas and 2) their use of the conventions of the English language. Revising ideas involves adding, cutting, reordering, moving, and changing parts of the composition to make ideas accurate and clear. Editing or proofreading involves locating errors and correcting such items as punctuation, capitalization, indenting, usage, grammar, spelling, and handwriting within a meaningful context.

A few things to remember about revising

Quantity vs. Quality—Until students become comfortable writing, channel their creative talents into many short, easy writing assignments. Frequent (daily) writing is more important than one or two perfect writings. During this early stage students should not have their compositions "red pencil" corrected, nor should they be pressed to revise. Writing, like speaking, develops with use. Frequent (daily) writing is more important than one or two perfect writings.

Real Audiences and Purposes—One important part of a teacher's role is to create real reasons for students to speak and write. When students want to communicate, revising becomes a meaningful task. For example, when writing to a senator to convince him/her to vote for/against solar energy, getting the message across is important. On the other hand, when the only purpose for writing is to learn to be a writer and the only audience is the teacher as a grader, many students fail to see a reason to improve their compositions.

Meaning Takes First Priority—Each lesson has a number of idea and convention outcomes. If a student has not achieved several idea and convention outcomes, the meaning or message of the composition should be given first priority. This is particularly important when working with beginning writers, since they learn best when faced with only one or two improvements per lesson. If convention outcomes are important, then it is wise to lower the difficulty level of the idea objectives so that students can focus successfully on applying the conventions of the English language.

Publishing

Writing is a form of communicating. Therefore, teachers need to set up authentic communication situations. Just as students need real purposes for writing (rather than just learning to write) and real audiences (instead of the teacher as the grader), they also need real publishing opportunities. It doesn't make any difference whether this step is called "Presenting," "Sharing," "Celebrating," "Showing-off," or "Publishing." For writing to be meaningful, students need a chance to present their finished products to various audiences. Such opportunities are a primary motivation for students to write and speak. They also benefit the teacher who does not have time to read and respond to every composition.

Creating real communication situations—Teachers must be alert to communication opportunities. Authentic communication opportunities include a real reason to write and a real audience. Reasons for communicating in written form are to convey information, to request something, to extend memory, to organize ideas, to clarify feelings, and to entertain. Audiences can range from family members, other supportive trusted adults in students' lives, classmates, and self to the world of unknown readers. Writing for family and peers is easier than writing for an unknown audience because students have communicated with these people and know how they will respond.

Publishing methods—Another aspect to consider is how the final composition is published. There are at least 250 documented publishing methods. These include school newspapers, greeting cards, accordion books, and broadcasting over the school public address system. One valuable reference for teachers is *75 Creative Ways to Publish Students' Writings* also by Cherlyn Sunflower (New York: Scholastic Inc., 1993).

Teachers often ask two questions:

Should poor or weak writing be published?

Give every student the opportunity to publish. Take time to educate students, parents, fellow teachers, and administrators that differences are normal. Help these people understand that writing is a developmental process and that errors are signs of growth.

Should students recopy their rough drafts?

Do not require a "clean" final copy until students have become skillful writers. Beginning writers of all ages are rarely motivated to recopy their revised drafts. Beginning writers and low achievers often view rewriting as a meaningless task.

Consider saving the requirement of a clean, corrected final copy with excellent handwriting, for very special occasions. Once students learn keyboarding and word processing skills, a clean final draft will become more rewarding. Until then, if a clean copy is needed, consider having another student be a low achiever's secretary.

Modifications

At the end of every lesson you will find two special sections: 1) Modifications to Encourage Beginning Writers and 2) Modifications to Challenge Advanced Writers. While these ideas are intended for students in your classroom with special needs, they can also be used for a variety of younger and older writers.

Two kinds of modifications can be made to assure that all your students succeed: 1) modify one or more parts of the composing process and 2) modify your expectations.

1. Process Modification—One easy, but very successful, process modification is a comprehension check. After group composing, when average or higher achievers are sent back to their seats to begin brainstorming and composing on their own, keep the less mature writers with you. Then ask questions to see if they understand:

- what they need to brainstorm,
- how to organize their ideas, and
- how to apply the necessary conventions of the English language.

Instead of just repeating the information modeled during the Brainstorming and Group Composing steps, check students' comprehension with specific questions such as:

- After the decision to have school parties twice each year, what do you need to brainstorm next?
- Which words in your title will need to be capitalized?

If students don't know the answers, you now have their attention and an opportunity to reteach. Comprehension Checks cut down on raised hands and such questions as "What do I need to do now?" You'll find Comprehension Checks and other process modifications in the section Modifications to Encourage Beginning Writers.

2. Realistic Expectations—Besides modifying the process, the other key to promoting growth is to set realistic expectations. After planning what objectives you want the class to accomplish, consider individual differences among the class members. At times it may be necessary to lower requirements to a point that you know is at students' instructional level instead of at their frustration level. For example, if your objective is "Students will write a three-paragraph science report including hypothesis, materials, procedures, and results," you could reduce this standard for a low achiever. The student could be expected to write a one-paragraph report built from three pattern sentences:

I thought ＿＿＿＿＿＿ would happen. (hypothesis)

I did ＿＿＿＿＿ using ＿＿＿＿＿. (procedures and materials)

I found out that ＿＿＿＿＿＿＿＿＿＿＿＿.

Likewise some students might need a greater challenge than the group as a whole. For example, you might ask a high achiever to add a fourth paragraph telling how the results of a science experiment could be used in a similar situation. You'll find other expectation modifications in both Modifications to Encourage Beginning Writers and Modifications to Challenge Advanced Writers.

Whether requirements are raised or lowered, realistic expectations help reduce stress and boredom and are the keys to your students' long term growth and success.

Section 1

EASY WRITINGS TO GET STUDENTS STARTED

EASY WRITINGS

TO GET STUDENTS STARTED

There are two relatively easy levels at which students can write: the word or phrase level and the sentence level.

Word or Phrase Writings

Word or phrase compositions frequently consist of nouns that label or identify an object or picture. Other word-level writings may be lists such as grocery lists, wish lists, and "To Do" lists.

Sentence-Level Writings

Sentence-level compositions fall into three categories: simple pattern, complex pattern, and complete sentences. Question sentences, just like declarative or telling sentences, are composed using the same three basic patterns.

1. **Simple Pattern Sentences.** A simple pattern sentence consists of a sentence in which one part is omitted. The teacher supplies most of the sentence and the student provides the rest of the idea. For example, if the pattern sentence contains a noun and a verb (I like), the student could provide the direct object (dogs). Similarly, in a simple question sentence, one part is left out, as in "What did _____ do?" or "Can a tree _____?"

2. **Complex Pattern Sentences.** A complex pattern sentence consists of a sentence in which two or more parts have been omitted, as in "The _____ ran quickly through the _____." Examples of complex pattern questions include "Where will _____ _____?" and "Which _____ did _____ in the _____?"

3. **Complete Sentence Pattern.** A complete sentence pattern occurs when the student provides all the ideas for the sentence, but the teacher supplies the sentence structure. For example, a sentence structure consisting of article, adjective (what kind of), noun (what), action verb (did what), adverb (how), and prepositional phrase (where) could

2

be brainstormed, and the student could create a sentence such as "A huge hawk flew rapidly over the pasture." For question sentences, supply question words such as *who, what, when, where, why,* and *how* along with the sentence structure.

Some Forms of Word- or Sentence-Level Writings

"Things to Do" Lists	"Miss you" Cards
Birthday Messages/Cards	New Year's Resolutions
Labels	Pet Peeves
For Sale Ads/Notices	Phone Messages
Found Item Ads/Notices	Rules/Regulations
"Get Well" Messages	Telegrams
Introductions	Thought for the Day
Invitations	Valentine Messages
I Owe You's	Want Ads
Lost Item Ads/Signs	World Records

LESSON 1

DESCRIPTIVE NAME TAGS

Writing name tags may not at first seem like a way to involve children in a meaningful and purposeful kind of writing. But creating name tags with additional information can do just that. Descriptive name tags can be helpful for the beginning of school, back-to-school night, a field trip, or for a new student or a substitute teacher.

OBJECTIVES

Students will create a descriptive name tag. To do this, they will:

- Print their first name in the center of a 4" by 6" index card in letters two inches tall (so the name can be read at a distance).
- Write five or more "ing" words that describe their interests, hobbies, and personality traits. Correctly form each word.
- Spell at least four of the five descriptive words correctly.

MOTIVATORS

1. Bring in a bag containing five objects that tell something about you. Explain that today you are going to share some things about yourself that students may not know. As you remove and show each object, use an "-ing" word to describe yourself. For example, you might remove a pencil from the bag and say you like "writing" or remove an apple and explain that you like "snacking."

2. Show students a name tag you made for yourself. Read the descriptive words that surround your name. Explain how each word describes you. Tell the students that they will be making name tags to help them get to know each other.

3. Have students draw pictures of themselves doing some of their favorite things.

BRAINSTORMING

Activities	Hobbies	Sports	Personality
waiting	painting	running	trying
casting	collecting	kicking	helping
reading	trading	dribbling	sharing
eating	telling jokes	playing tennis	listening
watching		serving	
playing piano		skiing	
		ice fishing	

Key Questions

Point out to students that they can get to know each other by telling other students something about themselves.

1. *What is an activity that you enjoy doing in your free time? What is one of the things you do during that activity?* (As students answer, help them turn what they do into an "ing" word. For example, "waiting" would be an "ing" word for something people do when they fish. Allow plenty of time for students to think. As students reply, respond positively and write their ideas on the chalkboard.)

2. *What is one hobby you have? What "ing" word can you use to describe what you do?* ("Collect stamps" and "collecting" are sample answers.)

3. *What sport do you like to participate in? What "ing" word describes something you do when you play that sport?* ("Kickball" and "running" are sample answers.)

4. *What is something special about your personality? What "ing" word describes that part of your personality?* (Share that on your name tag you wrote *laughing* because you like to laugh. Allow students time to think. This is more difficult than questions 1, 2, and 3. Elicit answers such as "sharing, helping, joking, hurrying.")

GROUP COMPOSING

Tell students that they are going to make a sample name tag together as a class before they make their own.

1. Draw a name tag on the blackboard. In the center of the name tag write the class's name (your name) in large letters. Tell students that you wrote your name in two-inch letters so people will be able to read the name tag at a distance. If students know the music teacher, P.E. teacher, principal, librarian, or janitor, well enough you could create a name tag for one of them instead of doing one for the class as a whole.

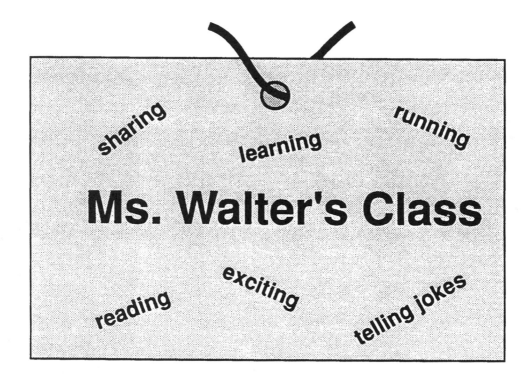

2. Inform students that they will need five or six "ing" words to describe the class. Have them use the list of "ing" words they brainstormed earlier to find words about sports or hobbies that describe the class. Write the words on the name tag in smaller letters.

3. Encourage students to suggest other "ing" words that would tell others about the activities of the class.

4. Ask students to suggest personality words to describe the way the class acts.

5. Finally ask students to read the name tag together. Start by reading the name and then read the describing words, moving around the name tag clockwise. An example is "Ms. Walter's Class, sharing, learning, running, telling jokes (joking), and reading."

6. Pass out 4" by 6" index cards and ask students to create their own individual name tags.

RESPONDING TO STUDENT WRITING

1. As students brainstorm descriptive words for their name tags, circulate around the room. Hold short conferences with students who are having trouble coming up with an "ing" word or who need assistance correctly forming an "ing" word.

2. If you want students to self evaluate, make **positive comments** about "ing" words that really describe students accurately such as "Katie 'sharing' is a good way to describe yourself because it tells readers about your personality."

   - To help students generate "ing" words, **ask questions** such as "What is something special or unique about your personality?"

   - Comment positively on legible handwriting. Explain that if handwriting is easy to read it will help others get to know them quicker.

3. When students have finished, ask them to read their name tags out loud to a partner. Ask revising partners to count and make sure they have five or more descriptive "ing" words.

PUBLISHING

Tell students that they are going to wear their name tags all week to help them get to know a little about each other.

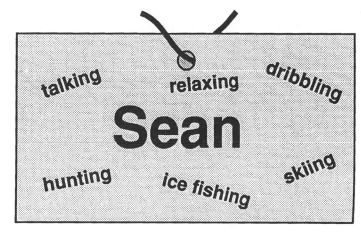

1. Use a hole punch to punch a hole in the center of each name tag about ½" to ¾" from the top edge. To help the name tags last longer, have them laminated before continuing.

2. String a piece of yarn about 2 feet long through the hole.

3. Tie the two ends of the yard in a knot, forming a loop big enough to slip over the student's head. (For short term use, safety pins can be used instead of a hole and yarn.)

After the name tags are completed, give students time to walk around the room, read each other's name tags, and learn people's names. If you want more structure, ring a bell each time students need to move on to talk with another person.

MODIFICATIONS TO ENCOURAGE BEGINNING WRITERS

- Have students dictate their "ing" words to you. Write the words on a list so that students can choose ones to write on their name tags.
- When someone gives a word that does not end in "ing," follow up with a question that will lead to an "ing" word.
- Model how to spell "ing" words during the group brainstorming. Display the rules for adding "ing" to words during composing for students who aren't good spellers. These two rules may help.

Rule 1: When adding "ing" to a word with a final "e," drop the "e" and add "ing."

Example: hope - hoping

Rule 2: When a word is only one syllable long and has a consonant at the end preceded by a vowel, double the last consonant and add "ing."

Example: hop - hopping

MODIFICATIONS TO CHALLENGE ADVANCED WRITERS

- Ask students to be more selective in choosing words that truly describe them.
- Encourage high achievers to think of more words that describe personality traits.
- Have students brainstorm words with "ful" or "able" suffixes. Examples are careful, faithful, truthful, deceitful, thoughtful, agreeable, dependable. "Ful" endings are easier than "able" endings.

LESSON 2

COUPON GIFTS

Coupons are easy to write and fun to use. This particular lesson is built around Mother's Day, but almost any time a special gift is needed, coupons can be created. As an alternative, have students write reward coupons for when they have been especially good. You can find more on reward coupons at the end of this lesson.

OBJECTIVES

Students will write three to six coupons for their mother. (Note: Some children may not live with their mother. In such instances the coupon gift can be made for a grandma, aunt, step-mother, or other adult figure.) To do this, they will:

- Write one message naming a task that each coupon is good for. The task or favor should be one that will be appreciated by the child's mother such as "one free hug," "setting the table," "taking out the garbage," or "cleaning my room."
- End each message with a period.
- Add an expiration date in which the month is capitalized and a comma is placed between the day and the year.

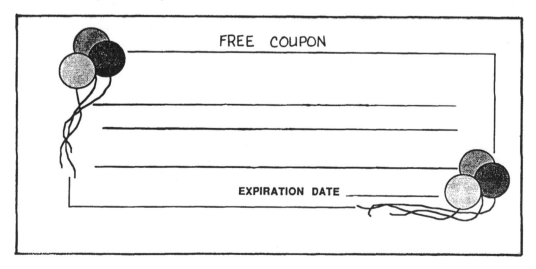

9

MOTIVATORS

Day One

1. Inquire what special holiday is coming up. (Mother's Day) Point out that on this day, they can tell their mothers, stepmothers, aunts, or grandmothers how special they are and thank them for the many things that they do for them. Share a list of things like the one below that many moms do. Ask students to listen and reflect on these jobs.

   > Loads the dishwasher, mops the kitchen, drives you to school, shovels snow, buys clothes, feeds the pet, takes you to the doctor, plays with you, vacuums the house, bakes cookies, and lots more.

2. Ask how many students like to go shopping with their mom or dad. Show them a variety of food, service, and other coupons. Inquire how many of their parents use coupons when they go shopping.

3. Inform students that they are going to make some special coupons as a Mother's Day gift. Explain that before they can make their gift, they need to do a little research. Ask students to watch what their mother does this afternoon, this evening, and tomorrow morning. Tell students to make a list of jobs and then think about small things they could do to help their mom with each one. Give students a special piece of paper on which to write their observations and thoughts. The reproducible page is at the end of this lesson.

The Next Day

Ask students to get their lists out. Praise students who did their research whether or not they have their notes. Explain that their research will provide ideas on ways they can help their mother.

Ask volunteers to share some jobs from their lists. As students answer, respond positively and write their ideas on the chalkboard. Continue brainstorming "jobs mothers do" until you have a long list.

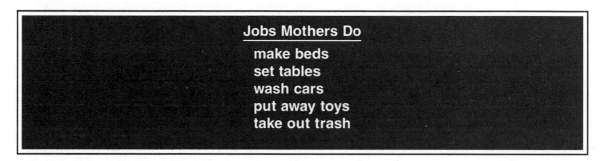

Jobs Mothers Do

make beds
set tables
wash cars
put away toys
take out trash

BRAINSTORMING

Key Questions

1. *What are some things that you could do around the house to help your mom?* (Write student's ideas on the chalkboard.)

2. *What are some other ways you can help your mom?*

3. *What are some things your mother likes you to do, but that you don't do very often?*

4. *What can you do to make your mother feel loved?*

Ways I Can Help

dust	clean my room	wash car
baby sit	fold towels	mow lawn
hug her	make my bed	get mail
vacuum	wash dishes	feed dog
mop	set table	make supper
	bake cookies	shovel snow
	load dishwasher	

(For each question elicit easy and simple ways the student can help. Encourage small things that require thought rather than lots of time and effort. If children promise too many large tasks, the coupon experience can turn them off to helping.)

GROUP COMPOSING

Tell students that they have to come up with some good ideas to help their mothers. Explain that the class will fill out one or two coupons together before they start on their own coupons.

1. First ask the class to choose a job or favor to put on the coupon. Then tell them they must decide what message to write.

    For example, if their mother makes their bed and they want to take on that job for one day, how could they write that on a coupon? If they wanted to make a coupon for washing the car, how would they word that? Lead students to express what the coupon is good for. Respond positively, for example, "This coupon is good for 1 free car washing." is a great way to word a coupon.

2. Draw a coupon on the chalkboard and write the message on the coupon.

3. Ask students what they need to add to the coupon to tell how long it is good for. (an expiration date) Help students select a realistic date in the near future. Write the date on the coupon and ask what goes between the day and the year and why. (A comma; so the numbers don't run together.)

4. Explain that the coupon needs one more thing to make it realistic. Ask how they can show who is giving the coupon away and who will do the work. (The person who makes the coupon needs to put his/her name on it.)

Tell students that before they make their own coupons, they need at least ten of their own ideas that their own mother will appreciate. Ask students to write their ideas down as fast as they can think of them. Remind them not to worry about their handwriting or spelling because this will be their rough draft. Tell students that they'll choose their best ideas later. Remind students that they will create coupons *especially for their mother.* When students finish, encourage them to star or circle their best ideas.

RESPONDING TO STUDENT WRITING

1. As students write their coupon messages, walk around the room. Visit individually with students who need special attention.

    - Give **positive feedback** on thoughtful favors/tasks students can do for their moms such as "I bet your mother will appreciate your cleaning off the dinner table, especially if you don't usually do that" or "After a hard day at work, I'm sure your mother would love a great big hug from you. Good thinking!"

    - Ask **questions** to help clarify the messages on the coupons such as "What is something that your grandmother would like you to do for her?" or "What other chores could you do for your mother that would make her very happy?"

2. Be particularly alert to unrealistic coupon ideas. A helpful article to read is "Encourage Your Students to Lend a Helping Hand," *Learning,* Nov./Dec. 1986, p. 43.

3. Ask students to read their coupons to a partner. Have students ask which coupon messages the partner thinks their mom will appreciate the most. They may then change or delete any messages if they wish.

PUBLISHING

1. Give students some precut strips of paper for their coupons. Instruct them to print their coupon messages, the expiration date, and their name neatly on the strips.
2. Remind students to use their best handwriting so their mothers will be able to read the coupons. Suggest that if they have time, they can decorate or make a border around the edge of each coupon.

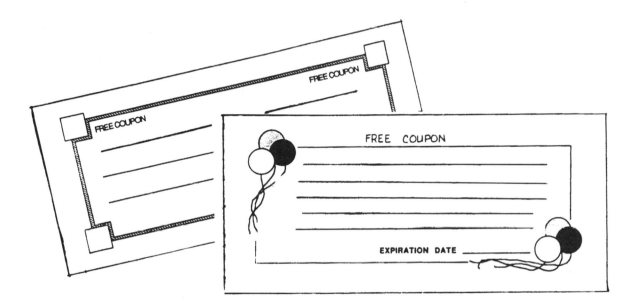

Suggest that students deliver their coupons to their mother on Mother's Day, leaving them by her place at the table on Sunday morning or delivering them personally. Tell students that their mother is sure to appreciate the special thought put into the gift and that she can trade in the coupons whenever she wants help.

Alternative Publishing Idea: Shaped Coupons for Special Occasions

Students can also create shaped coupons for various occasions such as a student's birthday, Valentine's Day, Father's Day, Secretary's Day, or for a new student who needs to get acquainted.

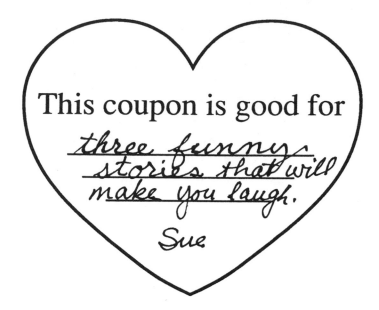

Alternative Publishing Idea: Gift Certificates

Students can create gift certificates instead of coupons. Often gift certificates are larger than coupons and on special paper with a gold seal. Gift certificates have the price of the object or service even though it is free to the recipient. The gift certificate should tell what it is good for and include an expiration date. Large and small reproducible gift certificates are supplied at the end of this lesson.

$15 Value	**$15 Value**

Gift Certificate for

a car wash on a

sunny day.

From *Jason*

9/29/95
Expiration Date _____

MODIFICATIONS TO ENCOURAGE BEGINNING WRITERS

- Realize that some students may not carry out the research on their mothers. Praise students who have done the research, but don't call attention to students who have forgotten.

- Require a student to create only one coupon or have this student dictate his/her ideas to an older student or aide.

- Begin each coupon message with a pattern sentence such as "This coupon is good for _____." Skip the expiration date.

- Allow students to skip a rough draft and to write their ideas directly on the coupons.

MODIFICATIONS TO CHALLENGE ADVANCED WRITERS

- Ask students to write an additional message such as "I hope you will redeem this coupon soon" or write how many times the coupon is good for.

- Have students write a closing like "Love, _____" or "With all my love!" before signing their name.

REWARD COUPONS

If your students need to improve their behavior, reward coupons can help. Instead of coming up with ideas for rewards yourself, let your students do the work. Of course, you retain final control as to whether or not a certain coupon is used.

Suggested Brainstorming Categories for this lesson might be "Responsible Behaviors" and "Rewards."

Key Questions for "Responsible Behaviors" might be:

What is one thing you could do to help a new student?

What can you do on the playground to help keep everyone safe?

What good deed could you do every day?

What is one responsible behavior we all need to work on?

What is one problem we have in this class? What would be a positive behavior you could replace it with?

How could you earn a reward in this class?

How could you earn a reward while you are in the cafeteria?

Encourage students to come up with responsible behaviors such as the following:

Lend a helping hand.   Follow class rules.

Be a good sport.   Try hard.

Complete all homework.

Be a good listener.

Use legible handwriting.

Stay with the class during a field trip.

Clean up after self in cafeteria.

Key Questions for "Rewards" could be:

What special treat might you enjoy when all your class work is done?
What reward could you use on the playground?
What reward would you like when you have lots of work to do?
What special treat might you receive at lunch?
What other rewards could you earn?

Encourage students to come up with experience rewards such as the following:

Eat lunch with the teacher.

Receive a round of applause from peers.

Get time to spend in the library.

Take a note home to parents about good behavior.

Be teacher's assistant for a day.

Help in a lower grade class for the afternoon.

Earn 10 minutes of free time for the whole class.

Bring a game to play with peers during free time.

Have no homework tonight.

Group Composing could be structured around two pattern sentences such as the following:

This Reward Coupon is awarded to _____

for/because _____.

You have earned _____.

Once all the coupons have been made, collect them and put them in a small box. Tell students that when you notice a responsible behavior or a good deed, you will give them one of the Reward Coupons they have made. You may want to set up some rules about using coupons such as the following:

1. They may be used when the teacher designates.
2. Coupons must be turned in to the teacher when used.
3. Students can't get credit for lost coupons.
4. Students are not allowed to trade coupons.

MOM

Jobs Mom does:

1. _____

2. _____

3. _____

4. _____

5. _____

Ways I could help:

1. _____

2. _____

3. _____

4. _____

5. _____

(2-2)

Gift Certificate for

$15 Value

$15 Value

From _____

Expiration Date _____

Gift Certificate for

$15 Value

$15 Value

From _____

Expiration Date _____

$15 Value

$15 Value

Gift Certificate for

From _____

_____

Expiration Date _____

$15 Value

$15 Value

LESSON 3

ADVICE FOR YOUNGER STUDENTS

People of all ages love to give advice. It makes them feel important and helpful and also helps to build self esteem. This lesson provides an opportunity for students to give helpful advice.

OBJECTIVES

Students will write six to eight sentences of advice based on what they have learned over the last school year. To do this, they will:

- Complete the pattern sentence "Successful third graders should/shouldn't _____."
- Spell the word "should" or the contraction "shouldn't" correctly.
- Begin each sentence with a capital letter.
- End each sentence of advice with a period.

MOTIVATORS

Note: Adjust this lesson to the grade level of your students. For the purpose of this lesson, fourth and third graders have been used as examples.

21

1. Remind students that next year they are going to be fourth graders and there are many things they can tell the incoming third graders that will be helpful.

2. Put on a name tag that says "Third Grader" and ask students to pretend you are a new third grader. Tell them to think about the things that third graders should and shouldn't do.

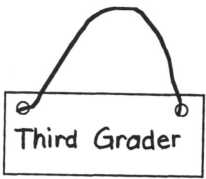

3. Read a book on manners. A funny one with pictures that appeal to older students is *Mind Your Manners* by Walter Chandoha, Middletown, Connecticut: Weekly Reader Books, 1985.

BRAINSTORMING/GROUP COMPOSING

Point out that the new third graders unfortunately won't know the rules. Explain that they will be making a list to remind the new third graders what they should and shouldn't do. State that they'll begin each sentence with the words, "Successful third graders . . . ."

Suggest that since they are writing sentences about what successful third graders should and shouldn't do, they will need to use the word "should" and the contraction "shouldn't." Write these words on the blackboard.

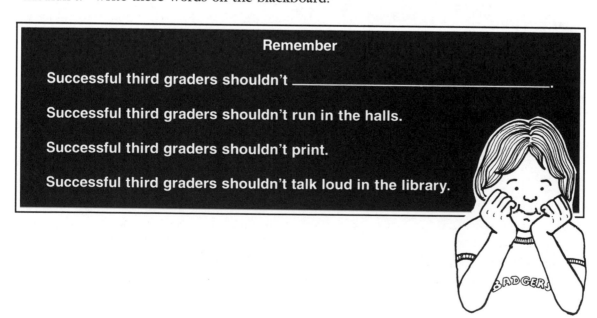

Remember

Successful third graders shouldn't _____.

Successful third graders shouldn't run in the halls.

Successful third graders shouldn't print.

Successful third graders shouldn't talk loud in the library.

Key Questions

1. ***What is something third graders shouldn't do?*** (As students reply, give a positive response such as "Good point! Successful third graders shouldn't run in the hall.") ***How should I spell the word "shouldn't?" What is the mark between the letters "n" and "t" called? What does it show?*** (By asking for help as you spell the word, you give students practice in spelling the contraction. Reinforce that the apostrophe shows where a letter is missing. Write students' suggestions on the chalkboard. Continue brainstorming until you have many ideas listed.)

2. ***What is something that a successful third grader should do?*** (Add the ideas to the list on the chalkboard.)

3. ***What have you learned this year that you would like to share?***

Tell students that now it's their turn to create their own advice for successful third graders. Explain that when they are finished, their ideas will be saved and given to the new third grade class next year.

RESPONDING TO STUDENT WRITING

1. As students compose their advice for the third graders, walk around the room. Visit individually with as many students as possible. Give positive feedback and/or ask questions to help students to "re-see" their advice from the point of view of a younger student.

   - **Advice**

     If the student has written good advice, make a comment such as "Successful third graders shouldn't skip their homework" is great advice because it clearly tells the third graders something that will really help them in school.

     If a student is stuck and can't think of a rule, ask a question such as "What did you learn you shouldn't do this year?" or "What rule did you have trouble remembering yesterday going to lunch?"

     If a student has come up with some poor or dangerous advice, ask the student a question to help him/her reevaluate it. For example, ask "How good do you think your mom/dad/coach would think this advice is?" Follow up with another question such as "How might this get the third grader in trouble?" Then reinforce the new understanding by saying something like "Those third graders sure are lucky you have thought so hard about what advice to give."

   - **Contraction and Apostrophe**

     If the student has remembered the apostrophe, make a comment like "I'm glad you put the apostrophe after 'n' because that shows the letter 'o' has been left out."

     If the student has forgotten the apostrophe, ask questions such as "Where has a letter been left out of the word 'shouldn't'?" and "How do we show that a letter is missing?"

2. When students are finished, ask them to read their advice slowly to someone. Ask students to listen to see if each piece of advice makes sense. Then tell them to choose their

best six or eight pieces of advice and circle or star them. Demonstrate this by going to the chalkboard and circling or starring a piece of advice that the class chooses.

PUBLISHING

When students are finished, have them write at the end of their list "From a future fourth grader" or "From a successful third grader" and sign their name. Explain that you will give their advice to your class at the beginning of next year so they will start off the year well.

MODIFICATIONS TO ENCOURAGE BEGINNING WRITERS

- Require students to write only one to three pieces of advice.
- During the motivation and group brainstorming, have students pull their chairs up close around you. This will help create an intimate environment for sharing. This will also allow you to ask any disruptive students to return to their desk until they can act appropriately.
- Pair students who tire easily when reading or have poor handwriting with students whose handwriting is legible.

MODIFICATIONS TO CHALLENGE ADVANCED WRITERS

- Ask students to construct other pieces of advice such as "Successful third graders always _____" or "Successful third graders don't _____."
- Suggest students create a say no pledge similar to the one below.

THE "SAY NO" PLEDGE

I pledge not to try drugs.
I want to be healthy and happy.
I will help my friends say "No"!
I pledge to stand up for what I know is right.

- Have students disregard the pattern sentence and create their own sentences such as "Save energy by _____" or "Reuse _____."
- Give students who have finished writing and revising early a Revising Checklist and ask them to help other students revise and proofread their advice.

Revising Checklist

_____ Does my advice make sense?

_____ Is the advice good advice?

_____ Does each sentence begin with a capital letter?

_____ Does the contraction shouldn't have an apostrophe between the "n" and the "t"?

_____ Does the sentence end with a period?

LESSON 4

WISE SAYINGS OR
NEW WORDS OF WISDOM

Wise sayings, words of wisdom, and proverbs are all forms of advice that have been passed down from one person to another for many generations. Whether we realize it or not, many people use this information to guide and explain events in their lives.

OBJECTIVES

Students will write three wise sayings that are thoughtful, positive, and full of good advice. To do this, they will:

- Create with new endings for old sayings.
- Begin each new wise saying with a capital letter and end it with a period.

MOTIVATORS

1. From a container pull out a slip of paper on which you have written a wise saying. Read the saying. A list of popular wise sayings your students might know appears toward the end of this lesson. Ask students what they think the person who wrote the saying was trying to say. Pull other slips of paper with wise sayings out of the box and ask students to explain the advice. Example:

> ## A penny saved is a penny earned.

2. Ask the class what a wise saying is. Point out that wise sayings and proverbs are forms of advice that have been passed down from one person to another for many years. Ask students who has given them some advice lately and what the advice was.

3. Read excerpts and show the illustrations from Judith Frost Stark's book *Don't Cross Your Bridge Before . . . you pay the toll.* Examples are:

> A penny saved is "not much."
> 'Tis better to be safe than "punch a sixth grader."
> If at first you don't succeed, "get new batteries."
> Don't bite the hand that "looks dirty."

Then ask your students what the original sayings were. Inquire whether all wise advice needs to come from grown-ups. Share that you believe that students of all ages can give wise advice.

BRAINSTORMING

If at first you don't succeed, _____ .

> go home and cry
> smile and say "I really wasn't trying"
> say "I'll try harder next time"
> ask your mom or dad for help

Don't count your _____ before _____ .

presents	Christmas
baseball cards	trade them
pencils	sharpen them
friends	you need them

Key Questions

1. *One wise saying that I like is "If at first you don't succeed, try try again." What does this mean to you?* (Allow time for students to think. As students reply, respond positively.)

2. *What new wise ending could we give for "If at first you don't succeed, _____"? What should children do if they fail? What positive solution can we give?* (Allow plenty of time for students to think. As students reply,

respond positively and write their ideas on the chalkboard. Continue brainstorming until many new endings are listed.)

3. *Another wise saying is "Don't count your chickens before they hatch." What does this mean to you?* (Allow plenty of time for students to think.) *Let's think of a new ending that would be terrific advice.*

4. *What new ending could we give for "Don't count your* _____ *before* _____*"? What shouldn't a child count? Before what?* (Continue brainstorming until many new endings are listed. If necessary, brainstorm endings for additional wise sayings to make sure students are catching on.)

GROUP COMPOSING

Tell students that they have brainstormed many interesting ways to end the wise sayings. Now they need to go back and pick one new ending for each.

1. Ask students to vote on which wise saying to write first. Put a star by the one students choose.

2. Next ask them to choose one of the up-to-date endings they brainstormed. Circle their choice.

3. As you write the saying and new ending on the chalkboard, ask how you should begin the wise saying (with a capital letter), and what punctuation mark is needed at the end. (Period.)

4. Repeat group composing for a second wise saying.

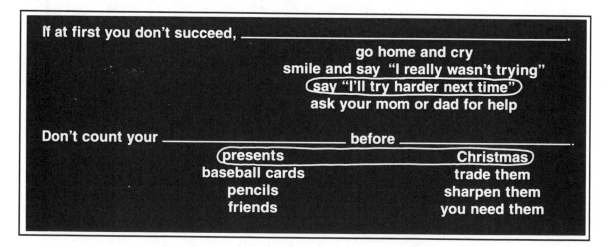

RESPONDING TO STUDENT WRITING

1. As students work on their new words of wisdom, walk around the room. Hold mini-conferences with those who need assistance or attention. Read back a student's new

words of wisdom so that he/she can hear whether the new advice sounds positive, thoughtful, and wise.

2. If you want students to work towards particular learner outcomes, focus your positive comments and questions to help each student self evaluate one or two of the outcomes. For example, if a student has written an appropriate alternative ending, you might say "I really like your ending. That's good advice."

3. Have students read their sayings to a partner and ask whether they think the advice makes sense.

PUBLISHING

Tell students that they are going to take or send their new words of wisdom to a class at a lower grade level so that the students can benefit from their advice. Students who wish to may illustrate their sayings.

MODIFICATIONS TO ENCOURAGE BEGINNING WRITERS

• Make sure students fully understand the wise sayings they will rewrite.

• Expect a more concrete response. For example, "Look before you leap" might become "Look before you jump in a hole."

• Do a **comprehension check** before students begin to compose.

MODIFICATIONS TO CHALLENGE ADVANCED WRITERS

- Allow students to rewrite all of the old saying not just the ending. For example, "When the cat's away, the mice will play" might become "When Mom goes shopping, we can have a blast."

- Contract with students to rewrite five old wise sayings with really thoughtful new endings. Let them select their wise sayings from the list at the end of this lesson. Reproducible pages are also supplied for publishing.

POPULAR WORDS OF WISDOM

A bird in the hand is worth two in the bush.

A friend in need is a friend indeed.

A penny saved is a penny earned.

A miss is as good as a mile.

A stitch in time saves nine.

A watched pot never boils.

Absence makes the heart grow fonder.

Actions speak louder than words.

An apple a day keeps the doctor away.

All that glitters is not gold.

All is well that ends well.

An ounce of prevention is worth a pound of cure.

Beggars cannot be choosers.

Better late than never.

Birds of a feather flock together.

Beauty is only skin deep.

Children should be seen and not heard.

Curiosity killed the cat.

Don't bite the hand that feeds you.

Don't count your chickens before they hatch.

Don't cut off your nose to spite your face.

Don't put all your eggs in one basket.

Early to bed, early to rise makes a person healthy, wealthy, and wise.

He/she who hesitates is lost.

If at first you don't succeed, try again.

It is always darkest before the dawn.

It takes two to tango.

Leave no stone unturned.

Love all, trust none.

Laugh and the world laughs with you. Cry and you cry alone.

Look before you leap.

Make hay while the sun shines.

Money is the root of all evil.

No news is good news.

Never underestimate the power of persuasion.

Never put off till tomorrow what you can do today.

Out of sight, out of mind.

People who live in glass houses shouldn't throw stones.

Still waters run deep.

Strike while the iron is hot.

Sticks and stones will break your bones, but words can never hurt you.

The early bird catches the worm.

The pen is mightier than the sword.

The squeaky wheel gets the oil.

There are two sides to every story.

There's no fool like an old fool.

There's a time and a place for everything.

There's no place like home.

'Tis better to be safe than sorry.

To err is human, to forgive is divine.

Too many cooks spoil the soup.

Two's company, three's a crowd.

Two heads are better than one.

Walk softly and carry a big stick.

When the cat's away, the mice will play.

Where there's smoke, there's fire.

You are what you eat.

You can choose your friends, but you can't choose your relatives.

You can lead a horse to water, but you can't make it drink.

You can't teach an old dog new tricks.

You get out of something what you put into it.

New Words of Wisdom

from _____

_____

Words of Wisdom

by

_____

_____

_____

_____

_____

_____

_____

_____

_____

_____

LESSON 5

"SECRETS ABOUT ME" SIMILES

Similes and metaphors can enliven speaking and writing, but few students know how to use them. In this lesson you will learn along with your students the descriptive power that similes can provide when you want to compare two objects.

OBJECTIVES

Students will use the pattern "I am as _____ as a/an _____" to create a list of secrets called "Secrets About Me." To do this, they will:

- Write at least eight comparisons between themselves and an object, using a characteristic of the object that describes them.
- Use the article "a" in the pattern in front of words that begin with a consonant and the article "an" in front of words that begin with a vowel.
- Begin each comparison with a capital letter and end each one with a period.

MOTIVATORS

1. Relate that you are going to share some secrets about yourself with your students. As you read your own list of secrets that you have composed ahead of time, hold up an object or picture as each statement is read. Some examples are:

   I am as bright as a light bulb.
   I am as bubbly as a cola drink.
   I am as strong as a drop of glue.
   I am as natural as a box of oat cereal.
   I am as clear as plastic wrap.
   I am as soft as a beach towel.
   I am as colorful as a sunset.
   I am as sly as a cat.

   Ask students what they learned about you that they didn't know before.

2. Ask students what words were repeated in each statement. (I'm as _____ as a _____.) Explain that a statement that compares one thing to another using *like* or *as* is called a simile. Tell students that they will use similes to make their own "Secrets About Me" book.

 Inform students that you'll put your book of secrets on the bookshelf so that they can read and look at it when they have some spare time.

3. Share these poems written by two sixth graders.

SECRETS ABOUT TIM

I am as noisy as a rock band.
I am as intelligent as a wizard.
I am as funny as my dad.
I am as strong as a tornado.
I am as rough as a football player.
When I play football, I'm as powerful as lightning.
When I play hockey, I'm as quick as a jack rabbit.
I am as crazy as a blind bat.
I am as wild as a party animal.

SECRETS ABOUT SONYA

I am as gentle as a purring kitten.
I am as friendly as a robin.
I am as colorful as a unicorn's horn.
I am as stubborn as a mule.
I am as fast as a thoroughbred (at times).
I am as clean as a picture on a wall.
I am as brave as a soldier.
I am as smart as a dolphin.
And I am as quiet as a leaf falling at night.

BRAINSTORMING/GROUP COMPOSING

Explain to students that before they write their own "Secrets About Me" similes, you'll help them write some similes about the class. Point out that to make a comparison, they will first have to think of a characteristic of the class. Then they will have to decide what thing or object has that same characteristic.

Our class is as _____ as a _____.

quiet	rock
attractive	flamingo
smart	computer
active	
playful	
funny	
friendly	

Key Questions

First Simile

1. *What is one characteristic of our class?* (Write the characteristic, e.g. quiet, on the chalkboard.)

2. *To make a simile, we need to say "our class is as (quiet) as something else." What could our class be as (quiet) as?* (Verbally recognize and praise the students' ideas but hold off writing these ideas down.)

    What else could our class be as quiet as? (Give a positive response such as "Great, 'Our class is as quiet as a rock,' is another powerful comparison to make of our class.")

3. *Which comparison do you want us to use?* (Write the particular comparison on the blackboard.)

4. *Why did we use the article "a" in front of the word (rock)?* (Allow time to think. If no one knows, explain that the article "a" goes in front of words that begin with a consonant. The article "an" goes in front of words that begin with a vowel because it sounds better that way.)

Additional Similes Continue this pattern of brainstorming characteristics and matching objects until eight comparisons are made. As you write each comparison, ask which article is needed before the last word. Comment that students have eight similes that compare their class to objects or things with similar characteristics. Then remark what a powerful tool a simile can be for describing.

Ask students to come up with about twelve similes in their rough drafts, so they can pick out the ones that best describe themselves.

RESPONDING TO STUDENT WRITING

As students write their secrets, walk around the room. Visit individually with students who need special attention.

- Give **positive feedback** on students' ideas such as "'I am as happy as a butterfly' really gives us a clear picture of how you feel" or "'Active' is a characteristic that certainly describes you well."
- Ask **questions** to get students thinking when they are stuck such as "What is another characteristic that describes you?" or "What object or thing could be gloomy?"
- Make **positive comments** when students use the article "a" or "an" correctly such as "Great, you used the article "a" before a consonant sound."
- Ask **questions** to get students to self evaluate when they use the article incorrectly such as "What article would sound better in front of "elephant" than "a"?

Ask students when they have completed their similes to slowly read them out loud to a partner to see if they make sense. Suggest they put a check or star beside the eight similes that describe them best. They should then switch and listen to their partner's similes.

PUBLISHING

Tell students that they are going to publish "Secrets About Me" so that others can try to guess who wrote them. See the reproducible page at the end of the lesson. Have students glue their list of secrets to a sheet of construction paper and write their name on the back.

Display the "Secrets About Me" lists somewhere in the room or post them on the bulletin board. Or have each student read a randomly selected list to the class as other students try to guess who the similes describe.

MODIFICATIONS TO ENCOURAGE BEGINNING WRITERS

- Have students write eight secrets without using a simile.

    "I am ＿＿＿＿＿＿." (I.e. "I am tall" instead of "I am as tall as a horse.")

- Require only four similes.
- Give low achievers a basket of small objects such as a comb, a shoe lace, a magnifying glass, a plastic flower, and a toy truck and walk them through some special instructions.

    1. Have students pick an object and write the name of that object in the third blank in the sentence.

        "I am as ＿＿＿＿＿＿ as ＿＿＿ _truck_ ."

2. Have them say "a" and "an" in front of the object. Ask which sounds best.

3. Provide feedback and have them write the correct article in the second blank.

"I am as _____ as __a__ __truck__."

4. Now ask students to think how they are like the objects. Make a positive comment and ask them to write the describing word in the first blank and read the sentence to see how it sounds.

"I am as __fast__ as __a__ __truck__."

Make a positive comment such as "That's an excellent secret about you."

Repeat this procedure with at least two more objects.

- Provide a special form for students to use during composing.

Secrets About Me

I am as _____ as ____ _____.

I am as _____ as ____ _____.

I am as _____ as ____ _____.

I am as _____ as ____ _____.

I am as _____ as ____ _____.

I am as _____ as ____ _____.

I am as _____ as ____ _____.

I am as _____ as ____ _____.

MODIFICATIONS TO CHALLENGE ADVANCED WRITERS

- Ask the student to choose their similes quite carefully so that each one accurately reflects true characteristics.

- Suggest students write similes using "like" instead of "as."

- Encourage students to rewrite some of their similes as metaphors. For example, if they wrote "I'm as fast as a bird in flight," they could rewrite it "I'm a bird in flight."

Name: _____

Date: _____

Secrets About Me

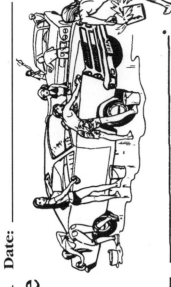
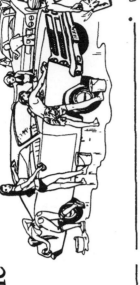

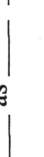

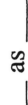

I am as _____ as _____.

I am as _____ as _____.

I am as _____ as _____.

I am as _____ as _____.

I am as _____ as _____.

I am as _____ as _____.

I am as _____ as _____.

I am as _____ as _____.

CAR WASH TODAY

LESSON 6

"I USED TO BE" MEMORIES

Recalling memories of what used to be is a captivating pastime. Your students will enjoy thinking back on what used to be and contrasting it with what is happening currently in their lives. This lesson can also be used to help teach the concept of antonyms.

OBJECTIVES

Students will write seven compound sentences following the pattern "I used to _____, but now I _____." To do this, they will:

- Complete the first clause of each sentence with what they used to be, do, have, etc.
- Complete the second clause with how they are different now.
- Begin each sentence with a capital letter.
- Separate the independent clauses with a comma before the connecting word "but."
- End each sentence with a period.

MOTIVATORS

1. A few days before this lesson, send letters home to students' parents requesting a baby or early childhood picture and a current picture of the student. If desired, this lesson can be tied into the arrival of individual school pictures taken of each student by a professional photography company.

2. Show the students some photographs of you as a child. Next, share some more recent photographs of you doing some activities. Then, share some memories similar to the following.

> I used to crawl, but now I walk.
> I used to throw food on the floor, but now I eat it.
> I used to be a brat, but now I'm an angel.
> I used to be short, but now I'm tall.
> I used to cry, but now I think problems through.
> I used to ignore directions, but now I am a good listener.
> I used to be good at jacks, but now I like to play racket ball.
> I used to think I was dumb, but now I teach school.

3. Have students take out the two pictures that they brought from home. Ask students to look at their pictures as you ask the following questions. Wait about 30-60 seconds between questions.

> *What did you used to like when you were a baby?*
>
> *How have you changed since your earlier picture was taken?*
>
> *How are you different now?*
>
> *What are some things you used to do that you don't do anymore?*
>
> *What things do you do instead?*

BRAINSTORMING

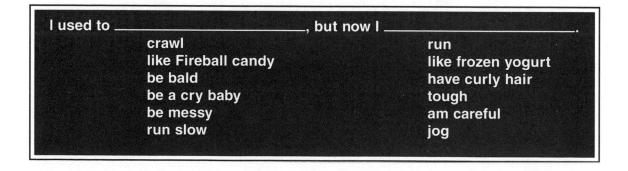

I used to _____, but now I _____.

crawl	run
like Fireball candy	like frozen yogurt
be bald	have curly hair
be a cry baby	tough
be messy	am careful
run slow	jog

Key Questions

1. *What are some things you did when you were younger?* (Write students' ideas on the blackboard. Respond with a positive comment such as "Yes, many of us used to crawl.")
2. *What did you like?*
3. *What did you look like?*
4. *Now you need an ending for each idea that tells how you have changed.* (Read back one previous statement at a time and ask what students do now instead. Get several possible answers.)

Group Composing

Tell students they now need to put their ideas of how they used to be and how they are now together in one sentence.

1. Ask what word they can use to connect the ideas. (Elicit that "but" is a good connecting word in this situation because it signals a change in thought.)
2. Write "but" after the first statement on the chalkboard, and write an ending statement that students agree on.
3. Tell students the sentence needs one more thing to be correct. Ask what punctuation mark you should place before "but." Add the comma. Explain that this separates the 2 clauses in the compound sentence.
4. Proceed in a similar manner with the remaining statements.

Tell students they will write ten sentences of their own using the pattern "I used to _____, but now I _____." Suggest they look back at their pictures if they can't think of an idea.

RESPONDING TO STUDENT WRITING

1. Walk around the room as students write their memories. Make positive comments and ask questions to help students resee and evaluate their memories.
   - **Memories**

     If the first or last or both parts of the memory make sense and fit the student, make a comment such as "I like how you used the word 'terrific' to express how you currently feel about yourself."

     If the student is having trouble thinking of a memory, ask a question such as "What is something you are doing in your baby picture that you don't do anymore?" or "What is something you are wearing in your baby picture that you don't wear anymore?"

- **Mechanics**

   If the student has correctly used the comma, make a comment such as "The comma after your clause 'I used to cry' helps me pause and think before I read your new statement."

   If the student has forgotten the comma, ask a question such as "What punctuation is needed before the word "but" to separate your two ideas?"

   If the student has remembered a period, make a comment such as "The period after your first statement and before your next statement helps me separate these ideas."

2. Ask students to reread each of their "I used to be . . ." sentences silently and put a check or star by their seven best memories. Explain that they will publish only their best ideas.

PUBLISHING

Tell students they are going to make individual books for their memories. Explain that later they can enjoy trading books with friends. Show them an example of a book cover.

1. Distribute two pieces of construction paper to each student.

2. Instruct students to write the phrase "I Used to Be" in large letters at the top of one piece of construction paper.

3. Under the words have them glue their baby picture. Under the baby picture they should write the words "But now I Am" and under those words glue a more recent picture.

4. Provide fourteen pieces of lined paper for each student. Instruct them to stack the lined paper carefully on top of the blank piece of construction paper, add the cover, and then staple all these papers three times on the left. (Demonstrate.)

5. Tell students to write one clause on each page. Give an example such as "I wrote 'I used to be skinny,' on my first sheet of lined paper. On my second sheet of paper I wrote the rest of that statement 'but now I'm overweight.'" (Show students your book.)

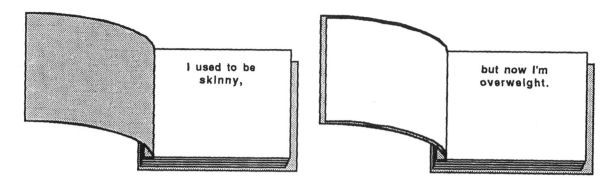

6. Explain that once they've written their seven best memories neatly in their book, they can illustrate each one.

MODIFICATIONS TO ENCOURAGE BEGINNING WRITERS

* Ask students to write only one memory and illustrate it.
* Write the sentence pattern with blanks "I used to _____, but now I _____." on students' papers. These students can then participate in the same lesson without having to manage all the mechanical aspects of the task.

> I used to _____, but now I _____.
>
> I used to _____, but now I _____.

* During revising provide a checklist so that students can more easily evaluate their own writing.

> **Revising Checklist**
>
> _____ 1. I wrote ten "I used to _____" sentences.
>
> _____ 2. I reread each sentence out loud to a friend to see if it made sense.
>
> _____ 3. Each of my sentences begin with a capital letter.
>
> _____ 4. Each sentence has a comma before the "but now I _____" clause.
>
> _____ 5. Each of my sentences end with a period.

* Post a list of opposites such as the ones below:

easy-hard, walk-run, short-tall, heavy-light, open-close, smooth-bumpy, big-little, short-long, smile-frown, love-hate, straight-crooked, full-empty, clean-dirty, win-lose, mean-nice, outside-inside

MODIFICATIONS TO CHALLENGE ADVANCED WRITERS

• Require that each descriptive "pair" be antonyms. (See list on page 45.)

• Have students create their own patterns such as the following:

> Sometimes I _____, but later I _____.
>
> Yesterday I was _____, but today I am _____.
>
> I like to be _____, but I don't like to be _____.
>
> Sometimes I feel _____, but other times I feel _____.
>
> I want to _____, but I should _____.
>
> I like _____, but she/he likes _____.

• Write a rap on the power of positive thinking such as the following:

> When you think (say) no, I think (say) yes.
>
> When you think bad, I think good.
>
> When you think empty, I think full.

• Ask students to create an illustrated book of opposites to share with younger or students.

> Page 1 could be up.
>
> Page 2 could be down.
>
> Page 3 could be in.
>
> Page 4 could be out.
>
> Page 5 could be soft.
>
> Page 6 could be hard, etc.

LESSON 7

"WHY DO" QUESTIONS

"Why" questions are particularly captivating to students as they explore and try to understand their world. This lesson can entertain, provide emotional relief from difficult situations, or form the start of serious research efforts.

OBJECTIVES

Students will write five questions following the pattern "Why do/does _____ _____?" To do this, they will:

- Complete the first blank with a noun (subject).
- Complete the second blank with a verb.
- Capitalize the first word in each question.
- Put a question mark at the end of each question.

MOTIVATOR

Share that recently you went somewhere (for example, to the zoo or to a baseball game). Tell students that you had a wonderful time despite the "Why do's" floating in your head. Inquire if they know what "Why do's" are. Pause for responses.

Explain that "Why do's" are those frustrating questions no one can answer. Share some examples of "Why do's" that have occurred to you. Here are a few to get you started.

1. At a baseball game:

    "Why do the Twins always lose in the ninth inning?"

2. At the zoo:

    "Why do elephants have long trunks?"

    "Why do frogs hop instead of walk?"

3. While driving home:

    "Why do people drive so crazy?"

    "Why do I always get lost when I drive in the city?"

47

BRAINSTORMING

Explain that the class will write some "Why do's" together. First they will brainstorm words they can use as subjects of their "Why do's."

Why do/does _____	_____?
do shoe salesmen	wear ugly shoes?
does a priest	wear black?
do parents	never give big allowances?
do teachers	make so many rules?
does a baby	
do animals	
do big kids	

Key Questions

1. *Who does something you don't understand? What person, animal, or object does something you don't understand?* (Write the pattern sentence on the chalkboard. Then, as students give you subjects, write the subjects in a column under the first blank.)

2. *What is something you would like to ask about each of these subjects? What do these people, animals, or objects do that you don't understand or can't explain?* (List responses in a column under the second blank. Responses should contain a verb and any other words that are part of a predicate.)

GROUP COMPOSING

Tell students they will now use their brainstorming ideas to write some "Why do" questions together.

1. Involve students in deciding whether "do" or "does" is needed for each sentence. Explain that if the subject names one thing (for example, a baby) the singular verb "does" is needed. If the subject names more than one thing (for example, birds) the plural verb "do" is needed. Write "why" and the verb that students suggest for the first subject.

2. Ask a volunteer to read the first sentence as you complete it to see if it makes sense. Then ask what kind of sentence it is (a question) and what kind of punctuation mark goes at the end of a question (a question mark). Write a question mark after the predicate.

3. Repeat steps 1 and 2 for each subject and predicate.

Tell students that they will now get to compose three to five of their own "Why do" questions.

RESPONDING TO STUDENT WRITING

As students think and write their "Why do" questions, circulate around the room. Hold one- or two-minute conferences with students.

- Read a particularly interesting question out loud to a student so he/she can hear it. Then make a positive comment.
- Read out loud an awkward question so the student can reevaluate and revise it. If necessary, ask a question to help the student clarify his/her idea.

PUBLISHING

When students are finished, ask them to share their favorite questions with the class so everyone can enjoy listening to each other's questions. Some students may want to offer answers to other students' questions. Encourage students who would like to research the answer to a particular question to do so.

MODIFICATIONS TO ENCOURAGE BEGINNING WRITERS

- Allow students to use ideas from the group brainstorming.
- Tell students to raise their hands or ask another student when they need to know whether to use "do" or "does."

MODIFICATIONS TO CHALLENGE ADVANCED WRITERS

- Ask students when they are finished to circulate around the room and read the "Why do" questions of other students out loud and make suggestions on how to improve each question.
- Suggest that students compose ten questions around one serious topic. Contract with a student to "track down" answers to at least two of their questions.

LESSON 8

TONGUE TWISTERS

Tongue twisters are challenging to read and say. And they're even more fun to write. While learning to write tongue twisters, students can learn a lot about writing good sentences and understanding nouns, verbs, adjectives, adverbs, and prepositional phrases.

OBJECTIVES

Students will write four original tongue twisters. To do this, they will:

- Include in each tongue twister a noun as subject (who or what), an adjective (what kind of subject), a verb (what the subject did, does, or will do), and one or more adverbs or prepositional phrases (telling how, when, and/or where).
- Begin at least five main words in the tongue twister with the same sound.
- Begin each tongue twister with a capital letter and end it with a period.
- Capitalize the proper names of people, places, or things.
- Illustrate at least one of the tongue twisters.

MOTIVATORS

1. Ask students to close their eyes and listen to a silly statement that you found. Say this or another tongue twister slowly: Peter Piper picked a peck of pickled peppers. Then say the same tongue twister faster and faster. Ask what the special name is for what you just said.

Then show students four more tongue twisters on a chart or overhead. Have students read the first tongue twister slowly together. Point out to students that tongue twister #2 on the chart demonstrates that not all of the words in a tongue twister have to begin with the same letter.

Brenda bought a billion big black Buicks.

Gorgeous George got goose bumps as he put a giggling goat in a green truck.

Funny Fred fixed frozen french fries for his friends.

The seven stupid snakes slid slowly into the soft savory slime.

Ask a volunteer to read the tongue twister as fast as possible. Praise the student's effort and ask if anyone can read it even faster. Read the next tongue twister slowly as a group and then choose a volunteer to read it quickly. Continue until all tongue twisters have been read.

2. Ask students what makes a tongue twister different from other sentences. (Most words in a tongue twister begin with the same letter.) Explain that is why it is difficult to say a tongue twister without getting tongue-tied.

   Point out that not all the words in a tongue twister have to begin with the same letter. Explain that most of the big or important words usually start with the same letter, but the small words do not have to begin with the chosen letter.

3. Read these tongue twisters written by a fourth grader.

   A poor polka dot pickle accidentally poked Paula at the picnic near Pam's painted porch.

   Darling David drowned during December in Darrel's dishwasher at the dump.

4. Read an alphabet book of alliterations titled *Animalia* by Graeme Base, New York: Abrams, Inc. 1986. Tell students that there is a special name for the use of words that begin with the same sound. It's called alliteration. Explain that experienced writers use alliteration in their writing even when they aren't writing tongue twisters.

BRAINSTORMING

Invite students to brainstorm some ideas for a tongue twister with you.

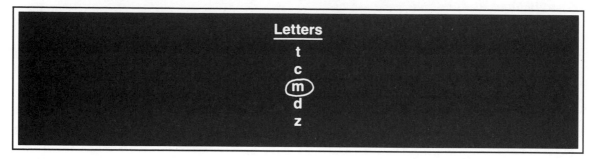

Key Questions

1. *First we need to choose a letter of the alphabet. What would be a good letter to use? What's another letter we could use?* (Positively reinforce suggested letters or explain why particular letters such as "z" would be difficult to do. Continue brainstorming letters.)

2. *Next we need to select one letter from the list to be the first letter of all the main words in our tongue twister. Which letter should we use?* (Remind them that some letters are more difficult to find words for. Give positive feedback for the choice of a good letter such as the letter "m.")

3. *Who or what should we write about? Remember that this person, animal, or object will be the subject of our tongue twister so it must begin with the letter we have chosen. What person or animal starts with our letter?* (Give a positive response such as "*Mouse* would make a good subject for our tongue twister because it starts with the letter 'm' and is an animal." Continue brainstorming until several subjects beginning with the chosen letter are listed.)

4. *Now we need to think of some words that describe our subject. What word beginning with our letter describes the subject?* (Respond positively and continue brainstorming until you have several adjectives that start with the chosen letter.)

2 What Kind	1 Who/What	3 Did What	4 How	5 When	6 Where
magic	mom	mixed	merrily	in March	in the meadow
moody	Mary Beth	milkshakes	easily	one morning	at the market
male	a monkey	made a mess	miserably	on Monday	under the
mighty	mother	met a mouse	slowly	at midnight	mailbox
merry	Mick	moved melons		in a minute	to Minneapolis
mad	mouse	munched		during May	
magnificent	monster				
mean	melon				
mixed-up					
mysterious					

5. *Every tongue twister needs a verb to tell what the subject does. What can we say our subject does or did?* (Make a positive comment to reinforce choice of verbs beginning with the correct letter. Continue brainstorming until several verbs are listed.)

6. *Now we need to decide HOW, WHEN, and WHERE our subject did something.* (Brainstorm these elements with students, providing an example of any adverb or prepositional phrase that begins with the chosen letter if necessary as a model.)

Note: At some point your students may be unable to think of a word for a particular category that begins with the chosen letter. Assure the students that this is okay. Explain that when a writer can't think of a word that starts with the chosen letter, they have two choices: skip the brainstorming category or use a word that doesn't start with the chosen letter. Both are okay.

GROUP COMPOSING

1. Explain to students that now they can put the tongue twister together. Tell them that you will write their tongue twister on the board as they compose it. Guide students to select one word from each group they brainstormed and to place the words in logical order in a sentence. For example, suggest that they put the describing word before the noun subject. Words that tell how, when, or where might go at the beginning, in the middle, or at the end.

2. Tell students there are some other things they need to do to their tongue twister before they are finished. Ask how they should begin their tongue twister sentence.

(With a capital letter.) Then ask what punctuation is needed at the end of the tongue twister. (A period.)

3. Have students read their tongue twister as a group. Tell them to take a deep breath first so they can read as quickly as possible. Give a positive response such as "Super! We've composed a very original tongue twister that sounds great. Did your tongue get tied up or twisted when we read it?"

Inform students they are ready to plan and write their own tongue twisters. Instruct them to fold a piece of notebook paper into 8 columns. Lay the paper lengthwise as shown.

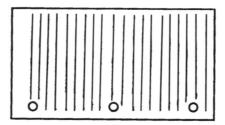

Fold your paper in half and crease it. Do this two more times to make 8 columns.

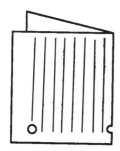 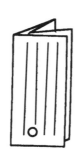 

Open the paper and press it flat with your hand. Please count the columns to make sure you have eight. (Wait as students count their columns.)

What Kind or How Many	Who or What	Did What	How	To Whom	Where	When	Why

Then instruct them to label the columns as follows:

Column 1—What Kind or How Many   Column 5—To Whom
Column 2—Who or What   Column 6—Where
Column 3—Did What   Column 7—When
Column 4—How   Column 8—Why

They can use the remaining columns for additional words if they need them.

Students should list their brainstorming ideas in the proper column. Then they should compose four tongue twisters from their lists.

Remind students that the first thing they need to do is choose a letter for their tongue twister. Ask them to write the letter they pick at the top of their paper and circle it.

RESPONDING TO STUDENT WRITING

1. As students are creating their tongue twisters, circulate around the room. Make positive comments and ask questions to help students add to or clarify their tongue twisters.

   If the student has captured a piece of a tongue twister particularly effectively, read that part out loud and make a **comment** such as "A 'meek machine' is an unusual kind of machine. Good thinking." or "Wow! I never realized so many adjectives began with the letter 's.' I particularly like the adjective 'spiny.' I can visualize a 'spiny' spoon."

   If a student is stuck on a particular part of his/her tongue twister, ask a **probing question** such as "What is something that starts with the letter "m" that a monster could do?" or "When did Freddy fix frosted frogs for his father?"

   • **Words out of grammatical order**

     If a student has placed a word incorrectly, reread the student's tongue twister out loud then make a comment such as "Where in your tongue twister is another place that you could put the word 'slowly'?"

   • **Periods at the end of a sentence**

     If the student remembered to place periods correctly, reread the student's tongue twister out loud then make a comment such as "I am glad you put a period at the end of this tongue twister. It lets me know now that I can stop and breathe!"

     If a student has forgotten the period, ask a question such as "What punctuation do you need at the end of your tongue twister to let your readers know that your tongue twister is over and that it is okay to breathe."

   • **Capital letters**

     If a student has forgotten to capitalize, ask a question such as "What should you do to the first word in your tongue twister to show you are beginning a new tongue twister?" or "When you use a person's name, what do you do to the first letter of the name?"

2. When students finish, ask them to find someone else who is done and quietly read their tongue twisters out loud to each other. Put these questions up on the board to help in revising.

Does the tongue twister make sense?   Yes   A little   No
Check off each of these parts the tongue twister has:
_____ a subject
_____ an adjective to describe the subject
_____ a verb
_____ at least one adverb telling how, when, or where
_____ five main words beginning with the same letter or sound
Does the tongue twister start with a capital letter?   Yes   No
Are the names of particular people, animals, and places capitalized?   Yes   No

Ask students to help their partner revise their tongue twister. Explain that if their tongue twister doesn't make sense, they need to decide if they need to add, change, or delete any words. After students have read and revised their tongue twisters, ask them to put a star by the two they like the best.

PUBLISHING

Tell students that they have written such "terribly terrific tongue twisters" that they are going to publish all of them in a book so that they can share them with the class and entertain their families and friends.

1. Give students four pieces of paper. Ask them to write one of their tongue twisters at the top of each page using their best handwriting.

2. In the center of each paper, ask them to make a large pencil illustration of the tongue twister.

3. Collect the finished pages, make copies of each, and staple the pages so that each person will get his or her own book.

4. Each day let three students read their tongue twisters to the class.

MODIFICATIONS TO ENCOURAGE BEGINNING WRITERS

- Shorten the task. Ask students to write only one or two tongue twisters and illustrate the best one.

- Limit the number of sentence parts that the tongue twisters must have.

- Guide students to choose one of the easier letters such as b, d, l, m, p, s, or t for the repeating sound and to stay away from vowels.

- Have the students write "Crazy Sentences." The brainstorming categories are the same, but no repeating sound is required. Here is an example.

     Who: Michael

     Did What: ate a million dead fish

     Where: on Main Street

     When: at 4:30 one dark and stormy night

     Why: because his feet were tired.

MODIFICATIONS TO CHALLENGE ADVANCED WRITERS

- Ask students to use the first letter in their first name for their first tongue twister, the next letter in their name for the next tongue twister, and so forth. Increase the number of tongue twisters students are asked to write.

- Direct a student to brainstorm a different letter and new lists for each different tongue twister.

- Ask students to write a tongue twister with ch, sh, wh, th, pr, sp, sw, tw, or other two letter beginnings. Example: "The cheerful child challenged the cheap chorus to chase a chilly chicken."

- Some students may not need to participate in the group composing. The group brainstorming may give these students enough structure to create good tongue twisters. You may only want to guide less able or less confident students through the group composing part of the lesson while allowing the rest of the students to begin earlier.

- More talented students may be able to brainstorm in their heads and may not need to fold notebook paper and write out all of the possible sentence parts.

- Ask a student who finishes early to put the class's completed tongue twisters in alphabetical order.

Index

Our
Terribly Terrific
Tongue Twisters

LESSON 9

CHECK WRITING

Even though check writing does not require putting thoughts into sentences or paragraphs, it is an important type of writing. Writing checks is very appealing to older students who see adults writing checks all the time. This lesson can be taught in conjunction with a math lesson or in your language arts program either as a short one day experience or spread out over a week or more.

OBJECTIVES

Students will write ten checks and keep track of expenditures in a check register. To do this, they will:

- Write today's date on each check.
- Write the full name of the person to whom the check is written.
- Capitalize proper names and titles of businesses.
- Write the amount of payment in both number and word form.
- Use legible handwriting.
- Write a reminder on the "memo" line telling what the check was for.
- Sign the check in cursive handwriting.
- Enter each financial transaction in the check register and keep a running balance.

MOTIVATORS

1. Ask students why people have checking accounts and why they write checks instead of using cash. (Good way to pay bills, safer than carrying cash, helps keep records of purchases/expenses.) Show your students your checkbook and how you keep track of the checks you write.

2. Tape a large check made out of a sheet of chart paper or butcher paper to the chalkboard and demonstrate writing a check for a really large amount such as four thousand sixty-eight dollars and thirty-two cents. Go through all six steps of check writing: date, to whom, amount in numbers, amount in words, memo, signature.

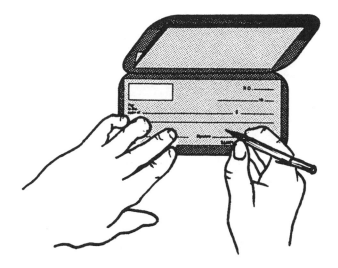

3. Have students construct their own checkbooks. Explain that they will get to write checks to "pay" for items and manage their own money.

Ahead of time duplicate 10 blank checks (two checks per day for one week), 3 check register pages, and 1 checkbook cover for each student. See reproducibles 1 and 2. Give each student the blank checks, check registers, checkbook cover, and a blank sheet of colored paper and provide the following instructions for constructing the checkbook.

(If you desire, checkbook covers can be made from sheets of colorful wallpaper instead of the copied forms. These covers look especially sharp! If you want this unit to last longer than a week, students can "purchase" new checks from you at a later date. Adding more checks now will make it very difficult to staple the checks to the checkbook cover.)

1. *Lay the blank sheet of colored paper on your desk and cover it with the checkbook cover.*

2. *Staple the checkbook cover and the colored sheet of paper together along both shorter edges.*

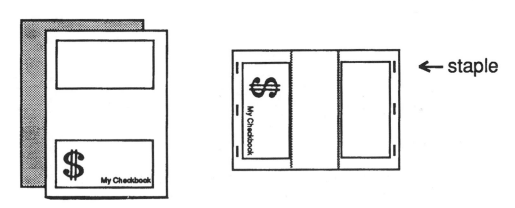

3. *Fold both sheets of paper together on the fold lines. Be sure that the checkbook cover always faces out. Crease the folds with your fingernail.*

4. *Fold the lower part of the checkbook up to make a pocket. Now staple along the right edge of the pocket three times. You should staple through all four sheets of the checkbook cover. Do not staple the left side yet. That's where the checks will be placed.*

5. *Next cut out your checks and stack them neatly.*

6. *Lay all of your blank checks on top of the pocket you made.*

7. *Next staple three times along the left edge through the checks and the two parts of the checkbook cover. Your checks must be loose on the right edge so that you will be able to tear them out.*

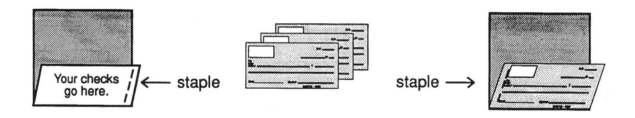

8. *Finally staple the check register pages to the inside of the checkbook cover above the blank checks.*

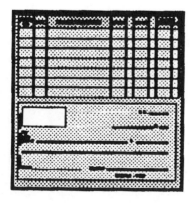

BRAINSTORMING

Tell students they will brainstorm ideas for checks they might write.

<table>
<tr><td colspan="2">To whom will the check be paid?</td><td>Memo</td></tr>
<tr><td colspan="2">Arnie Freeberg
Coast-to-Coast Hardware
Sun Mart Grocery
Stop and Go
Target</td><td>New ten speed bike
Movie tickets
Case of Diet Pepsi</td></tr>
<tr><td colspan="3">Amount of Check
$ 1.59 . . . . One dollar and fifty-nine cents
$76.00 . . . . Seventy-six dollars and no cents</td></tr>
</table>

Key Questions

1. *What is one item you would like to buy?*

2. *How much does the item cost? What will be the amount of the check? How many dollars? How many cents?* (Write the amount in numbers and words. Post a chart listing spellings of numbers and demonstrate using it. See Reproducible 9-3.)

3. *In what store might you buy the item? To whom will you make out the check?*

4. *Repeat this process for additional items and/or expenses.*

GROUP COMPOSING

Explain to students that you will help the class write a check, using the information from their brainstorming. Ask why they must use a pen and not a pencil when writing a check. (So that no one can change any information on the check.)

Writing the Check

1. Tell students the first thing they'll do is date their check. Ask what today's date is and elicit the correct way to write the date. (Capitalize month; comma after day.) As students supply information, fill in a sample check taped to the chalkboard.

2. Explain that on the next line (Pay to the order of _____) they will write the name of the person or business they are paying. Ask how they should begin a person's first and last name or the name of a business? (Capital letter.)

3. Have students choose an amount for the check. As you write the amount, explain that a dollar sign is written in front of the dollar amount and a decimal before the cents.

4. Explain that on the next line they will write the same amount in words. Point out that they should begin the amount with a capital letter. Have students look at a posted chart or a handout for the correct spellings of the numbers. Ask students why a check writer should begin the dollar amount as far left as possible. (So that no amount can be added in front of it.)

5. Elicit from students a word or phrase for the memo line that will help them remember how the money was spent. Ask what was the purpose of the check. What did they buy/purchase?

6. Ask what final thing is needed on their check. (A signature.) Explain that usually people write their signatures in cursive. Tell them that you will sign your own name because you must never write someone else's name on a check, not even for a joke. Tell them that is not legal.

NO. *500*

September 29, 19 *92*

Pay to the order of *K-Mart* $ *10.53*

Ten dollars and fifty-three cents

Memo _____   Signature *Darren Walker*

SAMPLE - VOID

Entering Information in Check Register

1. Explain that after they have written a check, they need to record the amount of the check they just wrote and subtract it from the balance so they can see how much money they have left.

2. Draw a check register on the blackboard or prepare a transparency showing the various parts: check number, date, financial transactions column, a payment or debit (subtracted out) column, a deposit or credit (added in) column, and a balance column.

3. Tell students that they will begin by depositing a payroll check of $200 which they have "earned." Show them how to enter $200 in the deposit column. Then enter today's date and add the deposit to the balance.

4. Next, demonstrate where the number of the check, the date, whom the check was written to (payee), and the amount should be recorded.

5. Finally, demonstrate how to subtract a check to get the running balance. Your students may need to calculate the subtraction problem on separate paper.

CHECK NO.	DATE	FINANCIAL TRANSACTIONS	PAYMENT		DEPOSIT		BALANCE	
—	2-31	Deposit Payroll Check	—		$200	00	$200	00
501	3-1	Stop and Go	$6	00			$194	00
502	3-6	Century Seven Theater	$4	00			$190	00
503	3-7	Moorhead Pet Vet	$27	00			$163	00

RESPONDING TO STUDENT WRITING

1. As students write their checks and record their transactions, circulate around the room. Hold mini-conferences with students who need assistance. As they complete one check and the corresponding register, ask them to double-check the number and word amounts they wrote, along with what they wrote and calculated in their check register. Bring together small groups of students to demonstrate this checking procedure.

2. If you want students to work toward particular learner outcomes, give each student a revising form designed to guide him/her to self evaluate. See reproducible Self Evaluation Checklist (9–4) at the end of this lesson.

PUBLISHING

Inform students that over the next week they will get a chance to deposit money in their checking account, pay bills by writing checks, and balance a checkbook register so they will know how much money is left.

MODIFICATIONS TO ENCOURAGE BEGINNING WRITERS

- Less able students often find more meaning and more motivation when check writing occurs in a simulation. Help students set up a weekly or monthly budget based on income and possible expenses. Then once or twice a day give them a chance to pay bills, deposit money to their account, balance their checkbook, and keep a register sheet to record transactions.

Set up and explain ways students may add money to their accounts such as weekly pay checks for work in each subject, bonuses for excellent assignments and tests, and rewards for good behavior and/or accurate records at the end of the month.

Also instruct students that they will have daily or weekly bills to pay such as rent for the use of their desks, fees for use of the pencil sharpener, and fines for turning in late assignments or talking out of turn and other misbehavior.

Begin by "giving" students a beginning balance of an even amount such as $90 or $400 and then make all their bills in even amounts.

MODIFICATIONS TO CHALLENGE ADVANCED WRITERS

- Ask high achievers to plan a budget including at least three of the following:
  - Where will you buy your food? Clothes? Toys?
  - How much will you spend on each?
  - How much will you spend for your home (or desk)?
  - To whom will you owe that?
  - What utilities will you need to pay?
  - Who will you pay these to?
  - How much will you spend for transportation?
  - To whom will you pay this?
  - How much for car/bike insurance?
  - What insurance company will you use?
  - How much will you put into savings?
  - Where will you put this money?
- Assign students to check the financial records of other students.

BLANK CHECKS

N O. _____

_____ 19 ___

Pay
to the
order of _____ $ _____

_____

Memo _____   Signature _____

SAMPLE - VOID

N O. _____

_____ 19 ___

Pay
to the
order of _____ $ _____

_____

Memo _____   Signature _____

SAMPLE - VOID

N O. _____

_____ 19 ___

Pay
to the
order of _____ $ _____

_____

Memo _____   Signature _____

SAMPLE - VOID

CHECK REGISTER PAGES

CHECK NO.	DATE	FINANCIAL TRANSACTIONS	PAYMENT		DEPOSIT		BALANCE	

CHECK NO.	DATE	FINANCIAL TRANSACTIONS	PAYMENT		DEPOSIT		BALANCE	

CHECK NO.	DATE	FINANCIAL TRANSACTIONS	PAYMENT		DEPOSIT		BALANCE	

Name: _____ Date: _____ (9-3)

WORDS FOR NUMBERS

One 1	Eleven 11	Twenty 20
Two 2	Twelve 12	Thirty 30
Three 3	Thirteen 13	Forty 40
Four 4	Fourteen 14	Fifty 50
Five 5	Fifteen 15	Sixty 60
Six 6	Sixteen 16	Seventy 70
Seven 7	Seventeen 17	Eighty 80
Eight 8	Eighteen 18	Ninety 90
Nine 9	Nineteen 19	One-Hundred . . . 100
Ten 10		

dollars   cents

69

SELF EVALUATION CHECKLIST

Reread your check and the record you made of it.

Check

1. Did you enter today's date?   Yes   No

2. Did you write the name of the person or business on the top line?   Yes   No

   Is the first letter of each part of the name capitalized?   Yes   No

3. Did you write the amount of the payment in number form?   Yes   No

   How clear and easy to read is your handwriting?   Hard to Read   Ok   Easy to Read

4. Did you write the amount of the payment in word form?   Yes   No

   How clear and easy to read is your handwriting?   Hard to Read   Ok   Easy to Read

5. Did you write a note to yourself telling what the check was for?   Yes   No

6. Did you sign your name in cursive handwriting at the bottom of the check?   Yes   No

Check Register

1. Did you enter your financial transaction in the check register?   Yes   No

2. What was your running balance? _____

   What did you find out when you double checked the balance?

   _____

I have carefully reviewed and revised my check and the check register.

_____

Signature

LESSON 10

CROSSWORD PUZZLES

Like adults, children of all ages enjoy doing crossword puzzles, but few have had a chance to make one. Composing crossword puzzles can be a challenge even though it requires only words and short phrases. While this lesson has been written to go with a science unit on the digestive system, use whatever topic your students have been studying in reading, science, social studies, or math. Crossword puzzles are a neat way to review information in a creative manner or to culminate a unit and share the knowledge acquired with others.

OBJECTIVES

Students will create a crossword puzzle and an answer key on a particular subject. To do this, they will:

- Choose 10 answers related to the particular subject.
- Generate several clues and choose the best clue for each answer.
- Enter the 10 answers on the crossword grid.
- Place approximately 5 answers going down and 5 across.
- Connect one letter of each answer to a previous answer.
- Spell each answer correctly.

MOTIVATORS

1. Bring in some crossword puzzles. Ask students if they have ever done a crossword puzzle. Explain that people enjoy crossword puzzles because they are fun, entertaining, and challenging.
2. Share a crossword puzzle that you have worked or have students help you work a crossword puzzle.

BRAINSTORMING

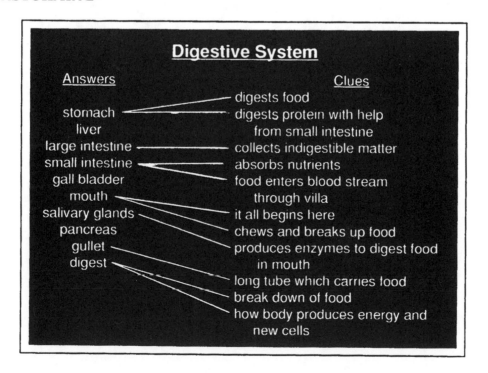

Key Questions

1. ***What have we been studying in*** _____***?*** (Inquire about whatever subject you want to review. As students reply, write their ideas on the chalkboard. Another approach would be to ask students for topics or hobbies in which they are interested.) ***If you could create your own crossword puzzle on anything you want, what would you pick?***

2. ***Since we have been studying*** the digestive system, ***it will be fun to make crossword puzzles to inform and entertain your friends. What are some of the pieces of the digestive system that we have studied? These will be the answers in our puzzle.*** (Allow plenty of time for students to think. As students reply, respond positively and write their ideas under "Answers" on the chalkboard. Continue brainstorming until at least *twelve ideas* are listed.)

   If students need more assistance, ask questions about different parts of the digestive system. If students have just studied the whole human body, you could brainstorm inner and outer body parts. For sports, you might use basketball, football, and volleyball as parts to brainstorm. If your students are studying Africa or another continent, brainstorming categories could be animals, resources, and countries.

3. ***Now we need to choose one of the answers and think of a clue for it. What clue can we give for*** _____***?*** (Allow plenty of time for students to think of clues. Continue brainstorming until at least two clues are listed for each answer. At first students won't know what makes a good clue. Gradually help students see that a good clue is one that is precise, yet does not give away the answer. At first when poor clues are given, respond positively and write the ideas under "Clues." Remember clues will be revised later.)

GROUP COMPOSING

Explain that a crossword puzzle has two parts: the answer key and the blank grid and clues that people use to solve the puzzle. Tell students that they need to create the answer key first.

Answer Key

1. Allow the class to decide which answers to include in the puzzle. Put a check or star by the ten answers they want to include. Explain that they have to spell answers correctly or no one will be able to work the crossword puzzle.

2. State that there are three rules for placing words on a crossword grid.

    Rule I: You are allowed to put only one letter in each square.

    Rule II: Each answer must share a common letter with another answer.

    Rule III: Use all capital or all lower case letters.

3. Point out that it is best to start with the long answers because they can be difficult to fit on the crossword grid. Have students choose a long answer from the list.

    Place the longest answer (large intestine) in the middle of a grid you have prepared. Model spelling the answer <u>without writing it</u> to see if the answer will fit. If there is room, print the letters in the blanks. Be sure to model writing in all capital or all lower case letters.

					S								
					M								
					A								
					L								
					L								
L	A	R	G	E		I	N	T	E	S	T	I	N	E
					N								
					T								
					E								
					S								
					T								
					I								
					N								
					E								

4. Remind students to put approximately the same number of answers horizontally as vertically. Explain that they need to connect as many answers as possible. This step sounds easy, but it isn't. Arranging the answers on the grid so that they overlap will be the most difficult part of this lesson. Help them with this step.

5. (Optional Step) Color in all the squares that are empty.

6. Next have students number all the answers. Start at the top and work left to right. Number the first answer #1. Put the number in the first square of the answer in the top left corner. Continue numbering all answers in that row no matter if they go down or across. Occasionally one number may serve two answers (i.e. a horizontal and a vertical answer).

Puzzle Grid and Clues

1. Tell students that now they can create the crossword puzzle grid. Lay another grid on top of the answer key. Trace the boxes with letters in them. Next trace over the numbers. Explain that the numbers will tell the puzzle readers where an answer begins for each clue. Tell them <u>not</u> to copy the answers because they want their friends to solve their puzzles.

2. Explain that next, they need to add clues to the crossword puzzle. Have students select a clue for each answer. Guide them to select clues that are correct but don't give the answer away. List all the down clues in order under the heading "Down." Then list all the across clues under the heading "Across."

3. State that the crossword puzzle needs a title. Add a title such as "The Digestive System." Under the title write "by Mr./Mrs./Miss/Ms _____'s Class."

The Digestive System
by
Ms. Jons 4th grade

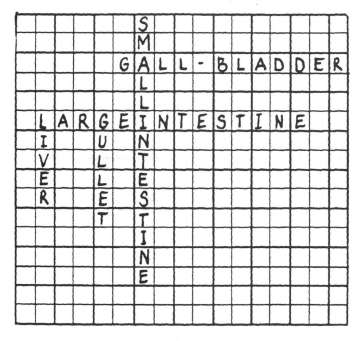

Clues

2. stores bile excreted from liver
3. collects indigestible materials

_____
_____
_____
_____

1. disolved food enters into blood stream here
3. secretes bile which helps in metabolism of fats
4. long tube for food to enter body

_____
_____

Tell students they now get to create their own crossword puzzle. Give each student or team of students two sheets of special graph paper. They will need at least a 16 by 16 grid for ten medium-sized words, see Reproducibles 10-1 and 10-2. Regular graph paper can be used by older students but is usually too small for elementary students' needs. Remind them to read their clues and answers to see if they match.

RESPONDING TO STUDENT WRITING

1. As students brainstorm, insert answers on their grids, and write clues, walk around the room. Encourage students to quietly try out clues on classmates to see if they get the desired answer. Ask them to make changes and corrections in the clues as needed.

Caution them not to change their answers on the crossword grid. Instead they should change the clue so it gets the correct answer.

2. If you want students to evaluate particular learner outcomes, give each student a peer revising form designed to help them with their evaluation. See Peer Revising Forms (Reproducibles 10–3 and 10–4) at the end of this lesson.

PUBLISHING

Tell students that they are going to share their crossword puzzles with each other and also with other students in the school. Inform them that three crossword puzzles will be published each week until everyone's crossword puzzle has been distributed. Explain solving each other's puzzles will be fun and will give them something to do in their spare time.

MODIFICATIONS TO ENCOURAGE BEGINNING WRITERS

• Have students insert only a smaller number of answers and clues (for example, four or five) on their grid.

• Require that only some answers connect on the grid. Encourage students to draw a shape around their grid that goes with the topic.

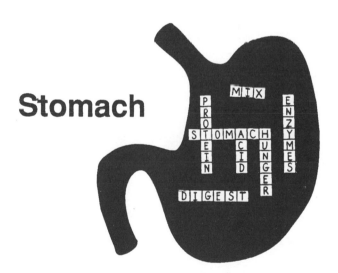

MODIFICATIONS TO CHALLENGE ADVANCED WRITERS

• Encourage students to create a crossword puzzle with 15 answers and clues.

• Suggest students put a word bank at the bottom of their crossword puzzle to help less able readers. The word bank should contain a list of all the answers needed for the crossword puzzle.

_____ 's Crossword Puzzle

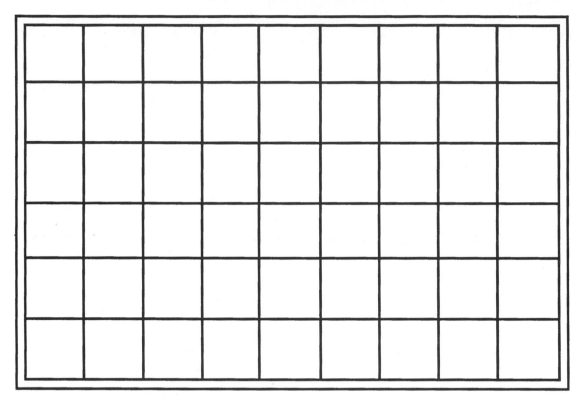

ACROSS:

_____

_____

_____

DOWN:

_____

_____

_____

Name: _____   **Date:** _____   (10-2)

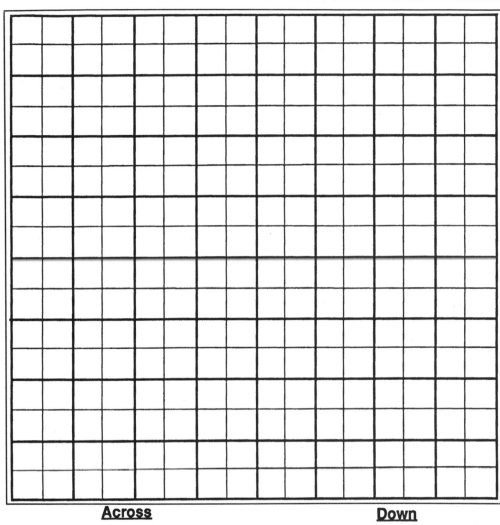

Across   **Down**

1. _____   1. _____

2. _____   2. _____

3. _____   3. _____

4. _____   4. _____

5. _____   5. _____

6. _____   6. _____

7. _____   7. _____

PEER EVALUATION CHECKLIST: ANSWER KEY

Read your classmate's answer key.

1. What is the subject of the crossword puzzle? _____

2. Are ten answers entered on the crossword puzzle grid? (Count them.)   Yes   No

3. Which answers are related to the subject? List them

Down	Across
1. _____	1. _____
2. _____	2. _____
3. _____	3. _____
4. _____	4. _____
5. _____	5. _____
6. _____	6. _____

4. Is one letter of each answer connected to another answer?   Yes   No

   Which answers are not connected? _____

   _____

5. Which answer or answers *may be* spelled wrong? _____

   _____

I have carefully studied my classmate's answer key for his/her crossword puzzle and have made some good suggestions.

_____
Signature of Classmate

I have carefully read what my classmate said about the answer key to my crossword puzzle, and I have used some ideas that I liked.

_____
Signature of Author

Name: _____ Date: _____ (10-4)

PEER EVALUATION CHECKLIST: CROSSWORD PUZZLE GRID AND CLUES

Read and rethink your classmate's crossword puzzle grid and clues.

1. What is the title of the crossword puzzle?

   _____

2. Is the author's name on the crossword puzzle?   Yes   No

3. Lay the crossword puzzle grid over the answer key. Are there enough squares for each answer to be spelled out?   Yes   No

   Which words need more room? _____

   _____

4. How easy to read is the crossword puzzle grid?   Easy to Read   OK   Difficult to Read

   What do you suggest to make it easier to read and more fun to work?

5. How many clues are listed down?   1   2   3   4   5   6 _____

   Which down clues are confusing?

   _____

   Which down clues are correct, but challenging? _____

6. How many clues are listed across?   1   2   3   4   5   6 _____

   Which across clues are confusing?

   _____

   Which across clues are correct, but challenging? _____

7. How easy to read are the clues?   Easy to Read   Ok   Difficult to Read

   What would make the crossword puzzle easier to read and more fun to work? _____

   _____

I have carefully studied my classmate's crossword puzzle and have made some good suggestions.

_____

Signature of Classmate

I have carefully read what my classmate said about my crossword puzzle, and I have used any ideas that I liked.

_____

Signature of Author

81

Section 2

NARRATIVE WRITINGS

NARRATIVE PARAGRAPHS

A simple narrative paragraph is a chronological sequence of events telling a story of something that may or may not have happened. Simple narratives consist of at least three events: a beginning, a middle, and an end. When writing a story, writers often use transition words and phrases such as "Long, long ago," "Suddenly," "A short while later," and "At last" to show time order.

A complex story consists of a longer and more complicated sequence of events. Complex stories usually have more than one character and often have both good characters (heroes) and bad characters (villains). Usually each of the main characters has a well developed personality. The main character confronts one or more problems and often makes a series of unsuccessful attempts to solve each problem. Finally a solution is found. Complex stories may also include a description of the setting, the characters' feelings, and a moral to the story.

Some Forms of Narrative Writing

Adventure Stories
Agendas
Anecdotes
Autobiographies
Biographies
Cartoon/Comic Strips
Chain-of-Events Stories
Choose-the-Ending Stories
Cliffhangers
Conversations/Dialogues
Creative Story Retellings
Fables
Fairy Tales
Family Histories

Fantasies
Folktales
Friendly Letters
Ghost Stories
Good News-Bad News Stories
Historical Novels
Jokes
Legends
Memoirs (Memories)
Movie Scripts
Mysteries
Myths
Novels
Parables

Parodies
Picture Story Books
Play Scripts
Puppet Shows
Science Fiction
Serialized Stories/Sequels
Short Stories
Slide Show Scripts
Spooky Stories
Surprise Endings
Tall Tales
Television Scripts
Time Lines

LESSON 11

HOW FAR WILL IT STRETCH?

Students enjoy stretching their imaginations as they write their own versions of this simple "journey." And they won't realize that they are learning to use prepositional phrases as descriptors. Note: In the modifications section, you'll find other journey formats that can be used.

OBJECTIVES

Students will write a story about stretching something. To do this, they will:

- Title their story "How Far Will It Stretch?"
- Begin the story with an introductory sentence such as "One day <u>main character</u> decided to see how far his/her rubber band would stretch."
- Tell where (place) the rubber band started to stretch in the second sentence.
- Use at least five prepositional phrases telling where the rubber band stretched.
- Conclude the story with an ending sentence such as "Then it broke! Ouch!"

MOTIVATORS

1. Read your students the story "How Far Will a Rubber Band Stretch?" by Mike Thaler (New York: Simon and Schuster Trade, 1990).
2. Bring in enough wide rubber bands for your students. Cut through one side of each rubber band so that the rubber band is one long piece. Give a rubber band to each student who agrees not to snap it or bother anyone. Ask students to hold each end of their rubber band with two fingers. Then use the following guided imagery.

    Close your eyes. Keep your rubber band loose until I tell you to stretch it. Imagine you're on our playground and you say "I wonder if this rubber band will stretch. I wonder if it will stretch around the swings." (Ask students to chorus "yes.") ***Everyone stretch your rubber band a little—just a little; we don't want it to break or fly away. Do you think it will stretch a little farther?*** (Ask students to whisper yes.)

Then continue this guided imagery past, over, through, between, and under things until students think the rubber band will break. At that point stop and collect the rubber bands before brainstorming.

Rubber Band

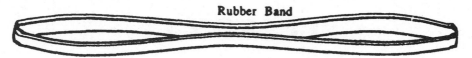

3. Get a long piece of string or a big ball of yarn. Wrap it over chairs, around desks, and between objects as you talk out loud. Say, *"I'm going to pretend this yarn is a rubber band and I'm curious how far it will stretch before it breaks. I'm going to go over to* (Insert a student's name) *chair, under _____ desk, through _____ two hands."* Continue in this manner using other prepositional phrases to explain what you are doing. Involve as many students and objects as possible. End by saying, "Oh No! It broke!" At the same time slowly pull the yarn back to you.

BRAINSTORMING

Explain to students that you will help them brainstorm ideas for a class story about a rubber band.

Key Questions

1. *Where could this story take place? Where could it begin?* (Allow plenty of time for students to think. As students reply, respond positively and write their ideas on the chalkboard. Continue brainstorming until many ideas are listed.)

> It all started _____.
>
> in my backyard
> at the zoo
> downtown while we were shopping
> in my brother's bedroom
> on a farm

2. *What object could we stretch the rubber band over?* (Write students suggestions under the heading "over.")

3. *What could the rubber band go around? Who or what could we wrap it around?* (Write suggestions under the heading "around.")

4. *What place could the rubber band go into? What could the rubber band squeeze between? What could the rubber band go behind?* (Write suggestions under the appropriate heading.)

over	around	into	between	behind
my dog	the stove	the kitchen	the two	the refrigerator
Mom's bed	the couch	a closet	bookcases	the clock
the TV	Dad's stereo	the dog food	the bikes	a toilet
a plant	the new lamp	the garage	the kitchen	the piano
the dining			chairs	
room table				

GROUP COMPOSING

1. Tell students that they'll call their story "How Far Will It Stretch?" Ask what they need to remember when writing the important words in a title and what punctuation is needed at the end of this title. (To capitalize; question mark.)

2. Begin the story by writing on the chalkboard "One day _____ decided to see how far his/her rubber band would stretch." Have students decide on a name to insert in the blank.

3. Next ask students to select a place from their list to tell where the story started.

How Far Will It Stretch?

One day _Tara_ decided to see how far his/(her) rubber band would stretch. _Tara_ started in her _brother's bedroom_ . It stretched _____.

over my dog,
around the new lamp,
into the garage,
between the bikes,
behind the piano

Then it broke! Ouch!

---

4. Focus students' attention on the lists of prepositional phrases on the blackboard. Ask them to think about what they would like to stretch the rubber band over. When students make a selection, write it in the sentence, "It stretched _____.

5. Guide students to choose one item from each of the remaining lists to tell what they want the rubber band to stretch around, where they want it to go into, what it should squeeze between, and what it should stretch behind.

6. Write the prepositional phrases in the sentence, explaining that commas are needed to separate them. Ask students what punctuation is needed at the end of this really long sentence to tell the reader he/she can breathe? (A period.)

7. Inform students that they'll end their story with "Then it broke! Ouch!"

Tell students that now they are ready to compose their own "How Far Will It Stretch?" stories.

RESPONDING TO STUDENT WRITING

1. As students write their "How Far Will It Stretch" story, walk around the room and make positive comments about creative and interesting places their rubber bands are going. Hold brief conferences with students who need assistance.

   - Read back portions of students' stories so that they can hear what they have written so far.

   - Make one or two positive comments and ask questions about who the main character is, where the rubber band started, and the prepositional phrases telling where the rubber band stretched.

2. As students move into the final stages of writing, ask them to find a partner and do the following:

   - Read their stories out loud to each other.

   - Listen to see if the writer gives a clear picture of who the character is, where the situation started, and to what places the rubber band was stretched.

   - Together think of any additions or changes they might make to help their story sound more interesting.

   - Proofread their story to check that the words in the title were capitalized, there are commas between the places the rubber band was stretched, and an exclamation mark was placed after the word "Ouch."

PUBLISHING

Tell students that they'll publish their stories on paper strips which will be pasted together to show how far their rubber bands stretched. Invite students to share their journeys with each other so that their friends can enjoy the stories and see how far each rubber band went.

1. Before class begins, duplicate and cut out 10 strips of pink, tan, or white paper about 1¾ inches wide and 11¾ inches long. A reproducible sheet to allow students to do the cutting has been included. See Reproducibles 11–1 to 11–3 at the end of this lesson. Note: If your students don't like to rewrite, give them these strips when they start to compose. Otherwise, have students rewrite the parts of their sentence on the strips now.

2. Instruct students to put glue on one end of a strip and then lay the end of a new strip so that it overlaps the first strip by about ½ inch. They should continue gluing the strips in order until all the strips of paper have been attached in one long line.

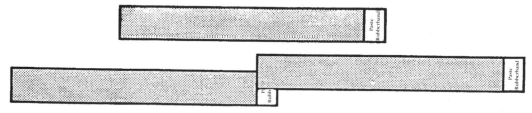

3. Lay the "stretched rubber bands" around the room so that people can read and enjoy.

Alternate Publishing Idea

Make copies of the lined reproducible sheet 11-1, 11-2, and 11-3 at the end of this lesson and have students write their story on them.

MODIFICATIONS TO ENCOURAGE BEGINNING WRITERS

- If the difficulty is in coming up with interesting objects for the rubber band to go around, under, through, and so on, give students a pad of paper and a pencil. Ask them to take a short walk around your room or school and write down five places where their rubber band could go.
- If the difficulty is in coming up with prepositions, provide students with a list of prepositional phrases.

Prepositions		
above	by	out
across	down	over
around	in	past
behind	in front of	through
below/beneath	inside/into	toward
beside	near	under/underneath
between	on top of	up

- Suggest that students draw a map of their story before beginning to write.

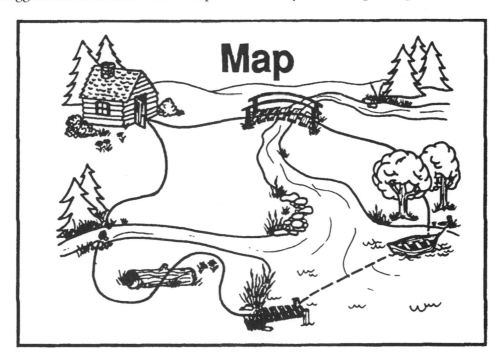

MODIFICATIONS TO CHALLENGE ADVANCED WRITERS

- Ask students what else could be stretched besides a rubber band and what animal or machine could do the stretching. Supply a list of prepositions.

- Suggest students write a different "journey format" story such as

    "_____ the _____ went on (an imaginary journey, a walk, a trip, a flight) past the _____, around a _____, into the _____, and arrived back in time for _____."

Example

Darrel the dog went on a walk around the lake, over the rocks, between the spruce trees, past the fire hydrant, under Mr. Drake's fence, into the flower bed, past the dog catcher and arrived back in time to watch *Those Crazy Animals* on cable television.

- Have students add a setting and how the character was feeling to their journey such as

    "One evening as the sun was setting there was a wolf who was feeling very hungry."

- Introduce a delightful book, *Klippity Klop* by Ed Emberley (Boston: Little, Brown & Co., 1974), which has a more complicated journey format.

    "_____ and _____ went for a *(trip or journey)*. They came to _____ and *(rode, walked, flew, swam)* over it. They came to a ____ and *(rode, walked, flew, swam)* across it. They came to _____ and *(rode, dove, walked, flew, swam)* under it." This keeps repeating until: They came to a _____ and looked in . . . and a _____ looked out . . . and YELLED at them!"

    At this point the characters reverse their ride until they reach home safely.

(11-1)

How Far Will It Stretch?

Paste rubber band here.	Paste rubber band here.	Paste rubber band here.	Paste rubber band here.	Paste rubber band here.
One day _____ decided to see how far his/her rubberband would stretch.	It all started in _____ .	It stretched		

(11-2)

Paste rubber band here.	Paste rubber band here.	Paste rubber band here.	Paste rubber band here.	Paste rubber band here.

Paste
rubber band
here.

Paste
rubber band
here.

Paste
rubber band
here.

Paste
rubber band
here.

Paste
rubber band
here.

How Far Will It Stretch?

by _____

_____

_____

_____

_____

_____

_____

_____

_____

_____

_____

_____

_____

_____

_____

_____

LESSON 12

COMIC STRIPS

Students all over the world enjoy reading comic strips. Now you can build on that interest and have your students write and publish their own comic strips for each other. Without realizing it, they will be learning to write their thoughts chronologically. You can use the pictures provided or cut out real comic strips with an action sequence and have students "white-out" the dialogue.

OBJECTIVES

Students will write a comic strip based on a three-picture action sequence. To do this, they will:

- Order three pictures chronologically to create a story.
- Write at least one sentence for each picture or frame.
- Use at least two transition words or phrases (such as "Early one morning," "All at once," and "Finally") to move the story along.
- Capitalize characters' names and the first word of each sentence.
- End each telling sentence with a period.

MOTIVATORS

1. Ask students what their favorite comic strips are. Have them cut out and bring in one of their comic strips to read to the group. Post these around the room.
2. Share one of your favorite comic strips with students. Before hand, "white-out" the dialogue, cut apart the frames and mix them up, and write a new sentence for each picture, incorporating transition words. As you read each sentence, ask students to tell which picture it goes with. If you wish, you may use these sentences and the comic strip.

> Early one morning Cleo saw her friend Jackie sitting on a fence. Cleo thought, "That looks like fun." Then she climbed upon the fence to talk to Jackie. Suddenly the fence collapsed. Crash! As Cleo fell to the ground, Jackie chirped

loudly, "Please! Don't crush me!" Soon Cleo left and Jackie thought, "Wow! That was a close one. I could have been smashed as flat as a pancake."

Ask students which words helped them figure out the order of events in the story. (Early one morning, then, suddenly, soon.) Point out that these words are called transition words. Explain that authors use transition words to tell the reader when things happen and to help move the story along.

3. Tell students they are going to make their own comic strips but first the class will write one together. Show a sct of three enlarged pictures or make an overhead transparency of a three part comic strip. Cut the pictures apart so that they can be moved around. See Reproducibles 12–1 and 12–2 at the end of this lesson.

   Ask students to study the pictures and suggest how they could be arranged to make an interesting story. Accept any suggested order with a positive comment such as "That order would make a terrific story!"

Request other ways to order the pictures that would make interesting stories. Finally have a quiet student choose one of the suggested orders for group brainstorming.

BRAINSTORMING/GROUP COMPOSING

Tell students they now need to think of some sentences to go with each picture. Ask questions to elicit ideas for each picture.

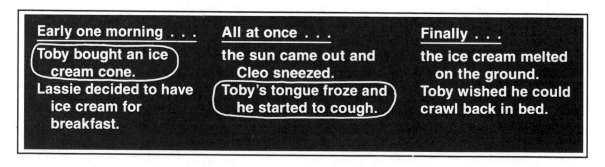

Key Questions

*1. **What do you think happened early one morning?*** (Allow wait time. As students answer, respond positively and write their ideas on the chalkboard.) ***What else could have happened early one morning?***

2. *Which one of these ideas should we use for the beginning of our story?* (Circle the idea students select.)

3. *All at once what happened?* (Elicit ideas for the second picture and write them on the board.)

4. *Which one of these events should we choose?* (Circle the idea.)

5. *Finally what happened?* (Write the suggestions for the third picture on the board.)

6. *Which one of these ideas should we use for our ending?* (Circle the idea, then go back and read the sentences in order. Ask students if they make sense and go with the pictures.)

Tell students they're ready to write their own comic strips. Give each student an envelope containing three pictures cut apart. You'll find reproducible pictures at the end of this lesson. (12-1 and 12-2)

Then ask students to write these brainstorming categories on their papers:

Early one morning . . .   All at once . . .   Finally . . .

Once students have written the categories, tell them they can start brainstorming a beginning, middle, and an end for their story.

RESPONDING TO STUDENT WRITING

1. While the students are writing their comic strips, walk around the room. Talk to those who need help. Focus especially on their ideas.

   • Make **positive comments** about students' ideas and use of transitions such as "Your transition words 'late one dark night' will certainly help your readers know when your story starts" or "The way you ordered your pictures is really clever."

   • Ask **specific questions** if students are having trouble coming up with ideas such as "Suddenly what happened?" or "What name could you give to the leopard in your story?"

   • Make specific **positive comments** and **ask questions** about correct use of mechanics such as "The period at the end of your first sentence helps the reader to pause before reading the next sentence" or "How should you start your character's name so everyone will know that it's her name?"

2. As students move into the final stages of their drafts, ask them to find a revising partner and follow these steps, which you have written on the chalkboard or a chart.

   • Reread your comic strip out loud to your revising partner.

   • Listen to see if your story makes sense.

   • Count how many transition words you used to signal the passage of time.

   • Decide whether you need to add more transitions to signal the passage of time.

PUBLISHING

Have students paste their pictures in order on a special sheet (see Reproducible 12–3) and write a sentence on the lines below each picture. Tell students that their comic strips will be placed on a special table in the school library so that students in other grades, teachers, and staff in the school can read and enjoy their comic strip characters.

MODIFICATIONS TO ENCOURAGE BEGINNING WRITERS

- Once students have ordered the three pictures, ask for only one sentence that tells what happened instead of three sentences.
- Provide the transition words for each sentence by writing time order words on the students' papers ahead of time.
- Write the cartoon about their favorite super hero or heroine.
- During the revising step, ask questions such as "What is the best part of your story?" This will help students with poor self images learn to reinforce themselves positively.
- For low achievers who tire quickly or students with poor fine motor control, plan to publish rough drafts instead of having them recopy on clean paper.

MODIFICATIONS TO CHALLENGE ADVANCED WRITERS

- Encourage students to write dialogue for each picture. During brainstorming, instead of asking "What happened?", ask "What did _____ say?" and "How did _____ respond?"
  Remind students that the characters exact words and thoughts will go into speech and sound bubbles instead of quotation marks.
- Provide four, five, six, or more pictures to order. Then require students to write one or more sentences for each picture. Make available additional transition words such as the following:

Beginnings:	Late one evening	Just after lunch	It all began
Middles:	Meanwhile	Ten minutes	Then
	Soon	Suddenly	Soon
	Just then	Afterwards	Next
	Later	But now	Later on
Endings:	Finally	At last	But tomorrow

- Show students some of these special speech, thought, and sound bubbles and ask them to incorporate them in their comic strips. Thought bubbles can contain pictures, words, or nonspoken thoughts. Wild words such as "crash" show action, strong emotion, or conflict. Spiked sound bubbles often indicate shouting. For additional information consult "Do Your Own Comics" by Herb Kohl. *Teacher Magazine,* Jan. 1977.

Thought Bubbles

Wild Words and Sound Bubbles

- Encourage students to create cartoons that cause readers to chuckle about real life problems.
- Suggest students write and illustrate their own action sequence comics. Cut long 3- to 5-inch wide strips of butcher paper or use adding machine tape. Have students use a ruler to divide the paper into rectangles.

COMICS

LESSON 13

PLAY DIALOGUE

Creating puppets is an excellent method for getting students motivated to write. Use the puppet patterns provided or have students create their own. As they are writing an ordered sequence of dialogue, your students will also learn to use quotation marks and commas correctly. Your students will love to publish their short plays by performing their compositions orally.

OBJECTIVES

Students will write play dialogue for two characters. To do this, they will:

- Write at least six sentences of conversation.
- Use four or more verbs (such as "exclaimed," "whispered," "replied," "shouted," "asked," or "pleaded") in the dialogue instead of the word "said."
- Place quotation marks before and after what's been said to indicate a particular character's exact words.
- Indent/begin a new paragraph each time a *different* character speaks.
- Capitalize the first word in each sentence and the first word in each quotation. Put periods and question marks inside the quotation marks.
- Capitalize the proper names of characters.

MOTIVATOR

Hold up two puppets you have made. Explain that today students will get to make a puppet of their own. Show reproducible puppets 13-1 through 13–10 at the end of this lesson. Tell them to think about what their puppet wants to say as they make it because later they will get to create their own puppet shows.

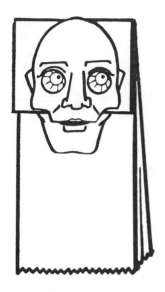

Give the following directions for making a puppet.

1. ***Choose one of these puppet faces.*** (Pass out several different puppet patterns. See Reproducibles 13–1 through 13–10.)

2. ***Color the two parts of your puppet's face and then glue them onto a piece of construction paper or tag board. While you are creating your own puppet, think about what its name could be and what it might want to talk about.***

3. ***Next, carefully cut out your puppet's face.***

4. ***Take a paper bag.*** (Get bags size #4 for 1–3 graders and bags size #6 for 4–6th graders. Size #8 bags are great for adult hands. Puppets fit all three sized sacks.) ***Lift the fold. Glue the puppet's mouth under the fold.*** (Hold up a bag and point to where to glue the puppet's mouth. It is important to glue the mouth piece on first so that the mouth will be properly aligned.)

5. ***Now glue the head to the bottom of the bag so that it lines up with the mouth piece.*** (Ask students to insert one hand into the bag and work the mouth of the puppet to see if the mouth was glued in the right place. Demonstrate. Finally tell students to put their puppets away for a while to let the glue dry.)

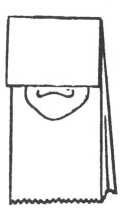

BRAINSTORMING

Put on the two puppets you showed your students earlier. Have the class brainstorm names for the puppets and a topic for them to talk about.

Key Questions

1. *What would be a good name for this puppet?* (As students answer, respond positively and write their ideas on the chalkboard. Continue brainstorming until you have several names.)
2. *What could we call my other puppet?*
3. *Out of all the ideas we came up with, which name do you like for our robot? What should we call the dinosaur puppet?*

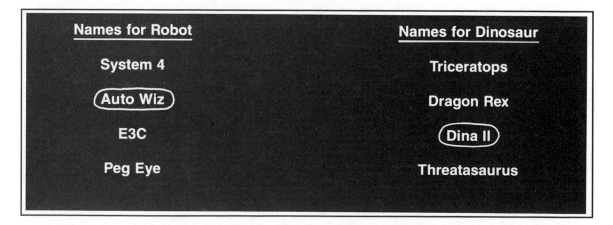

Names for Robot	Names for Dinosaur
System 4	Triceratops
(Auto Wiz)	Dragon Rex
E3C	(Dina II)
Peg Eye	Threatasaurus

4. *Our puppets would like to talk to each other but they don't know where to start. What can our puppets talk about?* (List topics on the chalkboard.)

5. Which topic do you like best?

GROUP COMPOSING

State that since names for the puppets and a topic for them to talk about have been chosen, the next step is to plan what the puppets are going to say.

1. Ask volunteers to suggest dialogue for the first puppet. Praise their ideas and write them on the chalkboard. Then ask what is needed to show that these are the exact words of the puppet. (Quotation marks.) Guide students in placing the marks correctly.

2. Point out that one more thing is needed to separate the words "_____ said" from the direct quotation. Place a comma after "said" and before the quotation.

3. Repeat the same steps for the second puppet, encouraging students to think of other strong verbs to replace "said" such as "whisper," "shout," "cry," and so on. Explain that students should start a new paragraph each time the speaker changes.

4. Continue eliciting dialogue until a short scene is completed. Then divide the class in half and have one half read aloud the first puppet's exact words and the other half read the second puppet's exact words.

(Title)

Auto Wiz said,   "Who are you?

                                                                          ?

      "Hey, I'm boss around here. Who are you?"   replied   Dina II   .

Auto Wiz whispered, "My space ship crashed a few microns by the stream."

      "Well, you can't stay here!   exclaimed   Dina II   .

Auto Wiz shouted,   "I want to go home!

Tell students they are now ready to create their own play. Ask them to find a partner with whom they can work quietly. Then suggest they use their puppets to help create the play dialogue. Each puppet should speak at least four times.

Instruct the teams when they finish their puppets' dialogue to quietly practice the play with their partner until everyone has completed their dialogue. Explain that later, if they choose, they will have an opportunity to perform in a class puppet show.

RESPONDING TO STUDENT WRITING

1. As pairs of students create their puppets' conversations, walk around the room. Visit first with teams who are having difficulty choosing a topic. Then hold short one- to two-minute conferences with the other students.

   • Read back portions of students' dialogue so that they can hear what they have created so far.

   • Give positive feedback for using powerful verbs like "screamed" and "shouted."

   • Assess whether or not the students' dialogue is connected in a meaningful sequence.

2. If you want students to self evaluate particular learner outcomes, give each student a revising form designed to guide self evaluation. See the Team Evaluation Checklist (reproducible 13–8) at the end of this lesson.

PUBLISHING

Put a table or two desks about two feet in front of a bookcase or wall. Drape the table with a large tablecloth or blanket.

Offer students a chance to entertain the whole class by performing their puppet show. Students may also want to perform their plays for a lower grade.

MODIFICATIONS TO ENCOURAGE BEGINNING WRITERS

- Give students a sheet that has words for "said" such as "suggested," "bragged," "demanded"; blanks for the dialogue; and punctuation assistance (quotation marks, commas, and end punctuation) already provided. Two types of reproducibles (13-11 and 13-12) have been included at the end of this lesson.

- Post a list of words for "said" on a wall during composing. Ask students to reread the list each time they need a word for "said." Or duplicate the list of words (13-11) for "said" at the end of this lesson.

Other Words for "Said"		
whispered	declared	replied
shouted	muttered	objected
chirped	cried	explained
exclaimed	insisted	hollered
whined	screamed	growled
denied	responded	answered
shrieked	called	echoed
complained	gasped	protested
mumbled	howled	announced
yelled	argued	vowed
barked	sighed	concluded
reported	roared	asked

MODIFICATIONS TO CHALLENGE ADVANCED WRITERS

- Ask for a longer conversation such as a total of ten comments from *each* puppet.

- Require that the conversation evolve around a problem the two characters have and how the problem is solved. Note: Students will need to brainstorm a list of problems and possible solutions before they begin writing the dialogue.

- Direct students to use at least three transition words or phrases in their dialogue to signal the passage of time. For example a student could write, "Suddenly Tricia screamed, 'Get out of my bedroom!'" When the play is presented, have a narrator read the parts that are not direct quotes.

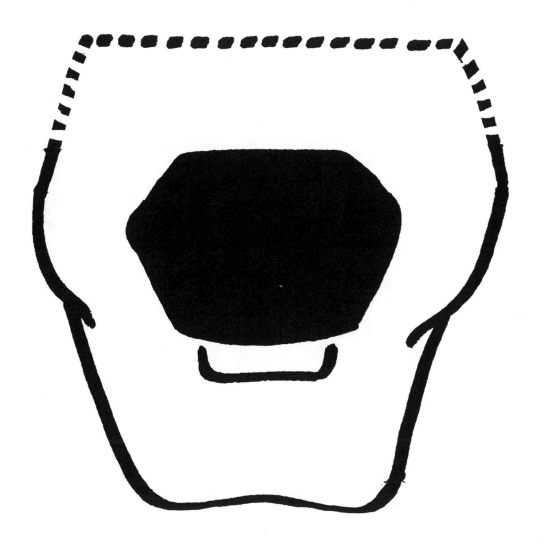

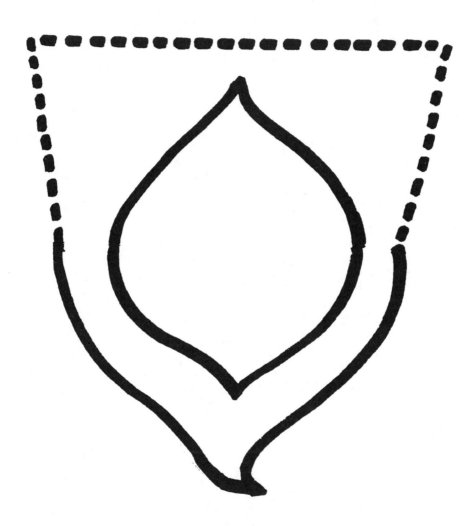

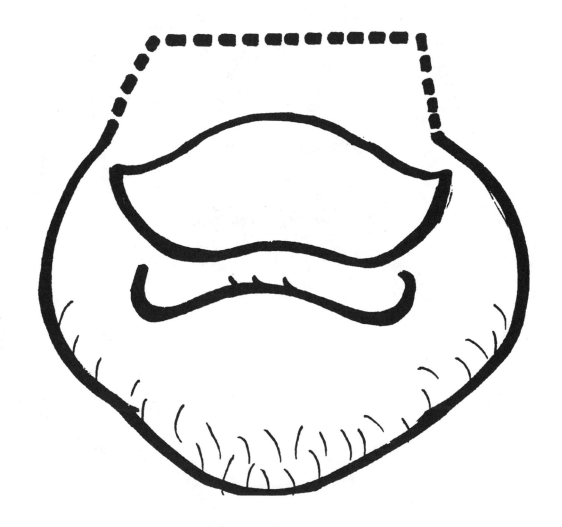

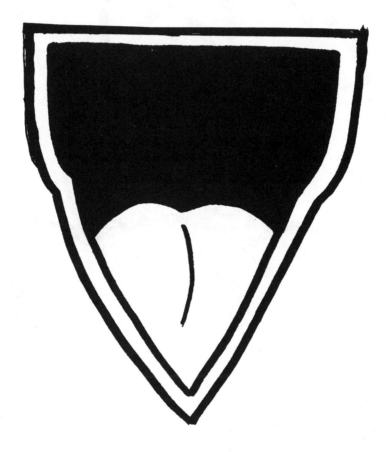

(13-5 continued)

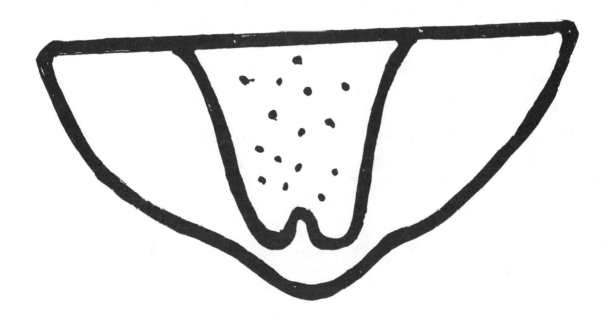

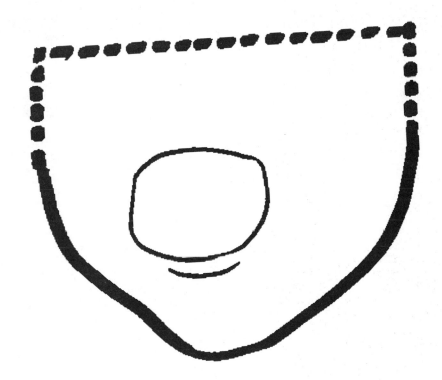

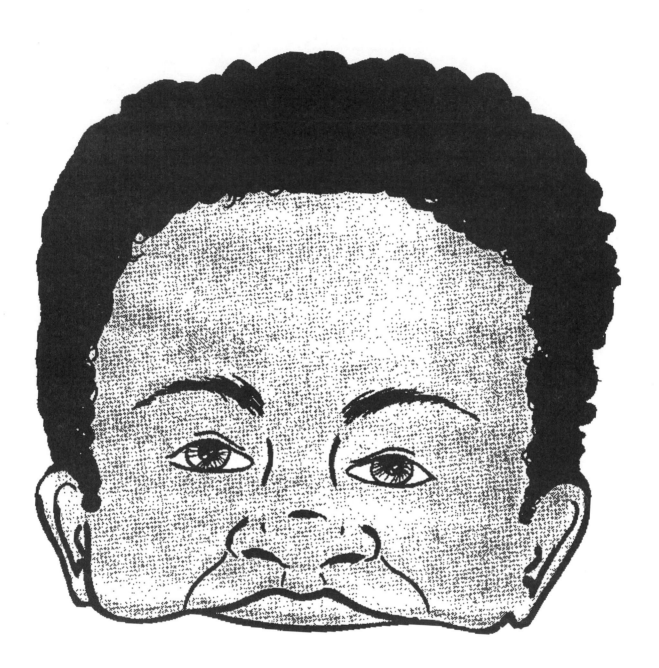

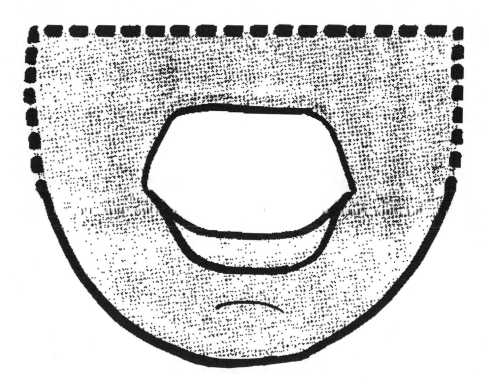

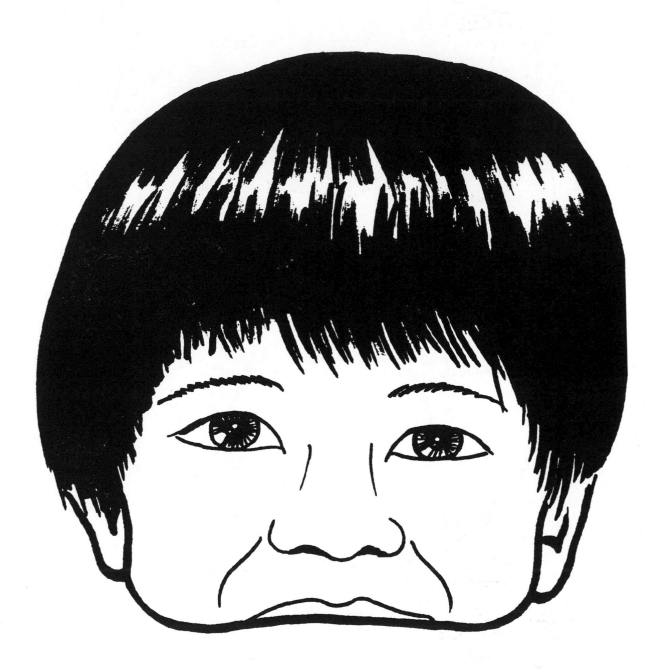

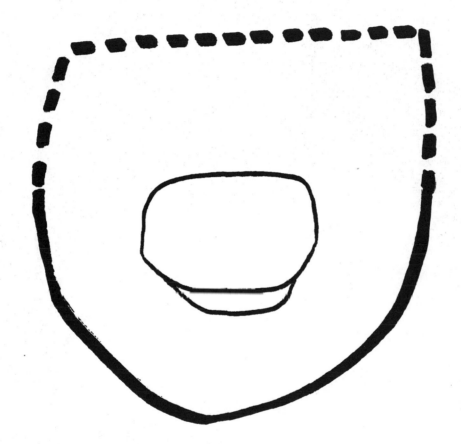

(13-9 continued)

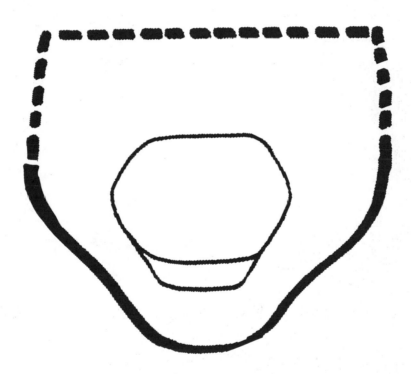

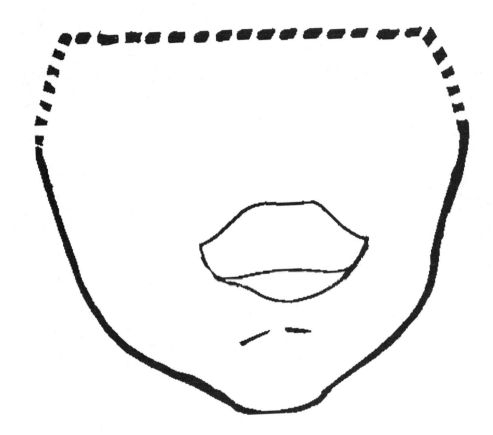

Other Words for "Said"

whispered	declared	replied
shouted	muttered	objected
chirped	cried	explained
exclaimed	insisted	hollered
whined	screamed	growled
denied	responded	answered
shrieked	called	echoed
complained	gasped	protested
mumbled	howled	announced
yelled	argued	vowed
barked	signed	concluded
reported	roared	asked

Other Words for "Said"

whispered	declared	replied
shouted	muttered	objected
chirped	cried	explained
exclaimed	insisted	hollered
whined	screamed	growled
denied	responded	answered
shrieked	called	echoed
complained	gasped	protested
mumbled	howled	announced
yelled	argued	vowed
barked	signed	concluded
reported	roared	asked

_____
(Title of Play)

_____ said, "_____

_____."

"_____

_____." replied _____.

_____ whispered, "_____

_____"

"_____

_____." exclaimed _____.

_____ shouted, "_____

_____"

"_____

_____!" screamed _____.

_____ sighed, "_____

_____"

"_____

_____." cried _____.

By _____ and _____

TEAM EVALUATION CHECKLIST

Reread and rethink your play.

1. What are the names of your two characters? How many sentences did character speak?

   _____ _____

   _____ _____

   Did you capitalize the name of each character?   Yes   No

2. What are the four verbs you used instead of "said" to make your play dialogue more interesting?

   _____ _____ _____ _____

3. Did you put quotation marks before and after the actual words of each character?
   Yes   No

4. Is the first word in every quotation capitalized?

   Yes   No

5. Did you begin a new paragraph and indent it each time another character spoke?

   Yes   No

We have carefully evaluated and revised our play.

_____

Signature of Playwriter

_____

Signature of Playwriter

LESSON 14

"VERY BAD DAY" STORIES

Everyone can relate to having a bad day. Putting our thoughts and feelings into words and telling others about it helps us feel better. This lesson can be adapted for writing about a sad day, a wonderful party, an exciting track meet, a lazy Saturday afternoon, or a fantastic holiday.

OBJECTIVES

Students will write a story about a very bad day. To do this, they will:

- Title the story "_____'s Terrible, Horrible, No Good, Very Bad Day."
- Write about at least four events that are ordered chronologically.
- Begin at least three of the four events with transition words (such as "Early one morning," "After breakfast," and "At supper") to move the story along.
- Follow each event with the repeating sentence "I could tell it was going to be a terrible, horrible, no good, very bad day."
- Indent the first line of each new paragraph.
- Capitalize the main words in the title and all proper names.

MOTIVATORS

1. Tell students that you have a favorite book that tells about a boy named Alexander who has a bad day. Read *Alexander and the Terrible, Horrible, No Good, Very Bad Day* by Judith Viorst (New York: Atheneum, 1972) to your students. Then ask, "What made Alexander's day bad?"

2. Share your own version of a very good or very bad day. Ask students to tell about a day that they have had recently.

3. Read this fourth grader's version of a bad day.

THE TERRIBLE, HORRIBLE, NO GOOD DAY

It all began in bed. Julie's covers got stuck to her bed. After that she knew that it was going to be a terrible, horrible, no good, very bad day. During breakfast she opened the milk and it squirted all over her blouse. She knew it was going to be a terrible, horrible, no good, very bad day. Later that afternoon all the kids that she was babysitting started to cry, all at once! That was the end of Julie's terrible, horrible, no good, very bad day.

BRAINSTORMING

Tell students the class will write a class story about a bad day before they write their own stories.

Key Questions

1. ***First we need to decide whose bad day we're going to write about. Who could our group story be about? Who else would make an interesting character for our group story?*** (As students answer, respond positively and write their ideas on the chalkboard.)

2. Which character should we choose for our group story?

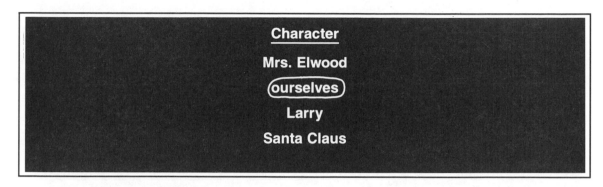

Character

Mrs. Elwood

(ourselves)

Larry

Santa Claus

3. When authors write stories, they use transition words to help their readers know in what order the events in the story occur. What words can we use to tell when the events in our story occur? (If your students are advanced writers, you may want to reread Judith Viorst's book and have your students jot down the various transition words she used. Or you could share a few of your own ideas for transition words and then lead your students to brainstorm others. With beginning writers it is best for the teacher to choose the transition words for them. Write transition words such as "Before school," "During lunch," "At recess," "On the way home," and so on, on the chalkboard.)

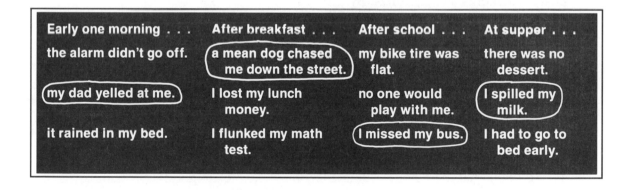

Early one morning . . .	After breakfast . . .	After school . . .	At supper . . .
the alarm didn't go off.	a mean dog chased me down the street.	my bike tire was flat.	there was no dessert.
my dad yelled at me.	I lost my lunch money.	no one would play with me.	I spilled my milk.
it rained in my bed.	I flunked my math test.	I missed my bus.	I had to go to bed early.

4. What is something terrible that could happen to you early one morning? (As students answer, respond positively and write their ideas on the chalkboard.) *What's one more event that could start your day off poorly?*

5. After breakfast what could happen to you on a very bad day?

6. On a horrible day what could happen at school?

7. What could happen after school on a terrible day?

8. At supper what could go wrong?

GROUP COMPOSING

1. Tell students that they need to choose a title for their story. Remind them of Judith Viorst's book *Alexander and the Terrible, Horrible, No Good, Very Bad Day* and ask how they might change that title to fit their story. (Our Terrible, Horrible, No Good, Very Bad Day). Explain that this is a good title because it really tells what their story will be about.

> ### Our Terrible, Horrible, No Good, Very Bad Day
>
> **Early one morning my dad yelled at me. I knew right then it was going to be a terrible, horrible, no good, very bad day** _____

2. Comment that students have brainstormed many events that could happen on a bad day. Now they must choose one from each list to include in their group story. Guide students to choose an event from the first list.

3. Remind students of the line that is often repeated in Judith Viorst's book. Add the repeating sentence next in the story.

4. Ask students to choose an event from the next list. Then have them read the repeating line out loud so you can write it.

5. Continue this procedure for the third and fourth events.

6. Ask students to recall the powerful conclusion that Judith Viorst used in her book. (Some days are like that.) Explain that this would be a good ending for their paragraph as well. It is an important part of the story because it teaches a lesson to remember when one is having a bad day. Add the concluding sentence.

7. Have students reread the group story to see if any changes should be made.

8. Tell students that their stories about a terrible, horrible, no good, very bad day need to include at least four events.

RESPONDING TO STUDENT WRITING

1. While students write their "Very Bad Day" stories, walk around the room. Individually confer with children who need help. Give positive feedback and ask questions. Focus especially on their ordering of events in a time sequence, the use of transition words/ phrases, and how each unfortunate event added to the bad day.

- Make as many positive comments as you can about students' strengths such as "I've noticed that you have used five transition words. This will really help your readers know when in the day your events occurred." or "You have all your events in order by time. That makes it easy to understand."
- Ask specific questions to get students thinking about improving ideas such as "What transition words could you add to the beginning of your story so we will know when your story begins?" or "Where is another place you could add the repeating sentence?"
- Make positive comments and ask specific questions to get students thinking about mechanics such as "Indenting the first line of your paragraph tells your reader you're starting a new idea." or "Which words in the title should you capitalize?"

2. As students move into the final stages of their writing, ask them to do the following.

- Have your partner read your story out loud to you.
- Listen to see if other people would get a clear picture of what events occur and when the events take place.
- Think of any changes you might make to make the story sound better.
- Read your partner's story out loud.

PUBLISHING

When students are finished, tell them that their stories will be posted outside your room so that they can read and learn about each other's bad days.

MODIFICATIONS TO ENCOURAGE BEGINNING WRITERS

- Have each student dictate one sentence for the group story. As a student provides a sentence, record the complete sentence in magic marker at the bottom of a large sheet of paper. When everyone has made a contribution, give each student his/her sentence to reread and illustrate. Later compile these sentences into a group book.
- Give students special sheets of paper with transition words such as "Early one morning," and the repeating sentence "I could tell it was going to be a terrible, horrible, no good, very bad day" already written on them.

Early one morning _____ _____ _____. I could tell it was going to be a terrible, horrible, no good, very bad day.	After breakfast _____ _____ _____. I could tell it was going to be a terrible, horrible, no good, very bad day.

- Ask students who have a lot of bad days if they would like to write about a wonderful, fantastic, truly awesome day. Before you make this assignment, be sure to help students brainstorm ideas such as "What is something wonderful that could happen before breakfast?"; otherwise you'll set in motion a chance for another bad day.

You might want to change the assignment so *all* your students write about one of the following:

A Wonderful, Fantastic, Truly Awesome Day

A Spooky, Creepy, Dark, Scary Halloween Day

A Slow, Lazy, Laid-Back Weekend

A New, Exciting, Very Special Track Meet

Here is an example:

SARAH'S WONDERFUL, MARVELOUS, FANTASTIC DAY

One morning, Sarah a friendly fifth grader found out that the class was going to see a puppet show. At that very instant Sarah knew it was going to be a wonderful, marvelous, fantastic day.

After lunch Sarah dropped her lunch box. A cute boy named Ryan rushed over and picked it up for her. At that moment Sarah knew it was going to be a wonderful, marvelous, fantastic day.

On the way home from school she was asked to Milly's birthday party. Right then Sarah knew it was a wonderful, marvelous, fantastic day.

When she got home, she found that her brother was sick. So she got to watch her favorite TV show, "Happy Days." Now Sarah was sure it was going to be a wonderful, marvelous, fantastic day.

Finally after supper her brother Jason barged into Sarah's room, but instead of taking her records he loaned Sarah her favorite tape. What a terrific day!

MODIFICATIONS TO CHALLENGE ADVANCED WRITERS

- Provide students with a list of transition words to choose from or help students brainstorm other transition words such as "On the way to school," "Just before the 9:00 bell," "During math," "As we walked down to the lunch room," "At recess," and so on. Ask students to write ten or twelve events for their rough draft and then choose the best eight to put into accordion books.

- Ask students to retell familiar stories. Here is a retelling written by a second grader and part of a story written by a sixth grader. The spelling has been corrected. The first is a "close" retelling. The second is a "creative" retelling.

CINDERELLA

Once upon a time Cinderella went to a ball. Suddenly the glass slippers and lovely dress disappeared. Cinderella ran home but the prince found her. Finally Cinderella got married.

PRESIDENT CLINTON

One day President Clinton found some bricks. He said, "Who
   will help me build a new health care system?"
"Not I," said the senators.
"Not I," said the tax payer.
"Not I," said the doctors.
"Then I will do it myself," said President Clinton.

LESSON 15

SPOOKY STORIES

The thrill of telling or reading aloud spooky stories has existed for a long time. If necessary you can modify this lesson to respect the religious beliefs of some students. For example, students could write a scary story without involving spooky Halloween-type characters (such as a story about almost drowning, being approached by a drug dealer or being lost.)

OBJECTIVES

Students will write a three-paragraph spooky story. To do this, they will:

- Introduce an adventuresome character, a spooky setting, and a scary problem in the first paragraph.
- Introduce a frightening character and one or more attempts to solve the scary problem in the second paragraph.
- Create a solution or a surprise ending in the third paragraph.

MOTIVATORS

1. Turn off the lights and light a candle. Then read a scary ghost story or a Halloween poem to your students such as "The Haunted House" from the book *Scary Stories to Tell in the Dark* by Alvin Schwartz (Harper Collins Publishers, 1981).

Use your voice to add excitement and suspense to the story. Your school librarian can help you locate a story or you might use one of these:

Thirteen Ghostly Tales edited by Freya Littledale (New York: Scholastic Books, 1965)

Spook by Jane Little (New York: Scholastic Books, 1966)

One-Minute Scary Stories by Shari Lewis and Lan O'Kun (New York: Doubleday, 1991)

2. Play some scary Halloween music or spooky sound effects. Ask your students to close their eyes and imagine they are outside a creepy, old, haunted apartment house. Ask them to walk up the front stairs, open the huge wooden door, and see three bats fly out. Continue the walk through the old apartment house. Stop frequently. Ask students what they hear and see.

BRAINSTORMING

Tell students that the class will write a spooky story together before they write their own stories.

Spooky Setting	Adventuresome Character	Scary Problems	Attempts
stormy night	Shelia	chased by a skeleton	throw water on it
old mansion	Mr. Rod	friend disappeared	run away
midnight	a dog	black cat stares at you	buy a dirt bike
pumpkin patch	our principal	ghost floats	
Spooky Sounds	Frightening Character	Feelings	Surprise Ending or Solution
whisper	ghost	petrified	befriend the skeleton
scream	skeleton	terrified	ghost snatches the black cat
howl	witch	lonely	
		frightened	

Key Questions

1. *When and where could our spooky tale or ghost story take place?* (Allow plenty of time for students to think. As students reply, write their ideas on the chalkboard. Also respond with specific positive feedback. Continue brainstorming until many ideas are listed.)

2. *The main character could be someone in our class. If not, who else could be our adventuresome character?*

3. *What frightening characters might also be in the story?*

4. *What scary situations or frightening problems might our adventuresome character face?*

5. *How should the character try (but fail) to solve this frightening problem? What can the character do to try to get out of this scary situation? Who, if anyone, helps?*

6. *What scary sounds or gruesome noises might our hero/heroine hear?*

7. *How might the character feel?*

8. *What could be a solution for our spooky story? What could be a surprise ending?*

GROUP COMPOSING

Model how writers can use information from the brainstorming categories to compose a spooky story.

A Spooky Story			
Transition Words	Early one rainy morning . . .	All of a sudden a ghost poked it's head out . . .	Just then . . .
Late one night	_____	_____	_____
Before dawn	_____	_____	_____
All at once	_____	_____	_____
After that	_____	_____	_____
Suddenly	_____	_____	_____
Then	_____	_____	_____
An hour later	_____	_____	_____
Now	_____	_____	_____
At last	_____	_____	_____
	_____	_____	_____

Paragraph One

1. Have students select a setting for their group story and guide them to compose a sentence describing the setting. Ask how they can signal readers that they are starting a new idea or paragraph. (Indent.)

2. Write the sentence on the chalkboard. Next have students choose a main character. Encourage volunteers to compose sentences describing the character.

3. Finally, ask students to choose a problem from the brainstorming list and decide how they should write that problem.

Paragraph Two

1. Ask volunteers to suggest what happens next. Suggest that they begin this paragraph with a transition word or phrase. (Supply examples.) Elicit that they should start the paragraph by indenting.

2. Guide students to tell how the character feels, what the character sees, and which solution the character tries to solve the frightening problem.

3. As students give their sentences, write them on the chalkboard.

Paragraph Three

1. Ask students how they should begin the final paragraph and why. (Indent to signal new idea.)

2. Have them select a final solution and compose a sentence telling how the problem is solved. Elicit additional sentences telling how the character feels, what he/she says, and what he/she will do to avoid ever having to face this problem again.

3. Have students read the completed story to see if it makes sense. Make any suggested changes.

RESPONDING TO STUDENT WRITING

1. As students write their spooky stories, walk around the room. Hold short one- to two-minute conferences with students who need assistance.

   • Read back portions of students' spooky stories so that they can hear what they have created so far.

   • Make one or two positive comments and then ask questions about the setting, the adventuresome character, scary problems, creepy sounds, or solutions.

2. If you want students to self evaluate particular learner outcomes, give each student a revising form designed to guide self evaluation. See Self Evaluation Checklist (15–1) at the end of this lesson.

PUBLISHING

Tell students that they will get to share their spooky stories with their friends during a Read-Around so everyone can enjoy them. Explain that you'll play some frightening music, turn the lights off, and let them read their stories by flashlight to make their stories especially scary.

If possible, have an aide, students from another class, or students who finish early type the stories on the word processor. Make copies so students can have a copy of everyone's spooky story. For your convenience reproducible book covers (15-2 through 15-4) can be found at the end of this lesson.

MODIFICATIONS TO ENCOURAGE BEGINNING WRITERS

- Ask students when and where their story takes place. Then make up a scary beginning sentence that includes those ideas. Suggest to students that they might want to begin the story in this manner.
- Ask students to dictate their stories to other students.
- Require that students' stories consist of one paragraph instead of three.
- Ask shy students if they would like to read their story into a tape recorder. That way when other students read their spooky stories to the class, these students can play their tapes, if they wish to share.

MODIFICATIONS TO CHALLENGE ADVANCED WRITERS

- Suggest that students add at least six eerie noises to their stories.
- Request that students use dialogue to show feelings felt by the main character.
- Encourage students to add vivid sensory details.

SELF EVALUATION CHECKLIST

Reread and rethink your spooky story.

1. In the first paragraph, have you introduced

an adventuresome character	Yes	No
a spooky setting	Yes	No
a frightening or scary problem	Yes	No

   What could you do to improve your characters, the setting, or the problem?

   _____

2. Have you introduced a frightening character?   Yes   No
   If not, how could you weave in a terrifying character into the problem?

   _____

3. What was your adventuresome character's first attempt to solve the problem?

   _____

   What was your character's second attempt to solve the problem?

   _____

   What other ways might your character try, but fail, to solve the problem?

   _____

4. Does the adventuresome character find a solution?   Yes   No
   How could you improve the ending to make it stronger?

   _____

I have carefully read and evaluated my story. _____
                                                              Signature

A
Spooky Story

by _____

A Spooky Story

by _____

Spooky Stories

LESSON 16

TALL TALES

Students of all ages like to compose and tell tall tales because they are free to exaggerate or stretch the "truth." While this lesson was written for students who are writing longer compositions, it can be adapted for students who are writing only three- to four-sentence narratives.

OBJECTIVES

Students will write a tall tale that is at least four paragraphs long. To do this, they will:

- Introduce the hero or heroine and describe the character's special exaggerated abilities in the first paragraph.
- Tell how the character solves a new problem by heroic means in each succeeding paragraph. Include a setting. (Optional.)
- Give the tall tale a title that motivates potential audiences to read the tall tale.
- Include the hero's or heroine's name in the story title. Capitalize all important words in the title.
- Capitalize the names of particular characters and places.
- Indent all four paragraphs.

MOTIVATORS

1. Tell your students that a tall tale is an untrue, inaccurate, or exaggerated report of events, incidents, or facts composed with the intent to entertain or amuse. Over several days read or have students read together three or four tall tales about such characters as Pecos Bill, Paul Bunyan, and John Henry. Your school librarian can help you locate such tales. Here are some suggestions.

   Tall Tales by Adrien Stoutenburg et al. (Boston, Massachusetts: Houghton Mifflin Company, 1989)

   Paul Bunyan and Babe the Blue Ox by Daphne Hogstrom (Brainerd, Minnesota: Bang Printing, no date)

Paul Bunyan Fights the Monster Plants by Wyatt Blassingame (Pleasantville, New York: Reader's Digest Services, Inc., 1974)

Paul Bunyan by Steven Kellogg (New York: Mulberry Books, 1984)

Cloudy With a Chance of Meatballs by Judi Barrett (Boston, Massachusetts: Houghton Mifflin Company, 1989)

2. Ask students what made the characters they read about special. How were they different from other people and what special traits did they have? (Elicit that the characters had abnormal strength or performed exaggerated feats.)

3. Begin the lesson by telling students a tall tale that you have created. Begin the tale without exaggerations. Gradually start exaggerating traits, actions, problems, and hardships of the heroine in your story. If you wish, you may use the following example.

ALBERTA THE TERRIFIC

My mother is not like most moms. Oh yes, she takes care of us, cooks meals, cleans our house, works in our garden, and even works ten hours a week at a gift shop in the hospital. She is especially fast at everything she does. Let me explain what I mean.

One day I arrived home a little earlier than usual. When I opened the kitchen door, I noticed by mother sitting at the dining room table. She appeared to be writing a list.

I kissed her on the cheek and asked her what she was doing. As she held up 10 sheets of notes, she said, "I'm making out my weekly grocery list."

Slowly I asked, "Do we have any vanilla ice cream left?"

Mom shook her head, "No, not a scoop, but I can mix some up."

Suddenly she jumped up and ran out the door. As she left, I heard her say she was going to the Stop and Run. She was back in three seconds with five gallons of milk and forty fresh eggs. As she cracked the eggs with her left foot, she poured the milk into a mixing bowl larger than a chair. Mom used her elastic arm to grab the vanilla and the other ingredients that she needed.

Just as I said, "Mom, please don't go to any trouble. I can wait until you go to the grocery store," she jumped into the freezer with the mixing bowl and a wire whisk. I hardly had time to blink when out she jumped. The ice cream was frozen solid. Mom said, "Here, try this," as she handed me a huge bowl of ice cream. It was the best ice cream I have ever tasted.

Ask students when they knew you were stretching the truth in your story. Have them list some of the unusual things your mom did to solve the problem of no ice cream and some special qualities your mother had.

Explain that you used exaggeration in your story. Exaggeration can provide entertainment by taking a humorous look at unusual characters dealing with impossible situations.

BRAINSTORMING

Tell students that they are going to create a group tall tale. Explain that many people enjoy creating tall tales because in tall tales it is all right to exaggerate or "stretch" the truth.

Key Questions

1. *Who was the heroine in my story? Who do you know that would make a good hero or heroine for a story? What famous person could be a hero or heroine? What make-believe character or animal could be written about in a tall tale?*
   (Record responses on the chalkboard and continue brainstorming until at least six ideas are listed. Have students select one character to be in their tall tale.)

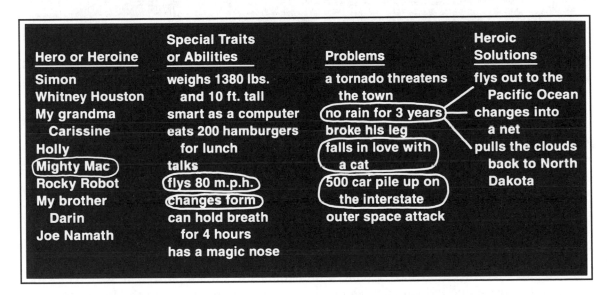

Hero or Heroine	Special Traits or Abilities	Problems	Heroic Solutions
Simon	weighs 1380 lbs.	a tornado threatens	flys out to the
Whitney Houston	and 10 ft. tall	the town	Pacific Ocean
My grandma	smart as a computer	no rain for 3 years	changes into
Carissine	eats 200 hamburgers	broke his leg	a net
Holly	for lunch	falls in love with	pulls the clouds
Mighty Mac	talks	a cat	back to North
Rocky Robot	flys 80 m.p.h.	500 car pile up on	Dakota
My brother	changes form	the interstate	
Darin	can hold breath	outer space attack	
Joe Namath	for 4 hours		
	has a magic nose		

2. *Next we need to brainstorm some really difficult problems, hardships, conflicts, or crises for our character to face. What difficult problem might* (Mighty Mac, for example) *confront? What terrible trouble could occur?* (Continue brainstorming until six to eight ideas are listed.)

3. *We need to choose three problems for Mighty Mac to solve. What is one problem Mighty Mac could encounter?* (Continue until three problems have been selected.)

4. *Now we need to come up with heroic solutions for each problem. How could Mighty Mac solve the problem of a three year drought? What unique talents or special abilities could Mighty Mac have that will help him solve the problem?* (Guide students to brainstorm appropriate traits or abilities for the solutions they suggest.)

5. It is not necessary to brainstorm solutions for the other two problems. Students can brainstorm ideas for their own tall tale at this time.

GROUP COMPOSING

1. Tell students that they need to come up with a title that has the hero's name in it and that will grab the readers attention. Write suggested titles on the chalkboard and choose a student to select one.

Titles

The Tale of Mighty Mac
Mighty Mac, the Farmer's Friend
Mac Flies to the Rescue

Topic Sentences	Good Tall Tale Beginnings
Mighty Mac was not like other dogs.	Long ago . . .
Mighty Mac had many unusual abilities that he used to help his friends.	Last year . . .
	It all began when . . .
Mac was a talented dog.	One hot summer day . . .

Paragraph One

1. Remind students that in the first paragraph they need to introduce the main character, describe the hero's special abilities, and describe the setting.

2. Help them compose a topic sentence such as "Mighty Mac was not like other dogs" to begin the tall tale. Point out that the sentence should tell readers they are going to describe Mighty Mac's special abilities.

3. Explain that since they have a topic sentence for the paragraph they now need to add details. Encourage individual students to compose sentences about the hero's abilities and about the setting.

Paragraph Two

1. Explain that now they need to tell about the first problem the hero faced. Remind them to use the ideas they brainstormed. Guide them to start with a good beginning such as "One hot summer day."

2. Encourage volunteers to compose detail sentences telling what the problem was, what the character did, and what the solution was.

Mighty Mac Flies to the Rescue

Mighty Mac had many unusual abilities that he used to help his friends. He could fly really high up into the sky at 80 miles per hour. He also had the ability to change his form even though he weighed 1380 pounds.
One hot summer day _____

_____

_____

Not long after harvest another crisis occurred. _____

_____

_____

Paragraphs Three and Four

Repeat the sequence in paragraph two with a second and third problem.

Tell students that they are ready to begin composing their tall tales. Give each student a six inch by three foot strip of white butcher paper or tape several sheets of paper together to form a long sheet. Direct your students to hold the paper vertically and write their tales on the strip. Later, the strip will be attached to a long brown tail.

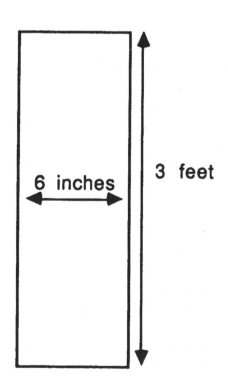

Responding to Student Writing

1. As students begin brainstorming and composing their tall tales, move around the room encouraging and coaching them as they get their ideas down on paper. Until a student has gained confidence in his or her writing abilities, respond only to the strong or exciting parts of the student's writing. Remember that frequent daily writing is more important to growth than one or two "perfect" writings per month.

    *   Make as many **positive comments** as you can about students' accomplishments such as "Swimming 300 mph is a special trait that will help your heroine solve many problems" or "Having a tornado threaten the Minnesota State Fair is definitely a problem that needs a heroic solution."

    *   **Ask specific questions** to get students thinking about improving ideas such as "How can the special trait of being able to see in the dark help your hero solve his problem?" or "To what might you compare your hero's size, so I could get a picture of him in my mind?"

    *   Make **positive comments** and **ask specific questions** to get students thinking about mechanics such as "You indented each paragraph. That helps me realize that your heroine is getting into a new problem." or "How could you make it clearer that your phrase at the top of your page is the title of your tall tale?" (Capitalize the words in the title.)

2. As students move into the final stages of their writing ask them to find a partner and do the following:

    *   Have their partner read their tall tale out loud to them.

    *   Listen to see if other people will get a clear picture of the events in the tall tale.

    *   Think of any changes they might make to make their tall tale even more exciting.

    *   Read their partner's story out loud.

Publishing

Inform students that they are going to glue their tall tales onto long brown tails and then hang them up in the hallway outside the room so that other students and teachers can read and enjoy their tall tales.

Give each student a strip of brown butcher paper or other colored paper 8 inches × 3½ feet. Provide these instructions.

1. To make a tail fold the paper in half the long way.
2. Lay a tail pattern on the folded paper and trace around it. (Hand out several precut tail patterns.)

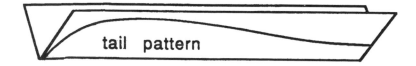

tail pattern

3. Keep the paper folded as you cut out one side of the tail.

4. Finally glue your tall tale in the center of the tail.

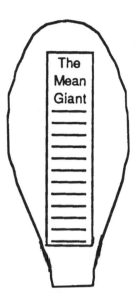

MODIFICATIONS TO ENCOURAGE BEGINNING WRITERS

- Require students to write a tall tale consisting of only three sentences. Each sentence should tell of one problem solved heroically by the character.
- Allow students to draw a picture of the character solving each problem. Once students have drawn the event, they will find it easier to compose the tall tale.
- Do not require the first paragraph introducing the character.

MODIFICATIONS TO CHALLENGE ADVANCED WRITERS

- Ask students to write a four-chapter tall tale instead of a four-paragraph tale.
- Require students to write at least 4 lines of dialogue to show readers the character's personality.
- Have students provide a setting describing when and where each problem occurs before each problem is related.
- Challenge students to create a clever or lively ending.

Section 3

DESCRIPTIVE WRITINGS

DESCRIPTIVE PARAGRAPHS

Writers can use a descriptive paragraph pattern to describe a person, place, thing, or event. The purpose of a description is to help a reader clearly visualize what is being described. Descriptions make use of adjectives (telling how many, and what kind), similes (comparing one thing to another), and adverbs (telling how, when, where, and to what extent).

Descriptive paragraphs consist of a topic sentence and two or more detail sentences. The type of details given depends on what is being described. Details in a sensory paragraph may consist of visual, auditory, olfactory, and tactile clues. Details in a factual paragraph may include who, what, when, where, how, and why. A comparison paragraph is another type of descriptive paragraph in which two people, things, places, or events are compared according to how they are alike and different. Descriptive paragraphs often end with a summary sentence.

Some Forms of Descriptive Writing

"All about" Books
Announcements
Autograph Books
Book Summaries
Business Brochures
Catalog Descriptions
Character Sketches
"Dear Abby" Problem Letters
"Dear Santa" Letters
Definitions
Eulogies
Fact Books
Fan Letters
Feature Articles
Field Trip Reports

Fortunes
Friendly Letters
Horoscopes
Job Application Letters
Lab Reports
Legal Contracts
Magazine/News Article
Math Story Problem
Messages
Minutes of a Meeting
News Bulletins
News Reports/Stories
Observational Notes
Pen Pal Letters
Post Card Messages

Predictions
Product Descriptions
Report cards/Progress Reports
Riddles
Science Articles
Sports Accounts/Articles
TV Program Summaries
Thumbnail Sketches
Time Capsules
Travel Brochures
Travel Log
Visitor's Guides
Wanted Posters
Weather Forecasts
Weather Reports

LESSON 17

WANTED POSTERS

Wanted posters can be used for many things besides finding criminals. One use is to advertise for something one desires—for example, to find a used bike or to trade old video games. Another use is to ask people to help with a project—for example, volunteers to pick up trash around the school or parents to help with a party or field trip.

OBJECTIVES

Students will create a wanted poster. To do this they will:

- Title the poster "Wanted."
- List the four information categories: Who (or What), Wanted For, Description, and Reward.
- Place a colon after each category label.
- Tell who or what is wanted, why the person or object is wanted, three or more details to describe the wanted item, and the reward offered.
- Write complete sentences in the description.
- Draw or glue a picture of the wanted person or object under the title.

MOTIVATORS

1. Bring in a sample of several wanted posters from the U.S. Post Office to show the students. After students have examined the posters ask what a wanted poster is used for. Discuss what kinds of people appear on wanted posters (criminals; lost or stolen children). Explain to students that they will write their own wanted poster to advertise for something they would like. To help them prepare to do this, the class will write one together.

2. Ask students to name the kinds of information found on wanted posters. Elicit the following categories and write them on the chalkboard: who or what is wanted, why the person or thing is wanted, a description of the wanted person or thing, the amount of the reward.

Brainstorming

Tell students they will brainstorm some ideas for each category.

Who or What	Wanted for	Description	Reward
kitten	He acts out	tall	$1,000
car thief	stories.	gray hair	no math
new friend	(He helps us find	glasses and	homework
line leader	great books.)	a smile	line leader
drug dealer	He gives good	carries lots	keep our
(Mr. Thomas)	grades.	of books	gerbil over
new lunchroom	He plays with	eyes twinkle	the summer
monitor	us at recess.	brown sweater	
kickball captain		old blue truck	

Key Questions

1. *Who or what would you like to find? Who would you like to have on our wanted poster?* (For example, students might think of a teacher or other school employee such as the librarian or janitor whom they would like to see return next year. List ideas under the appropriate heading.)

2. *Which one of these ideas should we use in our group's wanted poster?*

3. *Now why is (Mr. Thomas, for example) wanted? What are some reasons you want Mr. Thomas back next year as librarian?* (Coming up with reasons is a difficult mental task so allow students time to think.)

4. *Which one of these reasons should we put on the wanted poster?*

5. *How can we describe Mr. Thomas so other people will know how he looks? What one distinctive feature does Mr. Thomas have that would make it easy to identify him? What other traits make him unique?* (Elicit descriptive details and write them on the chalkboard.)

6. *Now that we have decided who is wanted and why, and have listed some descriptive details, we have only one category left. We must decide on a reward for the person who convinces Mr. Thomas to stay at our school. What reward should we offer? What can we afford as a reward?* (Guide students to think of something practical that they could offer.)

Group Composing

1. Tell students that now their ideas for the wanted poster can be put together. Project an overhead of a blank wanted poster pattern on the wall and add information to the poster as students select it.

2. First draw a crude picture of the wanted person and explain that they can get a real picture later. For the description category, guide students to combine some of the descriptive details they brainstormed into one or two sentences.

3. When they have filled in all categories, ask students to read the wanted poster together to see if it describes the person and to see if it sounds right. Explain that now students will get to make their own wanted posters.

RESPONDING TO STUDENT WRITING

1. While students are creating their wanted posters, circulate throughout the room assisting students who need special attention.

   • Ask students to read the wanted poster information that they have created so far. Comment positively on interesting ideas.

   • Ask questions to clarify students' descriptions, explaining that the clearer the description the better chance students have of finding what they want. For example, you might ask "What else can you tell me about a good substitute teacher?" or "What other rewards could you use besides money?"

   • If you want to comment on the mechanics of writing, say something like "You remembered to put colons after the 'Who,' 'Wanted For,' and other labels. This will make your poster easier to read" or "What punctuation do you need after the 'Wanted for' label but in front of the reason?" (A colon.)

2. When students have completed their wanted posters, tell them to find a partner and read their posters aloud to each other. Have students evaluate whether the posters

make sense and whether they create a picture of the wanted person or object. Have them revise their posters as necessary.

PUBLISHING

Tell students that when they have revised their wanted posters, they can mount them on some construction paper. Provide these directions.

1. Put rubber cement on the back of your wanted poster.
2. Then carefully center it on a piece of construction paper.
3. Draw or glue a picture of the person or object wanted on the wanted poster. (An alternative to drawing a picture or gluing on a picture is to tape on a 5" by 6" piece of aluminum wrap. This works well if they are trying to locate volunteers for something. Whoever looks into the foil sees his or her reflection.)

Students who finish early can make fingerprints to add to their wanted poster. Provide these directions.

1. Place a four-inch long strip of scotch tape on a table with the sticky side up. Tape that is an inch wide works best.
2. Rub a soft lead pencil on a piece of paper until a black spot has been created.

3. Rub your thumb back and forth across the lead on the paper.
4. Press your thumb on the sticky tape. Repeat for your other four fingers on your dominant hand.
5. Lift the tape carefully and stick it where you want the fingerprints.

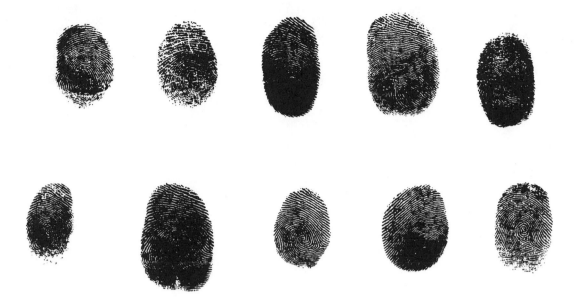

Instruct students to bring their wanted posters to you when they are finished, so you can tape them on the wall outside your classroom. Explain that the other students and teachers in the school will then know the people or things the class wants to find or keep. That way they can help find them.

MODIFICATIONS TO ENCOURAGE BEGINNING WRITERS

- Suggest that students draw the wanted person or item before writing the description.
- Ask students to complete each information category (Who, Wanted For, Description, and Reward) with only a one-, two- or three-word response. For example, the "Wanted For" category could be completed by the words "Saturday child sitting." The "Description" category could be completed by words such as "friendly, likes basketball, plays checkers." Give students Reproducible 17-1.

MODIFICATIONS TO CHALLENGE ADVANCED WRITERS

- Have students expand the description section of the wanted poster to a whole paragraph that includes many different types of traits such as physical traits, personality traits, type of criminal or positive activities, location of crimes or where the activity takes place, and so on.
- Encourage students to create an alias for the wanted person or item. Add whom to contact if the person or thing is located. Two other sections that can be added to a wanted poster are "Where Last Seen" and "Crimes."

WANTED

Who:
Wanted for:
Description:

Reward:

LESSON 18

FORTUNES

Very few people really believe in fortunes; nevertheless, most people enjoy having their fortune told. This lesson allows students to use their imagination to think about what might occur in the future.

OBJECTIVES

Students will write 3 one-paragraph fortunes. To do this, they will:

- Begin each fortune with a topic sentence such as "Today's your lucky day," "Tomorrow be prepared for some good luck and some bad luck," or "Next week will be difficult."
- Include at least three detail sentences about the person's fortune such as

    "You will find . . . " (completed with an object, animal, or place),

    "You are going to meet . . . " (completed with a person), and

    "You might become . . . " (an occupation, a person, or something else).

- Include at least one descriptive word in each detail that tells what kind, how many/how much, or which one.

- Capitalize the first word of each sentence and each proper noun.
- Put a period at the end of each fortune statement.
- Indent all three fortunes.

MOTIVATORS

1. Ask students to recall and share fortunate and unfortunate things that have happened to them or their families lately.

2. Bring in a fortune cookie for each student. Ask what they think is inside the cookie. Then let students open the cookies, read the fortunes, and eat the cookies. Ask some students to read their fortunes to the group.

3. Share a fortune that you have received. Then share what happened after receiving the fortune.

BRAINSTORMING

Tell students that today they are going to have a chance to write some fortunes. Explain that fortunes make a prediction about what might happen in the future.

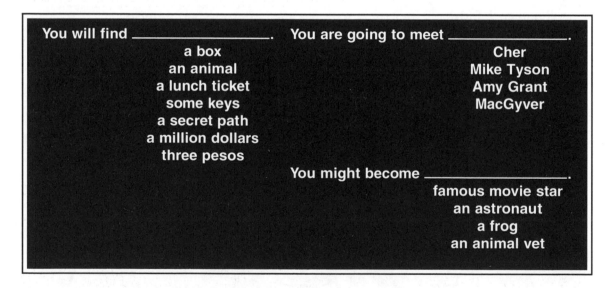

You will find _____.
- a box
- an animal
- a lunch ticket
- some keys
- a secret path
- a million dollars
- three pesos

You are going to meet _____.
- Cher
- Mike Tyson
- Amy Grant
- MacGyver

You might become _____.
- famous movie star
- an astronaut
- a frog
- an animal vet

Key Questions

1. *One type of fortune tells about finding something. What is something interesting or special that someone could find? What is something you would not like to find?* (Make a positive comment such as "Your lost lunch ticket would be useful to find.")

2. *Meeting an interesting, strange, or famous person is another kind of fortune. If you could meet someone famous or very interesting, who would you want to meet?*

3. *Some fortunes predict what someone might become in the future. What is an interesting occupation someone might have in the future? If we could turn you into someone or something else, who or what might you become?*

GROUP COMPOSING

1. Tell students that their brainstorming ideas can help them write some interesting fortunes, but first they need a topic sentence to tell what kind of fortune each one is.

   Point out that a fortune may be good news, bad news, or a combination. As you talk, write these three topic sentences or your own examples on the chalkboard:

> Today's your lucky day.
> Tomorrow be prepared for some good luck and some bad luck.
> Next week may be difficult.

2. Select a student to choose one topic sentence. Then ask students what they need to do to start a paragraph. (Indent.)

3. Have students select an idea to complete the detail sentence "You will find _____." Encourage them to add descriptive words to describe what will be found. Ask questions that elicit details of color, size, shape, and so on.

4. Ask students how to signal the beginning of each detail sentence in the fortune (a capital letter) and how to end each detail (a period).

> You will find __a box__.
>   shiny, old heartshaped ^
>
> You are going to meet __Mike Tyson__ in jail one sunny day in April.
>   a very disappointed ^
>
> You might become _____.

5. Next have students select an idea to complete the detail "You are going to meet _____." Have volunteers suggest details to add to the sentence to describe this person or tell when or where someone might meet her.

6. Repeat the same process for the third detail sentence.

RESPONDING TO STUDENT WRITING

1. As students write their fortunes, circulate around the classroom. Ask students to read you one or two of their best fortunes. Make positive comments and ask questions about things they could find, people they could meet, occupations they might have in the future, or people or things they might become.

2. If you want students to work toward particular learner outcomes, focus your positive comments and questions to guide them to self evaluate one or two of the following outcomes.

   • Write three one-paragraph fortunes each containing

   _____ Topic sentence such as "Today's your lucky day."

   Three detail sentences:

   _____ "You will find . . . " completed with an object, animal, or place

   _____ "You are going to meet . . . " completed with a person

   _____ "You might become . . . " an occupation, a person, or something else

   • Include at least one descriptive word in each detail sentence telling

   _____ what kind

   _____ how many or how much

   _____ which one

   • Use correct mechanics including

   _____ capital letter at the beginning of each sentence

   _____ capital letter at the beginning of each proper noun

   _____ period at the end of each fortune statement

PUBLISHING

Tell students that since they have written such interesting fortunes, they can exchange fortunes with their friends and make up new ones during recess.

As an alternative have students write their fortunes on strips of paper, fold the papers, and put them in a box. Have each student reach in and draw out a fortune and read it to the class.

MODIFICATIONS TO ENCOURAGE BEGINNING WRITERS

- Supply a sheet with a prewritten pattern such as the following.

Today you'll have _____ luck all day. You will find _____. You are going to meet _____. You might become _____.

Next week you'll have some good luck and some problems. You will find _____. You are going to meet _____. You will become _____.

Tomorrow you'll have an awful day. You'll find _____. You are going to meet _____ _____. You will turn into _____.

- If a student has a poor self image or is negative to peers, before you start group brainstorming, ask this student why people like getting good fortunes instead of bad ones and how a good fortune makes a person feel. Modify key questions to limit responses to only positive ones. Write each positive response on the blackboard. Ignore any negative ones.

MODIFICATIONS TO CHALLENGE ADVANCED WRITERS

- Require students to add when and where the fortune will take place in each detail sentence. For example: After your eleventh birthday, you will be allowed to ride your bike to town.
- Provide additional fortune detail patterns for students to complete. See the list that follows for more fortune patterns or have students come up with their own detail sentences.
- Suggest that students write real predictions such as "Minnesota farmers will produce a bumper crop of sugar beets."

ADDITIONAL FORTUNE PATTERNS

1. You are ___(What are you?)___   ___(How do you act?)___.

2. You will ___(What will you do?)___.

3. Your future holds ___(What does your future hold?)___.

4. ___(Who will do something?)___ will ___(What will that person do?)___.

5. Less ___(What?)___ will give you more ___(What?)___.

6. Your happiness depends on ___(Upon what does your happiness depend?)___.

7. Today you will ___(What will you do today?)___.

8. In your life, ___(What will happen?)___.

9. You will ___(What will you do in the future?)___ ___(Where?)___ ___(How?)___ ___(When?)___.

10. Before ___(What time?)___ your ___(To what could this happen?)___ will ___(What will happen?)___.

11. Try ___(What should you try?)___ before you ___(What should you do?)___.

12. A ___(Who/What can bring something?)___ brings ___(What will be brought?)___.

LESSON 19

"MYSTERY BAG" RIDDLES

People of all ages enjoy the mystery of riddles. Now your students can write their own riddles about any subject. In social studies they can write riddles about the American Revolution or a current event. And in science they can write riddles about the weather or cell structure.

OBJECTIVES

Students will write a riddle about the object in their mystery bag. To do this, they will:

- Write two or more sentences that describe the object.
- Write a third sentence that tells what the object can do.
- Write a fourth sentence that describes activities for which the object can be used.
- Write a question requesting the reader to solve the riddle.
- Begin each telling sentence with a capital letter and end it with a period.
- Begin each asking sentence with a capital letter and end it with a question mark.

MOTIVATOR

Have students sit on the floor up close to you. Use a mysterious voice to tell them that you have a Mystery Bag. (Ahead of time put an object in the bag and write a riddle about it.) Hold up the bag tied shut with a curly ribbon. Ask students to look at the Mystery Bag and see if they can find something that will help them figure out what is inside. When students notice the index card glued to the bag, read the first line of your riddle. Ask students what they think is in this Mystery Bag. Accept all guesses. Praise guesses that use the clues even if the answer is not correct.

Read the second line of your riddle and ask students if they still think their guess is correct. Allow time for them to think and respond. Again praise guesses that use the clues. If a student guesses the object, do not let on. Just accept it as any other guess.

Read the last clue, accept students' guesses, and then choose someone to open the Mystery Bag.

Explain that riddles give clues about an object without telling exactly what the object is. Tell students that your riddle was mysterious, because until they heard the last clue, it was difficult to be sure what the correct answer was.

BRAINSTORMING

Tell students that you brought in an object so they could write a class riddle. Explain that later they will get a chance to write their own riddles. Show students the object (spatula) you brought.

Key Questions

1. What are some words that describe how the spatula looks, feels, sounds, or smells? What could we say about the size of this spatula? (Give positive comments such as "About 10 inches long" is a good clue about size. Continue brainstorming a long list of descriptors for color, size, shape, texture, and so on.)

2. ***What are some things a spatula can do?*** (Remind students that a clue should tell about the object but not give the riddle away.) ***What else can a spatula do?*** (List suggestions on the chalkboard.)

3. ***What are some things you can use a spatula for? What common or uncommon use do people have for a spatula?***

GROUP COMPOSING

1. Write pattern sentences for riddles on the chalkboard. Tell students they need to choose two words from the first list for the first line of their riddle. Circle the two descriptors they select and then write them in the blanks of the riddle.

I am _____soft_____ and _____flexible_____.	
I am ___about 10 inches long and wooden___.	
I can ___stir jello___.	
You can _____.	
What am I?	

2. Have students choose two more descriptors from the list for the second line of the riddle. Encourage them to choose good descriptors, but point out that they should not make the riddle too easy. Write the descriptors in the blank in the second line.

3. Guide students to select clues that tell what the object can do and what it can be used for.

4. Explain that their riddle needs one more thing—a sentence asking readers to guess the object. Write "What am I?" on the chalkboard to complete the riddle.

5. Ask students to read the riddle out loud to see if it is too easy or too hard. Make any suggested changes. Comment positively and suggest students try the riddle out on their brothers and sisters or even their parents when they get home from school.

Tell students that now they will write their own Mystery Bag Riddles. Then bring out a basket of small objects. (Younger children can be given a bag with the object already in it. Older students can bring their own small object from home in a sack.) Have students come up one at a time and choose an object. Remind them to keep their objects hidden so no one will see them. Explain that after their riddles are written, they'll try to guess what is in each other's Mystery Bags.

RESPONDING TO STUDENT WRITING

1. As students write their riddles, move around the room helping those who need special attention. Make positive comments about good clues that describe the object but don't give it away. Ask questions to help students evaluate the quality of their clues.

   • four clues

   If the clues the student has chosen describe the object, make a positive comment such as "'Long' and 'black' give important size and color clues" or "'Float' is a super clue because it tells something your object can do without giving it away."

   If a student is stuck and can't seem to come up with another clue, ask a question such as "How does a cotton ball feel?" or "What other things besides tick can a watch do that won't give your riddle away?"

   • question asking reader to solve the riddle

   If a student has forgotten the question at the end of the riddle, ask "What goes after the clue sentences to tell readers it is time to answer your riddle?"

   • capitalization and punctuation

   If a student has remembered to capitalize each clue sentence, make a positive comment such as "Your capital letters at the beginning of each clue will help readers know you are telling about different clues."

   If a student has used incorrect end punctuation, ask a question such as "What kind of punctuation mark do you need at the end of an asking sentence?"

2. When students have finished, pair them with a revising partner. Ask them to take turns reading and listening to their riddles. Ask students to consider how many clues had to be read before their partner figured out their riddle. Ask them to decide if the riddle is too easy, too hard, or just right to solve.

PUBLISHING

Point out that you are really impressed with the fantastic riddles students have created. Inform them that students from a lower grade will come to class and have a lot of fun reading and trying to figure out the riddles.

Tell students that now they need to make their Mystery Bags. Give each student a 3 × 5 inch or 4 × 6 inch index card, a small paper bag, and some yarn. Provide these instructions.

1. Write your riddle on the card. Use your best handwriting so that younger students can read your riddles.

2. Next glue your index card to one side of the bag. Make sure that the riddle is not upside down.

3. Hide your object in your Mystery Bag.

4. Close the bag and tie it shut with the yarn.

When students have finished their Mystery Bags, have them come to the front of the room one at a time and read their riddles. Give each student a Guessing Sheet (Reproducible 19-1). After each student reads a riddle, ask the others to write their guesses on this sheet.

MODIFICATIONS TO ENCOURAGE BEGINNING WRITERS

• Ask students to write four descriptive sentences using these or other simplified pattern sentences: I am _____; I have a _____"; I can _____; You can _____; What am I?"

• Provide a special piece of paper with the brainstorming categories already written across the top.

I am _____.	I can _____.	You can _____.
What am I?		

MODIFICATIONS TO CHALLENGE ADVANCED WRITERS

• As students move into selecting from their brainstormed ideas, challenge them to select clues that are accurate but that don't give the riddle away too quickly. Tell them to make sure readers really have to think hard to solve the riddle.

• Have students write the first two describing sentences as similes.

I am as _____ as a _____.
I am as _____ as a _____.
I have _____ and _____.
You can _____.
What am I?

• Ask more able students to generate their own sentences instead of using the sentence patterns. During the individual brainstorming step, those students should be guided to turn their papers horizontally and write the following categories across the top: "Describing Clues," "Doing Clues," "How Used Clues," and "Possible Questions."

• Suggest students write a riddle about something that won't fit in a sack (such as a bank) or that can't be seen (such as friendship).

Mystery Bag - Guessing Sheet

1. _____

2. _____

3. _____

4. _____

5. _____

6. _____

7. _____

8. _____

9. _____

10. _____

11. _____

12. _____

13. _____

14. _____

15. _____

16. _____

17. _____

18. _____

19. _____

20. _____

21. _____

22. _____

23. _____

24. _____

25. _____

26. _____

27. _____

28. _____

29. _____

30. _____

Name of Riddle Guesser _____

LESSON 20

DREAM SCHOOL

Dreams are wonderful things. No matter how bad things are going, our dreams can bring us a moment of happiness. While this lesson deals with an ideal school, you can redesign it around any current topic that interests your students. If you are teaching bike safety, students may want to create their own ideal bikes. If you are teaching a unit on recycling, students could describe an ideal world where everyone recycles, reuses, and reduces waste.

OBJECTIVES

Students will write a paragraph describing their ideal school. To do this, they will:

- Begin the paragraph with a topic sentence such as "Wouldn't you like to see my dream school?"
- Include at least four details such as where it is, what it looks like, what it has in it, and what happens there.
- Indent the paragraph.

MOTIVATORS

1. Tell students about a new (imaginary) elementary school to be built this summer. Include aspects of your ideal school in your description.
2. Have students draw their dream school.

BRAINSTORMING

Where	Looks like	Has in it	What happens	How long there
Hawaii	bubble	pool	learning	6 hours
Wisconsin	football	T.V.	fun	15 minutes
		VCR		1 hour
		movies		

Key Questions

1. *Where would your dream school be built?* (Allow plenty of time for students to think. As students reply, respond with specific positive feedback and write their ideas on the blackboard. Continue brainstorming until many ideas are listed.)

2. *What would your dream school look like?* (Encourage imaginative responses.)

3. *What would be in your dream school? What kinds of things would a dream school have?*

4. *What happens in this school? What would you do at your dream school?*

5. *How long would you be at your dream school each day?*

GROUP COMPOSING

1. Tell students that they have brainstormed a lot of imaginative ideas. Now they will choose ideas and put them together in a class paragraph.

2. Point out that first they need a topic to begin their paragraph. Write the question "Wouldn't you like to see my dream school?" on the chalkboard.

3. Encourage individual students to compose sentences about where the school will be, what it will look like, what things are in the school, what happens there, and how long the school day is. Remind them to use the information they brainstormed.

> **My Dream School**
>
> Wouldn't you like to see my dream school? It would be located in Hawaii on the beach . . . _____
> _____
> _____
> _____

RESPONDING TO STUDENT WRITING

1. As students write about their dream schools, walk around the room. Hold mini-conferences with students who need assistance or attention. Individually read back descriptions so that students can hear what has been created so far.

2. If you want students to work towards particular learner outcomes, respond with positive comments and questions to help them self evaluate one or two of the following outcomes.

   • topic sentence

   If students have an excellent topic sentence, respond with a specific positive comment that tells why the topic sentence is effective.

If students want to create their own topic sentence, guide their thinking with a question such as "What is another question you could ask to get people interested in reading about your dream school?"

- 4+ detail sentences such as where, looks like, has, happens, how long

If students have included only two or three good detail sentences, respond first with a positive comment explaining how each detail will help future readers visualize this school. Then, if you expect four detail sentences, elicit additional ideas by asking questions such as "What do you want inside your dream school?" or "What will happen in your school?"

PUBLISHING

If students have not already made a drawing of their dream school, have them make one now. Tell them that they are going to share their drawings and descriptions with the principal, the school board and parents. Explain that they will hang their dream school descriptions and art work in the entrance hallway so that the principal, school board members, and parents can learn about their ideas.

MODIFICATIONS TO ENCOURAGE BEGINNING WRITERS

- Have students draw a dream school and then label important aspects of their school.
- Ask students to write one sentence for each of the following:
  1. important things that it will contain,
  2. how it will look, and
  3. where it will be located.

MODIFICATIONS TO CHALLENGE ADVANCED WRITERS

- Contract with students to write two paragraphs. One paragraph should include where their dream school will be located and how it will look. A second paragraph should include what will be in the school, what kinds of things will occur there, and how long each school day will be. Also ask these students to create a topic sentence to introduce each paragraph.

LESSON 21

DESCRIPTIONS OF OBJECTS

While this lesson has been written to go with a science unit on ocean life, you may choose any topic your students have been studying via a "hands-on" approach. Other possible topics include rocks, birds' nests, butterflies, leaves, bugs, volcanoes, cars, and the latest hairstyles. Categories of details for leaves might be type of edge, number of leaves, and veins. Categories for latest hairstyles might be length of hair, amount of curl, and where to part.

OBJECTIVES

Students will write a paragraph describing an object (seashell). To do this, they will:

- Start the paragraph with a topic sentence that tells what will be described.
- Write at least three supporting sentences telling color, shape, and size.
- Indent the paragraph.
- Begin each sentence with a capital letter.

MOTIVATORS

1. Tell students that since they have been studying ocean life, you have brought some of your favorite shells to class. Show the seashells and pass them around. Ask students to share experiences they have had at the beach.

2. Explain that you are going to describe one of your favorite shells. Ask students to listen and see if they can guess which shell is being described. Then tell them to raise their hands if they think they know which shell you described.

Use clues that relate to the color, shape, and size of the shell. Example: I have a beautiful shell. It fits in the palm of my hand. Its top looks like an ice cream cone. It is mostly white with brown spots.

3. Ask students what kinds of clues helped them decide which shell you were describing. Guide them to realize that the clues related to size, shape, and color of the shell.

4. Tell students they will each get to choose a shell from your collection and write a description of it. Share that you will put all the descriptions in a book and display the shells in a "Shell Showcase." Each shell will be numbered, and a matching number will be written on the back of its description. When people read the paragraphs, they can try to figure out which shell is described.

BRAINSTORMING

Tell students that the class will write about one shell together to help them learn how to write their own descriptive paragraph. Have the class vote on which shell they want to write about. Hold up the chosen shell.

color	shape	size
brown and pink	round	small
white spots	like a fan	as big as a golf ball
	wavy and rippled edges	as small as an egg

Key Questions

1. *What colors describe this shell?* (As students answer, give a positive response such as "That's right, it is brown and pink. Those are very good details," and write their ideas on the chalkboard. Continue questioning students about colors in the shell. Be sure to allow time for students to think.)

2. *What shape is this shell? What does it look like? What is the shell shaped like?* (Record student responses and tell them that the details they have brainstormed about shape will help people to picture the shell.)

3. *What could we say about the size of the shell? To what could we compare the size of the shell?* (Encourage or model answers that use a simile such as "as big as a golf ball" or "as small as an egg.")

4. *If we're going to tell someone about our shell, we first need to let them know what we're describing. We need a topic sentence to tell the reader what the paragraph will be about. We might say "Our shell is special for many reasons" or "Our shell has many outstanding features."*

What are some other sentences we could use to tell people what we'll be describing? (Allow plenty of wait time and record student responses.)

> **Topic sentences**
> Our shell is special for many reasons.
> Our shell has many outstanding features.
> My shell is awesome because of its shape, size and color.
> My shell has many special features.

GROUP COMPOSING

Remind students they have brainstormed a lot of information about the shell plus several strong possible topic sentences. Explain that now they must choose the information they want to use and put it together in a paragraph.

1. First have students decide which topic sentence they want to use. Ask what they need to do to signal readers that they are starting a paragraph. (Indent.)

2. Explain that since they have a topic sentence for the paragraph, now they need to add the details. Encourage individual students to compose sentences about the shell's color, its shape, and its size. Remind them to use the information they have brainstormed. As students give their sentences, write them on the chalkboard.

3. Ask students to read the paragraph out loud to see if it describes the shell and to see if they want to make any changes. What would they like to add, leave out, or change? (Make suggested changes.)

4. Tell students that there is one more sentence people will need when they read the paragraph in the "Shell Showcase." Write "Can you find this shell?" on the chalkboard to conclude the paragraph.

> Our shell has many special features. The shell is brown and pink with white spots. It is round and shaped like a fan. It is as big as a golf ball. Can you find this shell?

Have students select a shell and begin writing their own descriptions.

RESPONDING TO STUDENT WRITING

1. As students write their descriptions, walk around the room. Visit individually with students who need help getting started. Give positive feedback and ask one or two questions. Focus especially on different kinds of details and effective topic sentences.

2. If you want students to self evaluate particular learner outcomes, give them a revising form designed to guide them. See the Self Evaluation Checklist (Reproducible 21-1) at the end of this lesson.

3. Divide the students into groups of five. Have them put their shells together in a pile and exchange descriptions. Tell them that now they will get to see if they gave enough details to describe their shell. As each student reads a paragraph, others in the group should listen to see if they can find the shell described. After all the descriptions have been read, students should go back to their desks and add, change, or delete information to make their descriptions clearer and more precise.

PUBLISHING

Explain to students that they will put their shell paragraphs in a "Seashell" book. (See Reproducible 21-2.) Then you will display the numbered shells on a table. Let them know that their shell's number will be on the back of their paragraph.

Tell students that another class from their grade level and other visitors will read the shell paragraphs and try to guess which shell each paragraph was written about. Explain that the visitors can check to see if their guesses were right by comparing the shell's number with the number on the back of the description.

When all students have completed their descriptive paragraphs, assign each shell a different number. Set up a "Seashell Showcase" where all the shells will be displayed.

Bind the descriptions in a book and record the assigned shell number on the back of each composition.

MODIFICATIONS TO ENCOURAGE BEGINNING WRITERS

- Encourage students who have trouble finding words to express their thoughts to draw their shell before trying to describe it.

- Students who have difficulty brainstorming on their own can be given a special sheet to help them record their ideas.

TOPIC SENTENCES
#1 _____
#2 _____
#3 _____

COLOR
Descriptive words: _____
Descriptive sentence: _____
_____

SHAPE
Descriptive words: _____
Descriptive sentence: _____
_____

SIZE
Descriptive words: _____
Descriptive sentences: _____
_____

- Instead of having students write a paragraph, ask them to write three words or phrases to describe their shell. Examples are "pink," "shiny," and "shaped like a fan."

- If students are capable of more than words and phrases, but not ready for a paragraph, have them write a descriptive sentence such as "My shell is pink, shiny, and shaped like a fan" or "My shell is unusual because it is black, thin, and as small as a penny."

- The best way to motivate students is to organize the lesson around a topic in which they are currently interested. For example, if bikes are a "hot" topic, ask students to describe an ideal bike. Brainstorm details such as type of seat, special controls for speed, breaking mechanisms, speed, and cost. Students might then actually send their description plus illustrations to one or more of the companies that make children's bikes.

MODIFICATIONS TO CHALLENGE ADVANCED WRITERS

- Direct students to use at least two comparisons in their descriptions as in this example.

> My seashell is almost round. On the rim of the bottom is a dash of gold, mellon, and purple. The inside is rough. The top feels like a ripple chip. My shell is about two inches wide and about as tall as a dime standing up.

- Have students add additional sentences to the paragraph, describing details such as texture, hardness, or number of parts. Encourage them to think of other categories that could be included.

- Students who require a more challenging activity can write four paragraphs: an introductory paragraph, one paragraph on shape, one on color, and one on another feature.

Name: _____   **Date:** _____   (21-1)

SELF EVALUATION CHECKLIST

Reread and rethink your description.

1. Did you begin your paragraph with a topic sentence?   Yes   No

   What is your topic sentence? _____

   _____

2. A topic sentence tells what your entire paragraph will be about. How could you make your topic sentence better at introducing your description?

   _____

   _____

3. Did you indent the first line so your reader will know this is a new paragraph with a new idea?   Yes   No

4. Details provide readers with a picture of your object. What was the first detail that you described?

   _____

   _____

5. What was the second detail that you described? _____

   _____

6. What was the third detail that you described? _____

   _____

7. What other details did you add? _____

   _____

   _____

8. Did you begin each sentence with a capital letter?   Yes   No

I have carefully read and evaluated my story. _____
                                                            Signature

© 1994 Cherlyn Sunflower

Our Sea Shell Book

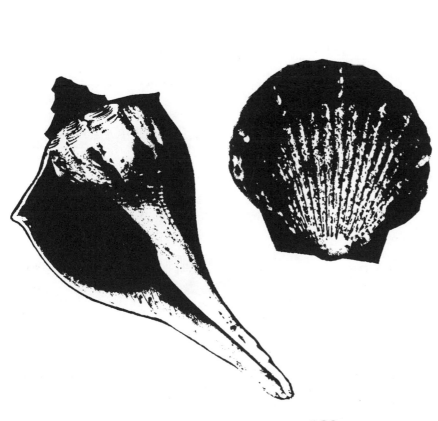

LESSON 22

TIME CAPSULES

Time capsules are an exciting way to communicate with ourselves or others in the future.

OBJECTIVES

Students will write a time capsule message. To do this, they will:

- Begin with a topic sentence that introduces the time capsule message.
- Indent the paragraph.
- Include at least six sentences containing two academic goals, two behavior goals, and two personal goals.
- Capitalize the month when the time capsule will be opened and place a comma between the day and year.

MOTIVATOR

Ask students to close their eyes and think about something special they did in school last year. Give them time to think. Then ask them to open their eyes and tell what they remember. Ask what made them remember those times. (Something important probably happened that helped them remember that day.)

Tell students that they are going to do something important that will help them remember today. Explain that they will write goals and put them in a time capsule. When they open the time capsule at the end of the school year, they'll see if they've accomplished their goals.

Pass out one self-sticking label and a small canister to each student. Explain that they will use these to make a time capsule. The canisters can be picked up at photo centers for free.

Have students write "Do not open until May 30, 19___" on their label, stick it on their canister, and set the canister aside until later.

BRAINSTORMING

Help students brainstorm some class goals for the coming school year to be put in the time capsule.

Academic Goals	Behavior Goals	Personal Goals
-get math problems right -read more books -learn cursive writing	-be friendly to everyone -work hard -share on playground	-win "Book It" pizza party -have fun while working -fill halls with published work

Key Questions

1. *What are some academic goals our class could have as a group?* (As students reply, write their ideas on the chalkboard and make a specific positive comment such as "Yes, getting more problems right in math is an academic goal we could have." Continue brainstorming until many academic goals are listed.)

2. *What is a goal that relates to how we behave or act?*

3. *What are some personal goals that our class might have? What are some things that we might want to accomplish?*

4. *Next we need to decide on a topic sentence for our time capsule paragraph.* (Remind students that a topic sentence tells what the whole paragraph will be about. Give students one possible topic sentence such as "We've set many goals for this new year" or "Our class has big plans for this year.")

How can we introduce our paragraph of goals? How can we open our time capsule message? What is another sentence that sums up our ideas about our goals? (Creating a topic or main idea sentence is difficult, so offer students one or two examples and then give them time to think. As students reply, write their ideas on the chalkboard and give specific positive feedback such as "'Our fantastic third grade class has many exciting goals for this school year' is a sentence that tells about the entire paragraph. Terrific idea for a topic sentence!" Continue brainstorming until two or three topic sentences are listed.)

Main Idea Sentences

Our fantastic third grade class has many exciting goals for this school year.

Our third grade class has big plans.

McKinley's third grade class has set many goals for this school year.

GROUP COMPOSING

1. Have students decide which topic sentence they want to use to begin their message. Ask what they need to do to show that they are starting a new paragraph. (indent)

Our Class Goals
Our fantastic third grade class has many exciting goals for this school year.

---

2. Explain that they now need to add detail sentences about their goals. Have the class select two academic goals from the list. Encourage volunteers to compose sentences stating these goals such as "We will work harder to get more math problems right" or "We plan to read more books." Write the sentences on the chalkboard. Repeat the process for behavior goals and personal goals.

Explain that now that they have chosen goals for the class for the coming school year, they can start thinking about their own personal goals for the coming year.

RESPONDING TO STUDENT WRITING

1. As students write their time capsule messages, walk around the room and visit individually with those who need help. Make as many positive comments as you can about students' useful goals and effective topic sentences.

   - **Ask specific questions** to help students think about improving ideas such as "Think of all the subjects you study in school. Which one do you most want to change? What is the change you would like to make?" or "What is one sentence that could introduce all your goals for this new school year?"

   - **Ask specific questions** to get students thinking about mechanics such as "What mark should you put after May 30 and before 1998 to make the date easier to read?"

   - **Make specific positive comments** to reinforce correct use of mechanics such as "You indented. That lets us know you are starting a new paragraph."

2. As students move into the final stages of their drafts, ask them to find a revising partner. Have them reread their time capsule message out loud to their partner to see if their goals for the coming school year have been clearly stated.

   Ask students to make any necessary improvements in their message. Explain that you will keep everyone's message in a safe place until next spring, when the time capsules will be opened to see if goals were met.

A chart like the following one may be helpful to you and your students.

Names	topic sentence	2 academic goals	2 behavior goals	2 personal goals	indented	cap. month	comma between date & year	comments

PUBLISHING

Tell students that they are now ready to put their goals into their time capsule. Explain that since the time capsules are small, they will have to fold their messages. Remind them to take a good look at their messages before they fold them because this is the last time they will see them until the end of the school year. Inform students that the next time they look at their messages they will decide whether or not they accomplished their goals.

Then have students put their time capsules in a bag. Tell students you will put the bag in a safe place until May. Then mark this date on your calendar.

MODIFICATIONS TO ENCOURAGE BEGINNING WRITERS

- Ask students to write a long list of ideas (quantity) instead of a few grammatically correct sentences (quality).
- Have students write only one academic, one behavior, and one personal goal. Suggest students use the topic sentence used in the group composition.

- Provide a specially prepared sheet of pattern sentences for students to complete such as "I have _____ goals for this coming school year," "I hope to _____," "I plan to _____," "I will _____," and "I won't _____." See reproducible 22-1 that follows.

My Goals for _____

I have _____ goals for this coming school year.

Academic Goals

1. I will _____.
2. I plan to _____.

Behavior Goals

1. I won't _____.
2. I will _____.

Personal Goals

1. I want to _____.
2. I hope to _____.

MODIFICATIONS TO CHALLENGE ADVANCED WRITERS

- Challenge students to add a reason for each goal. For example, if one academic goal was to "check out and read one library book each week," require that the student tell why he or she wants to accomplish this goal.

Name: _____ Date: _____ (22-1)

My Goals for _____

I have _____ goals for this coming school year.

Academic Goals

1. I will _____

_____

_____

2. I plan to _____

_____

_____

Behavior Goals

1. I won't _____

2. I will _____

Personal Goals

1. I want to _____

2. I hope to _____

LESSON 23

AWESOME MATH PROBLEMS

Writing word problems not only improves language arts skills but also helps students comprehend and solve word problems in math. While this lesson deals with writing addition word problems, with a few revisions to the brainstorming categories, the lesson can be adapted to subtraction, multiplication, and division word problems, as well as to money, measurement, and time problems.

OBJECTIVES

Students will write three addition story problems and supply the correct answers. To do this, they will:

- Include in each problem two characters, the objects they have, the actions they perform, and a location.
- Choose two three-digit numbers such as 371 and 509. (Tailor the numbers within each problem so that they correspond to your students' mathematical skills. For example, if students have learned to add two-digit numbers with no carrying, then ask for numbers that have zeros or small numbers in the one's place. Smaller or larger numbers can be used depending on the math skills of your students.)
- End each story problem with a question such as "How many are there all together?"
- State the mathematically correct answer to each story problem in a complete sentence such as "They had _____ _____ in all."
- Capitalize the first letter of a proper noun.
- Place a question mark at the end of the final question sentence.

MOTIVATORS

1. Give students a wild story problem to solve. Here's an example.

   Last night I was biking in Lindenwood Park, when all at once 300 mosquitoes started chewing on my arm! I squashed 237 of them, but then 784 more showed up on my leg. How many mosquitoes attacked me last night?

Require students to calculate the answer. (1084 mosquitoes attacked me.) Ask students where they think you found this math problem. Explain that you didn't find it in a math book; instead you made it up based on a real situation.

2. State that you have heard that some students think the problems in their math book are boring. Share that you think they can create better, more exciting story problems.

   Explain that today they're going to make their own textbook and answer key. State that when they are through, they'll take their textbook to another class and see if students can solve their awesome word problems.

3. If you want students to "invent" the addition story problem pattern, show them two similar addition story problems and ask how the two word problems are alike. For an example of how to do this see Lesson 40 on Cinquain Poems (Motivator 3). If you plan sample problems carefully, your students will deduce the following necessary elements: two characters who do something to a certain number of objects. An optional element is a setting.

BRAINSTORMING

Where	Characters	Action Words	Numbers	Objects
in a desert	Ryan	captured	322	space ships
at a shopping mall	Gayle	climbed	624	stairs
in outer space	Craig	swam across	913	lakes
in the lunchroom	Tyrone	juggled	700	books
	principal	ate	402	ice cream cones
	mean dog	built		robots
	CP4			
	Yun Pei			

Key Questions

1. *Where could a story problem take place? What is another exciting location for a problem?* (As students reply, respond positively and write their ideas on the chalkboard.)

2. *What are some names we could use? Who else could our story be about? What animal could be in a problem?*

3. *What do I need to do to the names?* (Capitalize them.)

4. *What could one of these characters do? What other actions could one of these people or animals perform? What could another character do?* (Elicit action words from students.)

5. *Next we need to think of what objects these characters could have.* (Review the objects or animals you used in your story problem. For example, "In my story I used

mosquitoes.") *What things do you want in our story? What is an object our characters could have?*

6. *Next we need to know how many objects. We need two numbers that can be added together.* (Decide ahead of time what types of numbers you want students to use.) *How many bones or tricks or fights does our character have? How many objects does the other character have?*

GROUP COMPOSING

Tell students that they have generated all the information necessary to create an awesome story problem. Have the following addition story problem pattern prewritten on a sheet of chart or butcher paper so you can quickly pull it out. It is important to keep up the momentum generated during the group brainstorming.

Story Problem Pattern

_____ _____ _____ _____ _____.
(1ST CHARACTER) (ACTION WORD) (NUMBER) (OBJECT) (WHERE)

_____ also _____ _____ _____.
(2ND CHARACTER)   (ACTION WORD) (NEW NUMBER) (OBJECT)

How many _____ did they _____ in all?
                (OBJECT)   (ACTION WORD)

<u>Answer</u>

They _____ _____ _____ in all.
     (ACTION WORD) (TOTAL NUMBERS) (OBJECTS)

---

1. Have students select a character to use in their group story problem. Ask what they need to remember when writing a person's name. (Capitalize it.) Circle the name and then write it in the first blank of sentence number one.

2. Next have them decide what action they want the character to do. Write the action word in the second blank.

3. Have students select an object, decide on the number of objects, and choose a location from their brainstorming lists. Circle the information and write it in the appropriate blanks.

4. Follow the same procedure for the second sentence.

    Remind students that this character does the same action with the same objects but the number of objects is different.

Story Problem Pattern

Yun Pei _____ _built_ _____ _322_ _____ _space ships_ _____ _at the shopping mall_ _____ .

_____CP4_____ also _____built_____ _____ _____ .

How many _____ did they _____ in all?

Answer

They _____ _____ _____ in all.

---

5. Inform students that next we need to complete the question to end their story problem. Fill in the object and action word. Remind students that a question mark is needed at the end of this sentence.

6. Point out that they need one more thing—the answer to the story problem. Ask students to figure out the answer now. Give them time to solve the addition problem. Use their response to complete the answer.

7. Ask students to read the story problem and answer aloud to see if it makes sense. Explain that now they will get a chance to make up five or six of their own addition story problems. Later they will choose their best three. Explain that they can use some of the ideas on the chalkboard or better yet, brainstorm some new ideas. Remind students that this is their rough draft or sloppy copy so it is okay to cross out and add ideas as they think.

RESPONDING TO STUDENT WRITING

1. As students write their own addition word problems, walk around the room. Visit informally with individual students who need special attention. Focus on the two information sentences, the one question sentence, and the five information categories: characters, action words, numbers, objects, and the location where the problem takes place.

   • Give positive feedback and ask questions such as "'Climbed' is a terrific action word for a word problem" or "What item might your character like to eat?"

2. Ask students who have finished their story problems to read each problem aloud to another person who is finished. Instruct them to listen to determine whether the problem makes sense.

   • Have them exchange papers and check their partner's answers. If they find an incorrect answer, they should ask the partner to recheck the answer.

   • After the math is checked, have them find a new partner, trade story problems, and then use the Peer Evaluation form (23-1) to improve their story problems.

   • Finally, have them reread their story problems and star three problems they think are the most exciting.

PUBLISHING

Tell students how impressed you are with their story problems. Then explain that they did so well that they are going to publish their exciting new math problems in a special way.

Publishing Idea 1: Looseleaf Notebook

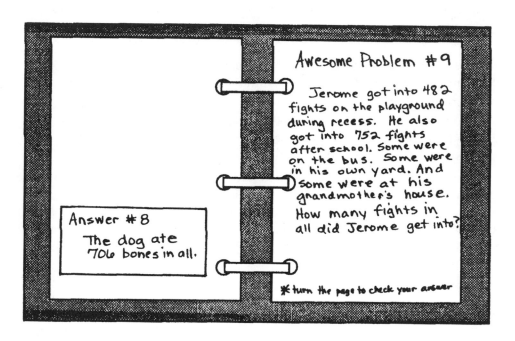

Awesome Problem #9

Jerome got into 482 fights on the playground during recess. He also got into 752 fights after school. Some were on the bus. Some were in his own yard. And some were at his grandmother's house. How many fights in all did Jerome get into?

*turn the page to check your answer

Answer #8

The dog ate 706 bones in all.

1. Give each student three problem sheets (23-2), three answer sheets (23-3), and one cover (23-4) for their best or most exciting problems.

2. Instruct them to write one story problem on each problem sheet. Remind them to print neatly so younger students will be able to read their problems.

3. Have them write one answer sentence on each answer sheet.

4. Finally, have them glue the correct answer sheet to the back of the math problem that it goes with.

5. Tell students if they finish early, they can draw a picture for each math problem below or beside the problem. Have them use a pencil to draw their picture so that when the awesome textbooks are duplicated the pictures will show up.

6. Tell students you will put all of their addition problems and answers into a looseleaf notebook and assign each one a number. Then they can take their *Awesome Math Textbook* down to a lower grade class so the students can try to solve the problems.

Publishing Idea 2: Math Bank

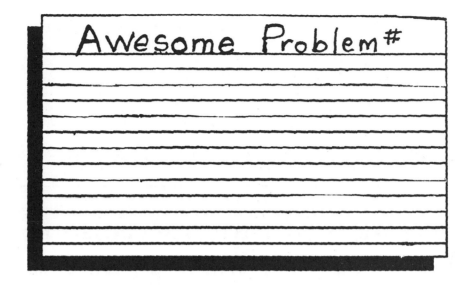

Give each student three 4 × 6 inch lined index cards and provide these directions.

1. Write "Awesome Problem #   " at the top of each index card.
2. Write one word problem on the lined side.
3. At the bottom write "Turn this card over to check your answer."
4. On the back write "Answer" at the top of the card. Then write your answer sentence.
5. At the bottom write your name so that people who solve this awesome problem will know who wrote it.

Store the cards in a file box or math bank. Students who finish their work early can select a card and solve the problem.

MODIFICATIONS TO ENCOURAGE BEGINNING WRITERS

- Ask students to write only one addition problem. Do not require them to add the location of the characters.
- Supply an action word (for example, threw, ate, caught, jumped, found) for each problem instead of having students generate these words.
- Ask the school secretary or a parent to type up the word problems and make copies instead of having students rewrite them.
- Provide academically weaker students with special sheets containing the "Story Problem Pattern" put on the chalkboard during group composing.

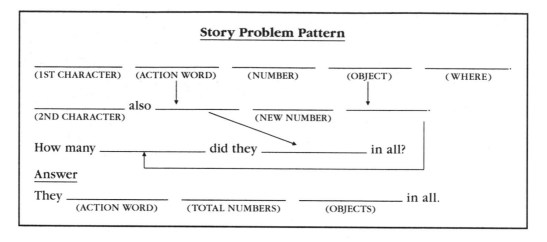

MODIFICATIONS TO CHALLENGE ADVANCED WRITERS

- Invite students to create their own information statements, questions, and answer statements instead of using the "Story Problem Pattern."

- Require them to add pieces of information to the story to make solving the problem more difficult. For example, if the story problem was:

> Gayle swam across 402 ponds.
>
> Tyrone swam across 297 ponds.
>
> How many ponds did they swim across?

The following information could be added:

> A 10 year old girl named Gayle swam across 402 ponds and walked around 17 large lakes. Tyrone liked to water ski so he skied across 107 lakes and swam across 297. Toby their dog swam across 15 ponds with them. How many ponds did Gayle and Tyrone swim across?

Name: _____ Date: _____ (23-1)

PEER EVALUATION CHECKLIST

Reread and rethink one of your partner's awesome story problems.

1. What are the names of the two characters? Are the names of each character capitalized?

_____ Yes   No

_____ Yes   No

2. What action word was used to make the problem interesting?

_____

3. What objects were in the story problem?_____

4. Where did the story take place?_____

5. Does this location make sense?   Yes   No

6. Does the story make sense?   Yes   No

7. What can be done to make the story more interesting?

_____

_____

_____

I have carefully evaluated one of my partner's story problems.

_____
Signature of Friend

I have carefully read what my partner found out about my story problem and I have tried to improve at least one thing to make my problem more interesting.

_____
Signature of Author

(23-2)

AWESOME PROBLEM

You may use this area for calculating your answer.

*Turn the page to check your answer.

Answer #

_____

_____

_____

_____

_____

_____

_____

Answer #

_____

_____

_____

_____

_____

_____

_____

Awesome

Math

Textbook

Copyright 19____

LESSON 24

PEN PALS IN THE 1990s

Millions of people have enjoyed having a pen pal. School children especially enjoy receiving letters from other children around the world. Another group that would appreciate hearing from your students are the millions of senior citizens in retirement homes. Many of these people would love to hear regularly from an elementary school student, and they would have the time to write back. Adjust the group brainstorming categories in this lesson to fit your students' audience.

OBJECTIVES

Students will write an introductory letter to a future pen pal.
To do this, they will:

- Put the day's date in top right corner.
- Include a greeting such as "Dear Sixth Grader," followed by a comma.
- Write one paragraph that gives information about the writer. Include an opening sentence such as "My name is _____" and at least 2 detail sentences about the writer.
- Write a second paragraph that requests information from the potential pen pal. Include a topic sentence and at least two questions for the pen pal, with question marks following each question.
- Include a closing followed by a comma and a signature.
- Capitalize the greeting, proper nouns, and closing.
- Indent each paragraph.

MOTIVATORS

1. Inquire what state or country your students would like to visit. Then tell them that they don't have to leave their own town because they can "visit" by exchanging letters with

207

a pen pal who lives in another state or country. Explain that through letters they can get to know a new person and learn many things about a new place.

2. Write a letter to your class explaining that they will be getting a pen pal. Duplicate enough copies for each student. If you wish, add a personal note to each student. Walk into the room carrying the letters in a "mail bag." As you call out students' names, deliver a letter to each student. Allow time for students to read their mail. Discuss how much fun it would be to get to know a pen pal and also how much they could learn from one.

(date)

Dear

    This year you are very lucky because you will get to have a pen pal. Your pen pal will be a (boy/girl/senior citizen) in (grade/town/other). Today we are going to write a letter introducing ourselves to our future pen pals. This way when your pen pals write back, they will know who you are and what you like to do.

    Maybe you'll want to tell your pen pal about your favorite activities, sports, hobbies, your family, pets, friends, our school, what you are learning, or other things. Soon you will be getting a letter back from your new friend. Won't it be fun to get a letter?

Your teacher,

---

3. Tell students about a pen pal that you have had. Show students a picture of your pen pal. Then read or tell them some of the things you and your friend write about.

BRAINSTORMING

Self	Hobbies & Sports	Family & Pets
age	water slides	size of family
name	playing dodgeball	favorite person in family
height	canoeing	parents occupation
hair color	piano	kind of pet
how earn $	basketball	tricks pet does
	climbing trees	

School & Friends	Town, State, Country	Other
name of school	where I live	have computer
grade level	special places	favorite food
number of classmates		favorite singer
favorite class		TV shows
teacher's name		hero/heroine
what do with friend		

Key Questions

1. *What will you tell your pen pal about your appearance? What personal information do you think your pen pal would like to know about you?* (Allow plenty of time for students to think. As students reply, write their ideas on the chalkboard under the category "Self." Continue until 5–6 ideas are listed.)

2. *To help your pen pal get to know you, what do you want to tell your pen pal about your favorite activities, hobbies, or sports? What do you like doing after school and in your spare time?* (Write ideas under the category "Hobbies and Sports.")

3. *What information might you tell your pen pal about your family? What special things do you do with your family? What might your pen pal want to know about any pets you might have?* (List ideas under "Family and Pets.")

4. *What might your pen pal like to know about our school? What's something that you like or dislike about school that your pen pal might want to know? What books do you like to read? Who are your favorite authors?* (Make a category "School and Friends.")

5. *What are some things you could tell your pen pal about your friends?*

6. *What do you think your pen pal will want to know about our town, state, or country?* (List ideas under "Town, State, Country.")

7. *What are some other things your pen pal might like to know that we haven't covered so far? What recent events have occurred? What events are coming up soon?* (List these ideas under "Other.")

8. *So far we've brainstormed a great deal of information about ourselves. What questions do you want to ask your pen pal? What questions do you have about your pen pal, his/her interests, family, or school?* (Suggest that students compose who, what, when, where, why, how questions to get the most interesting answers.)

**Who, What, Where, When, Why, How
Questions**

1. How old are you?
2. Where do you live? Please send me a map.
3. What is your school like?
4. What do you do for fun?
5. What do you look like?
6.

Ask students to write the six categories from the chalkboard across the top of the long side of a blank piece of paper. Have them fold the paper in half the long way. Have them open the paper and write the word "questions" below the fold. Allow students to brainstorm before moving to group composing.

Self	Hobbies & Sports	Family & Pets	School & Friends	Town	Other

Questions

GROUP COMPOSING

1. Ask students what they need to put in the top right hand corner of their letter (the date) and what punctuation mark is needed to separate the date and the year (comma). Write the date on the chalkboard.

2. Explain that next they need to write the greeting, using their pen pal's name if it is known or a general name such as "Sixth Grader." Ask what punctuation is needed after the greeting to show a pause (comma).

3. Explain that the body of a letter tells the message. Remind students that they have brainstormed lots of ideas. Encourage them to use one idea from each category so that the letter will sound interesting to a pen pal. Suggest they begin their letter "My name is _____ and I hope you'll become my pen pal."

As volunteers compose sentences from each category, add them to the letter.

March 3, 1995

Dear Pen Pal,

    My name is Cherlyn and I hope you'll become my pen pal. I play volleyball after school each day. I try to practice my piano but sometimes I'm too busy. I have three small dogs named Lacy, Lhong and Tilley. Tilley causes many PROBLEMS.

    I'm looking forward to getting a letter from you. Here are some questions to get you started.

4. Tell your students that they'll end the message part of their letter with a paragraph of questions for their pen pal. Suggest that they begin the paragraph "I'm really looking forward to getting a letter from you. Here are some questions to get you started!" Ask what they need to do to show readers they are starting a new paragraph. (Indent.)

5. Encourage volunteers to suggest questions to put in the class letter. Continue until you have added three or four questions to the second paragraph. Then ask what punctuation mark is needed after each question.

6. Explain that next they need to signal the pen pal that the letter is almost over. Tell students some people write "Sincerely," "Your future friend," or "Hope to hear from you soon." Have students select a closing and add it to the letter. Ask what punctuation goes after the closing to show there is a pause. (Comma.)

7. Remind students that after the closing they need to write one final thing—their name.

RESPONDING TO STUDENT WRITING

1. As students compose their pen pal letters, walk around the room and comment positively on interesting details and questions. Ask each student one or two questions to extend or clarify his or her letter.

2. If you want students to work toward particular learner outcomes, focus your comments and questions to help each student self evaluate one or two of the following outcomes.

   • Write an introductory letter to a future pen pal which includes:

   _____ the day's date in top right corner

   _____ a greeting such as "Dear Sixth Grader," followed by a comma

   • The first paragraph gives information about the writer and contains:

   _____ an opening sentence such as "My name is _____."

   _____ at least 2 sentences of details about the writer

   • A second paragraph requests information from the potential pen pal and includes:

   _____ a topic sentence

   _____ at least 2 questions for the pen pal

   _____ question marks following each question

- Remember to:
  - _____ add a closing followed by a comma and a signature
  - _____ capitalize the greeting, proper names, and closing
  - _____ indent each paragraph
3. As students finish, ask them to quietly read their letter out loud to a friend to see if it is interesting, sounds friendly, and gives clear information.

PUBLISHING

Ask students to write their pen pal's full name and address, if known, on the front of an envelope. Then have them fold their letter into thirds and put it in the envelope. See Reproducible 24-2. If students have a photo of themselves, they should include it with their letter. When everyone is done, gather all the letters in a large envelope and mail or deliver the letters.

There are several good resources for pen pals.

Learning Magazine

Has a Reader Exchange page each month where you can find or advertise for pen pals.

Student Letter Exchange
Info. Dept.
630 3rd Ave., 15th Floor
New York, NY 10017
1(212) 557-3312

Has provided pen pals for 53 years. Students can select the age, country, and sex of their pen pals. All pen pals can write in English.

International VideoPals
630 N. Tustin Ave., Suite 165
Orange, California 92667
1 (800) 843-7257

$15 registration fee. Tapes needing conversion cost $10. This non-profit whole class to one in another country by swapping videotapes.

Or write:

Attention Postmaster
Please deliver to any Elementary School _____ grade
in (give a town, state, and zip code)

Select a town from a state map. Smaller towns or cities are more likely to respond.

MODIFICATIONS TO ENCOURAGE BEGINNING WRITERS

- Require students to write only one paragraph that contains three details and one or two questions.

- Provide special paper that cues students where to place the different parts of a letter. See Reproducible 24-1 at the end of this lesson.

- Provide less able students with pattern sentences such as:

My name is _____.
I'm a boy/girl in _____ grade.
My school _____.
Two activities I'm involved in are _____ and _____.
My parents are _____.
I have _____ sisters and _____ brothers.
My pet's name is _____. He/she can _____.
My favorite subject in school is _____. My teacher is _____.
What _____? Where _____? When _____?

MODIFICATIONS TO CHALLENGE ADVANCED WRITERS

- Ask students to include a map with their letter. Have them find a map of the United States and locate their state. Then have them put a star on the map where their state or town is located so that their pen pal can see where they live.

- Contract with students who can write multiple paragraphs to expand each category (self, hobbies and sports, and so on) into a full paragraph. Guide these more advanced writers to use the category title to build a topic sentence and add two or three sentences of details from that category. For example:

> You probably want to know about my school and friends, too. I'm in the fifth grade at Govalle Elementary. Ms. Henrickson is my neatest teacher. She lets us write to real people instead of just practicing. The subject that I like best is math. In math we have been learning to divide. Cathie and Rita are my best friends. We talk on the phone at night and check our homework together.

Put stamp here.

LESSON 25

DIARIES

A diary is a safe place where one's private thoughts and feelings can be expressed and examined. Since students may not be used to writing to themselves, it may take time for them to get into this form of writing. One difficulty students may experience when they begin to write in a diary is a lack of vocabulary to express their feelings. For these reasons it is very important to provide the motivator and group brainstorming steps daily. Included here is one possible five-day series of lessons, which can be repeated several times.

As you teach this lesson, be sensitive about what students are willing to share and take care not to invade their privacy.

OBJECTIVE

Students will put one sentence (or one paragraph) of thoughts and feelings into a diary for at least 5 days.

DAY 1
MOTIVATORS

1. Tell students a diary is a place to write down the events of the day and personal feelings about them. People also use diaries to reflect on and clarify their own thoughts and feelings. Ask students to listen carefully as you read something that you once wrote in a diary and are willing to share.

2. Read your students a children's book written in the form of a diary. Point out that each diary entry begins with the day's date. Help students to see that a diary is more than a factual account of a day's

events. Ask your school librarian to help you find a book written as diary entries that your students will like. Examples are:

The Diary of a Church Mouse by G. Oakley (New York: Atheneum) (1987)

Dear M. Henshaw by B. Cleary (New York: Morrow) (1983)

BRAINSTORMING

Key Questions

1. *What kind of day have you had? What is one feeling you've had today?* (Since many students may not have language for their feelings, allow plenty of time for students to think. As students reply, accept each feeling and write it on the chalkboard. If a student has something to share but can't express it, go to questions 2, 3, 4, and 5. Then return to question 1. If necessary, supply several feeling words and allow the student to choose the one closest to his/her feeling.)

2. *When did you have this feeling?*

3. *Where were you?*

4. *What happened? What happened before that? After that?*

5. *Why do you think you felt this way?*

(Repeat the sequence of questioning until four or five types of feelings and related details are disclosed.)

Feelings	When	Where	What Happened	Why
sad	after lunch	on the playground	Carrie pushed me.	I had the ball.
proud	now	at home	My dad is going to watch my soccer game.	We might win the F-M league.
silly	yesterday	at my friend's house	We made Jello that felt like leather.	I only put in one cup of water.

GROUP COMPOSING

1. Point out that they should begin their diary entry with today's date. Ask what punctuation mark goes between the day and the year. (Comma.)

2. Ask students to select one thing they would like to write about in their diary today.

3. Remind students that a diary is a very private type of writing. Explain that if a student doesn't want to write about an event that happened yesterday or today and how they feel about it, they can draw a picture about it. Or they can write about something other than their thoughts and feelings. Remind them that this is their private diary. No one will read it unless they decide to share what they have written or drawn.

RESPONDING TO STUDENT WRITING

1. As students begin to reflect on their day, ask those who are having difficulty getting started to use the "How do you feel today?" pictures (Reproducible 25-1) or the "List of Possible Feelings" (25-2). Have students read through the faces or words listed and find one that is close to how they are feeling. During the first few days help students clarify their feelings and extend their thoughts.

2. Although working towards particular learner outcomes doesn't really go with this free, spontaneous type of personal writing, there are two outcomes you could set and monitor: how often and how much students will be expected to write. Set aside time on a daily basis. Five to ten minutes a day is sufficient at first.

3. As students write about events that occurred recently and about their personal feelings, take some time to write in your own diary. Remind students that what they write in their diaries is private. If a student wants to share a page of his or her diary with you, set aside time to do this later.

PUBLISHING

Many people use a spiral notebook for their diary, and they hide it so no one will find and read it. Your students may enjoy making a diary with a "lock."

Precut two 9- by 12-inch pieces of wallpaper or use construction paper for each student. Provide these instructions.

1. Lay one piece of wallpaper (horizontally for younger students and vertically for older students) face down in front of you.

2. Put eight sheets of lined paper on top of the wallpaper.

3. Next stack your diary entry for today on top of these sheets.

4. Now lay the "How Do You Feel Today" page on top of these sheets.

5. Lay the other piece of wallpaper face up on top.

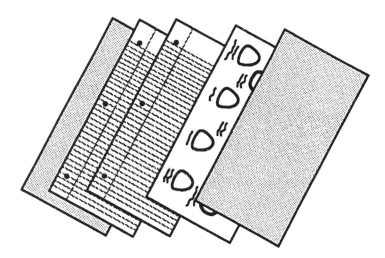

6. Hold all the sheets together as you staple at the top, middle, and bottom of the left edge.

7. On the right side of your diary opposite the staples and about 1 inch from the edge, punch a hole through the cover and all the pages.

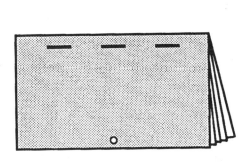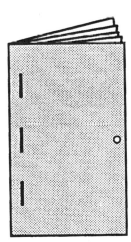

8. String yarn or heavy string through the punched hole and tie a bow or a loose square knot. This will help keep your diary PRIVATE.

9. Write "My Diary" or "_____'s Diary" along with the words "Keep Out" or "Private" on the cover.

MODIFICATIONS TO ENCOURAGE BEGINNING WRITERS

- Have less able students and students with language or learning disabilities draw in their diary <u>before</u> or <u>instead of</u> writing. It is fine to express one's inner thoughts and feelings in a picture since the real audience in a diary is oneself. (See Reproducible 25-3.)

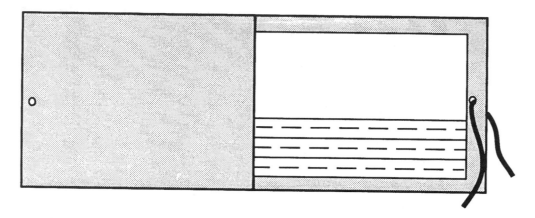

- Suggest students write shorter entries in their diaries. On day one have students put only two sheets of paper with all five days of the week on one sheet in their diaries.
- Give students 4½- by 6-inch paper to use in making their diaries. The smaller paper makes the blank page look less intimidating. Reproducible 25-4 gives you another diary page layout.

MODIFICATIONS TO CHALLENGE ADVANCED WRITERS

- Expect high achievers to write more often, gradually lengthen their writings, or put some of their thoughts and feelings into poetic formats. High achievers may want to continue writing after the diary unit is over. Ask them to purchase a spiral notebook to keep in their desks to use when they want to express their feelings or when their work is finished.

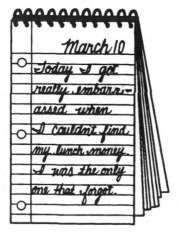

DAY 2
POSSIBLE MOTIVATORS

1. Tell about a horrible day you have had recently and why you decided to write your problems in your diary.

2. Inquire who has recently had something go wrong or had something happen that upset them. Discuss how they handled these feelings. Point out that many people find they can handle their problems more successfully after they have written their thoughts in a diary.

BRAINSTORMING

Brainstorm some problem situations with the class. Encourage students to share ideas for the following categories and list them on the chalkboard: a problem, how it began, who was involved, how the student felt, and how the problem could be solved.

Problem	How Began	Who Involved	Felt	Solution
brother hit me	playing on computer	Darin me	happy mean	Don't let him borrow my games.
cat disappeared	we left town	Jerry was supposed to feed Blackie.	sad angry	Walk around the block and look for Blackie.
mom and dad fight				

Key Questions

1. *What has upset you today? What problems have you had recently?*
2. *Which problem can we use for an example?*
3. *How did it begin?*
4. *Who was involved?*
5. *How did you feel? Why do you think you felt this way? How do you think the other person felt?*
6. *How could this problem be solved? What could you do to help solve the problem in a healthy way?*
7. *Repeat the #1-6 sequence of questioning until three or four types of problem situations have been disclosed.*

GROUP COMPOSING

Guide students to compose a diary entry using the information they have brainstormed. Encourage them to feel free to write about any of their thoughts and feelings, not just problems. Perhaps they would want to write about something they would like to change and their feelings related to it. Again remind them this is their private diary, and no one else is going to read it unless they decide to share a special paragraph or page.

DAY 3
POSSIBLE MOTIVATORS

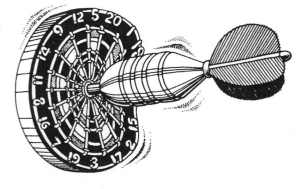

1. Share a recent accomplishment and one of your current goals. Explain that a person might want to put these thoughts and feelings in a diary so they won't be forgotten. For example, a goal might be to raise and sell Pekingese puppies and to lose twenty pounds.

2. State that people often write about their wishes and dreams for the future in a diary. Share one or two of your own special wishes or dreams as a child or some of your current ones. Especially share wishes and dreams that are not for objects so students will think about more important wishes. For example, a wish might be that someone who is sick will feel better soon.

BRAINSTORMING/GROUP COMPOSING

Brainstorm ideas for wishes and dreams or accomplishments with students. Also elicit what feelings were associated with the accomplishments or goals.

Wishes/Dreams	Accomplishments	Feelings
baby sister	won 2nd place in ice hockey	terrific; tired too
no more violence	taught my dog to fetch	proud
my mom finds a job		
my dad comes home soon	**New Goals**	**Feelings**
I want to read	get a bike route	rich
rain, rain, rain	be nice to my aunt	crabby
	learn a computer game	smart

Suggest that if students don't feel like writing about their dreams, goals, or accomplishments, they might write about their likes and dislikes or a pet peeve.

DAY 4
POSSIBLE MOTIVATOR

Share an important decision you have had to make recently. Then explain how writing in your diary helped you organize and clarify your thoughts and feelings so you could make a good decision. Give an example.

Next show students a sheet of paper divided into a "pro" and a "con" side. Tell about one decision you made and some ideas for and against it.

BRAINSTORMING/GROUP COMPOSING

Brainstorm ideas for decisions students have to make. For each one have students list 3 reasons for it and 3 against it. Explain that they should evaluate the reasons for and against to help them make a decision.

Decisions	Pros	Cons
Should I keep my newspaper route?	I can earn some spending money.	I'll have to get up at 5:30.
Should I tell on a friend who stole something?	It was a bad thing to do.	I promised I wouldn't tell.
Should I be best friends with "X"?	My friend needs help.	She/he won't be my friend any more.

Remind students they may write about something else if they wish to and that no one else will read their diary entry unless they decide to share it.

DAY 5
POSSIBLE MOTIVATORS

1. Explain that diaries can also be a place to write secret thoughts and feelings. A diary is special because no one else is allowed to read it unless the writer decides to share.

2. Share a special secret. Discuss why it is important to write and think about some secrets. Explain that family secrets and secrets about other people often should not be shared.

BRAINSTORMING

Instead of having students share their ideas orally, ask those who wish to share a secret to write it on a slip of paper. Collect the papers and read some of the ideas to the class. This allows students to share but remain anonymous. Request that students think before they share something that involves other people. Explain that many families have secrets that they should save for their personal diary.

When working with older students, you can question orally but have students think their responses instead of sharing with the group. Older students may have many more secrets that they will feel are very private. You'll want to honor this.

How do I feel today?

Angry or Mean

Wonderful, Helpful, Special, or Proud

Sad or Disappointed

Tired, Embarrassed, or Confused,

Astounded or Panicked

Stupid, Lonely, Hurt, or Exhausted

Naughty or Clever

Worried, Fearful, or Tense

Thoughtful or Bored

Calm, Brave, or Kind

How do I feel today?

LIST OF POSSIBLE FEELINGS

Abandoned	Eager	Jealous	Refreshed	Tempted
Affectionate	Embarrassed	Kind	Rejected	Tense
Angry	Energetic	Lazy	Relaxed	Terrified
Annoyed	Envious	Left out	Relieved	Tired
Anxious	Excited	Lonely	Sad	Ugly
Ashamed	Exasperated	Loving	Satisfied	Upset
Astounded	Exhausted	Mad	Scared	Valuable
Bad	Fascinated	Mean	Selfish	Valued
Bashful	Fearful	Miserable	Shocked	Wonderful
Betrayed	Foolish	Naughty	Silly	Worried
Bitter	Frustrated	Nervous	Sneaky	
Bored	Frightened	Nice	Special	
Brave	Free	Outraged	Strange	
Calm	Full	Overwhelmed	Strong	
Capable	Glad	Panicked	Stupid	
Caring	Good	Peaceful	Surprised	
Challenged	Grateful	Pleased		
Cheated	Greedy	Powerful		
Cheerful	Guilty	Pressured		
Clever	Happy	Proud		
Competitive	Hateful			
Confused	Healthy			
Cowardly	Helpful			
Crabby	Helpless			
Cruel	Homesick			
Crushed	Horrible			
Delighted	Hurt			
Determined	Ignored			
Different	Important			
Disappointed	Impressed			
Distracted	Inspired			

(25-3)

Dear Diary,

Monday ______________________________

____

____

____

Tuesday ______________________________

____

____

____

Wednesday ______________________________

____

____

____

Thursday ______________________________

____

____

____

Friday ______________________________

____

____

____

Dear Diary,

_____
_____
_____
_____
_____
_____
_____
_____
_____
_____
_____
_____
_____

Section 4

INFORMATIVE
"HOW TO" WRITINGS

DIRECTION/HOW-TO PARAGRAPHS

Writers can use a direction paragraph pattern to explain how something is done. Direction paragraphs begin with a topic sentence that tells what will be explained. Next directions or steps are given in chronological order. Each direction or step should contain a clear, precise action word.

The directions often begin with transition words or phrases (such as first, second, next, after that, then, finally) or numbers that signal the order in which the steps must be done. Most direction paragraphs also include necessary supplies and tools. These may be listed before the directions or simply within each direction.

Some Forms of "How-to" Writing

Advice	Recipes
Beauty Tips	Remedies
Explanations	Rules
Game Directions	School or Neighborhood Guides
How-to-do-it Manuals	Survival Manuals
Instructions	Travel Directions

LESSON 26

ART PROJECT

When students enjoy an activity such as an art project, encourage them to write down what they did so they can do it again later or share it with others who might like to do it. Pick any simple art project that appeals to your students. They will need to be led through many lessons of this kind before they become mature enough writers to really respond to this seemingly easy writing task.

OBJECTIVES

Students will write directions for doing an art project. To do this, they will:

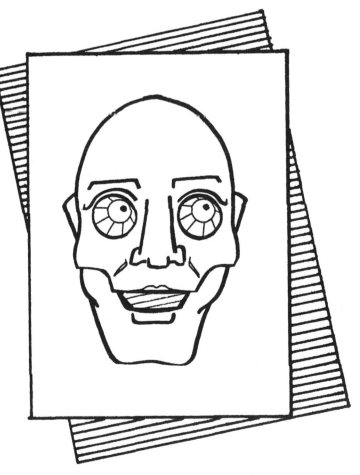

- Create a title that names the art activity and capitalize major words in the title.
- Give a complete list of necessary materials and tools.
- Give clear and complete step-by-step directions.
- Number each direction in chronological order.
- Start each direction with a capital letter and end it with a period.

MOTIVATOR

Show students several pieces of paper with different shaped holes in them. Ask them if they have ever wondered what you could do with a piece of paper that has a hole in it.

Explain that the other day you wanted to make something for a friend, but all your paper was ruined. Share that then you discovered how to make something out of a piece of paper with a hole in it. Show them a picture you have made from a hole.

Then tell students that they are going to make some special pictures from paper with holes in it. Give these directions plus any additional directions that you think will be helpful: *First cut a hole in the middle of your paper.* (Allow time for students to cut a hole.) *Now think about what the hole could be. Make your hole into a picture.* (Allow time for students to think and draw pictures.)

Tell students that other people might like to make pictures from holes, too, or they might want to do this again later themselves. Explain that before they forget how to do this, they need to write down some notes about what materials they used and list each step they followed. Then students will be able to share this information with other people who want to create pictures.

BRAINSTORMING/GROUP COMPOSING

Tell students that you will write their ideas on the chalkboard, but that they should also take their own notes. They should copy the ideas and steps on a piece of scratch paper as you write on the board. Explain that this will be their rough draft, so it's okay to cross out and make changes. Tell students that it doesn't matter if their notes are a little messy as long as they can read their own notes. Inform students that the notes on the board will be erased later on.

Key Questions

1. *What materials and tools did we need to make our picture?* (As students reply, give positive responses such as "Good, you remembered that we needed a piece of paper" and write their ideas on the chalkboard.) *What else did we need to make our picture?* (Continue brainstorming until the children run out of ideas.)

2. *What did we do first? What did we do next? What was the last thing that we did?* (List ideas on the chalkboard.)

3. *What could we call this kind of picture?* (Respond positively; for example, "'Cut Out Art' would be a great name for this art activity.") *What's another name for what we just made?*

Titles

Cut out art
Hole picture

You will need:
      paper
      scissors
      crayon
What to do:

  1. Cut out a hole in the midde of the paper.

  2. thought about what the hole could be.

  3. draw a picture with crayons.

RESPONDING TO STUDENT WRITING

1. In this step you will be modeling the revising process for students. Explain that since they have listed their ideas for how to do the art activity, they now need to self evaluate to see if the materials and tools are complete and if the directions are clear and in the right order.

   Instruct students to reread the directions. Then ask them where they see errors. Make changes on the chalkboard as students discover errors. Tell students to make corrections on their own notes. Also remind students that it is okay to cross out and make corrections because this is their rough draft. Inform students that they'll use their own notes to write their own directions.

Titles

O A

Cut ȯut ȧrt

Hole picture

You will need:

paper

scissors

crayon

What to do:

1. Cut out a hole in the midde of the paper.

think

2. ~~thought~~ about what the hole could be.

around the hole

3. draw a picture with crayons.

If students need help discovering errors and making improvements, ask some of these questions:

- Where will the person get a piece of construction paper?

- Where should the person cut the hole?

- What should we add to Step 3 to make it more complete?

- How could you start Step 2 to show it is a complete direction sentence?

- What do we need to do to the beginning of direction three?

2. Explain that it is time to give their directions one more check to make sure they are clear, complete, and in order. Put students in groups of two.

Instruct students to slowly read aloud their directions for the Hole Picture as their partner tries to make a new hole picture. Tell students to carry out only the directions they hear so their partner can decide if the directions are clear, complete, and in order. Tell students to make changes on their rough drafts that will make the directions easier to understand and will help create more exciting pictures.

PUBLISHING

State that directions like these would make a good gift for someone. Then ask students who might like to receive a Hole Picture and the directions for this easy art project. (Older or younger friends, parents, grandparents, brothers, sisters.)

Inquire whether they think the person who will receive the directions will want to read their notes the way they are. State that their notes probably look a little messy and ask what they can do to solve this problem. (Write their directions neatly on another piece of paper.)

Then pass out a special paper (Reproducible 26-1) designed to help organize the directions. Remind students to use their best handwriting. Walk students through the following directions.

1. The first thing you will do is write the name you picked for your art project on the line at the very top of this paper.

2. Next in the space beside the words "You will need:" copy from your rough draft the list of materials you will need to make the Hole Picture.

_____
(title)

You will need:

What to do:
1. _____
2. _____
3. _____
4. _____
5. _____
6. _____

---

3. Then, on the numbered lines under the heading "What to do:" copy from your paper each step to follow to create the picture. Be sure to carefully check the numbers of each step and make sure they are in order because you may have changed some numbers when you revised.

4. Finally, paste your directions on the back of your picture.

MODIFICATIONS TO ENCOURAGE BEGINNING WRITERS

• Do <u>not</u> require students to take notes. Instead be sure to involve them orally in the group brainstorming, group composing, and group revising. When the time comes to rewrite the directions on special paper, ask them to help you by writing down the ideas from the board.

MODIFICATIONS TO CHALLENGE ADVANCED WRITERS

• Have students write down the directions for a different art activity. Be sure to create a real audience and purpose; for example, suggest that other students might like to try this new idea during their free time.

(26-1)

_____
(title)

You will need:

What to do:

1. _____

2. _____

3. _____

4. _____

5. _____

6. _____

7. _____

8. _____

9. _____

LESSON 27

SCIENCE REPORT

Encourage students who are involved in a science experiment or activity, to write it down so they can repeat it later or share it with others. Adapt this language arts lesson to coordinate with your own hands on science program. Students will need to be led through many different writing lessons before they become mature enough writers to repeat this seemingly easy writing task on their own.

OBJECTIVES

Students will write a science report. To do this, they will:

- Include a title, a list of necessary supplies, directions, and results for an activity or experiment.
- Put the directions in chronological order.
- State accurately the results (findings) in at least three complete sentences.

- Number each direction.
- Start each direction with a capital letter and end each one with a period.
- Capitalize the major words in the title.

MOTIVATOR

Tell your class that they are all going to be involved in an important science activity.

Have students form a semi-circle around the table where you will be working so they can all observe what happens. Tell students that you have gathered some supplies that are needed to perform the experiment. Point to matches, a wide, heavy candle, a large clear container, a clear glass or jar, water, food coloring, and a utensil for stirring. Talk out loud as you work.

> *First, I'll pour approximately one inch of water into the large clear container. Now, I will put two or three drops of food coloring in the water. After I do this, I will simply stir the food coloring and the water together until it is all one even color. Next, I'll put the candle into the water container and light it carefully with a match.*

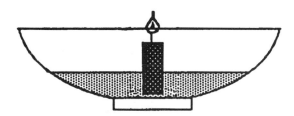

> *Now, the exciting part of the experiment is about to happen! What do you predict will happen if I put the glass over the candle?* (Call on a few students. Provide positive feedback such as "That's a possibility. Yes, that might happen.")

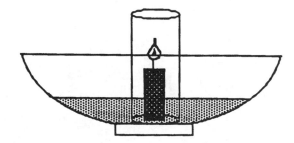

> *Now, I'll place the glass over the candle. Watch what happens. What happened? Why did the candle go out?* (Wait for responses. Reinforce students' ideas about what happened with comments such as "Yes, the candle went out because the flame didn't have oxygen to burn.")

What caused the water to rise inside the glass jar? (Allow plenty of wait time so students can think. Guide students to understand that because the air was used up, the water was pulled in. A vacuum was created.)

Get students thinking about the importance of preserving directions for important experiments and activities. Share a story of a time when you wanted to remember some directions but forgot to write the directions down. Here's an example.

Tell students you really like chocolate. Then explain that you were at a picnic once and someone had brought a pan of chocolate s'mores that were delicious. Relate that you asked for the recipe and were told what was in them and how to make them. Explain that the recipe sounded so easy to make you didn't write it down because you thought you could remember it. Confide that now you can't remember all the ingredients or the directions for making the bars and are really disappointed.

BRAINSTORMING/GROUP COMPOSING

Inform students that they can record the experiment just conducted so that if they want to repeat it later or share it with others, they will remember how to do it.

Tell students that as they recall the experiment, you will write down what they say on the board. Tell students they will also need to take their own notes on notebook paper. Their notes will be their rough draft so it is all right if they need to cross out and make any changes. Explain that a rough draft can be messy as long as they can read what they wrote.

1. *What is one thing we need to remember? What else do we need to include when we write our report on a vacuum? What is one more thing we need to remember so that we can do this experiment again later?* (Elicit the categories, necessary materials, results, and steps in the experiment from students and write them on the chalkboard.)

Necessary supplies	Steps	Results
1. candle	1. Put water in container.	The water rose in the glass.
2. matches	2. Add food coloring.	The candle went out.
3. food coloring	3. Stir water.	The fire used up the air oxygen.
4. spoon	4. Put in the candle.	
5. water	5. Light the candle.	This created a vacuum.
6. tall slender jar		
7. large clear container		

2. *Let's begin with the results of our experiment.* (Brainstorm results first because this is the most important part, but insert this information in the last column.) *What happened in our experiment?* (The water rose in the jar.) *What else did we*

notice? (Repeat out loud what each student says as you write it on the board. Continue until the results are stated in several ways.)

3. *Why did we think this happened? Why did the water rise in the jar?* (Elicit that the loss of oxygen created a vacuum. Add this information to the last column.)

4. *Next we need to recall how we began the experiment. What did we do first? What did we do after that? What did we do next?* (Continue brainstorming until all steps have been recalled. Accept all ideas.)

5. *What supplies did we need in order to perform the experiment? What other equipment did we need?*

RESPONDING TO STUDENT WRITING

1. Model the revising process for students. Guide students to review the writing to determine if the results of the experiment are clear and necessary supplies are complete. Remind students to check their steps to be sure they are clear and in the right order.

    Make changes as students discover errors or think of improvements. Remind them to make changes to their notes because later what is written on the board will be erased. Remind students again that it is okay to cross out and make corrections because this is their rough draft.

2. If students need help discovering errors and making improvements, ask specific questions such as the following:
    • What caused the water to rise up in the glass?
    • What would be a title that lets everyone know this experiment is about vacuums?
    • What was the most exciting finding?
    • Why did we need to use colored water?
    • What can we add to Step 2 in the "What did we do?" column to make it clearer?
    • What do you need to do to the first word of each step to show it is a new sentence?
    • If you don't know how to spell an important word like vacuum, what can you do?
    • What punctuation could you put after Step 3 to show where the thoughts stop?

Necessary supplies	Steps	Results
1. candle	1. Put 1 inch of water in container.	The water rose in the glass.
2. matches	2. Add ^(2 to 3 drops of) food coloring.	The candle went out.
3. food coloring		
4. spoon	3. Stir ^(the) water and food coloring.	The fire used up the oxygen
5. water		
6. tall slender jar	4. Put ⫶X̶ the candle in the water.	This created a vacuum.
7. large clear container		
	5. Light the candle. with the matches.	

3. Read the group report out loud to students or ask a student to read it. Direct students to listen to see if supplies are complete, the directions are clear, concise, and complete, and the results are accurately stated.

PUBLISHING

Tell students not to worry if their notes look rather messy because these are their rough drafts. Give them a special sheet on which to write their final copies. (See Reproducible 27-1.) Then inform students that they will put their science report in a special science notebook so they won't forget the experiment and their findings. (See Reproducible 27-2.) Provide these directions.

1. *On the top line, place the title of our science experiment. What should we name our experiment?* (Accept various titles.)
2. *After "Necessary Supplies," list all the supplies we used.*
3. *On the lines under the heading "Steps," write each step in the order that we followed to complete the experiment.*
4. *Then after "Results" write what we found out.*

Creating a Vacuum

Necessary Supplies: Water, Candle, Clear container, Clear glass, Food coloring, Matches, Spoon

Steps:

1. Put 1 inch of water in the container.
2. Add 2 to 3 drops of food coloring.
3. Stir the water and food coloring.
4. Put the candle in the water.
5. Light the candle with the matches.
6. _____

Results:

_____
_____
_____
_____

Inform students that they have now completed the first page of their Science Experiment Book. Explain to students that they will be adding pages for different experiments throughout the whole year. Instruct them to punch holes along the top (long) side of the report and cover and fasten them together using yarn or brass fasteners.

MODIFICATIONS TO ENCOURAGE BEGINNING WRITERS

- Involve students who get into trouble frequently in helping you assemble materials for the science experiment. Alert the other students that you will pick someone who is listening and sitting quietly to help you with the experiment. If possible, select a student who really had to "work hard" to sit still to help with the activity by putting the glass over the candle.

- Allow students with poor attention spans or ones who have difficulty following oral directions to participate in the group composing by listening. Do not require them to take notes. Involve these students orally in the group brainstorming and group revising. When the time comes to rewrite the directions in the students' special science notebooks, ask them to help you by writing down ideas from the chalkboard in their science notebook.

MODIFICATIONS TO CHALLENGE ADVANCED WRITERS

- Have students write the directions for a different science activity. Be sure to create a real audience and purpose; for example, suggest that other students might like to do this experiment during their free time.

Necessary Supplies: _____

Steps:

1. _____

2. _____

3. _____

4. _____

5. _____

6. _____

_____

Results: _____

_____

_____

_____

_____

27-2

Science Experiment Book

LESSON 28

HOW TO PLAY MY FAVORITE GAME

Your students will find that the ability to teach other people games adds a plus to their social lives. These directions can also be modified for other types of "How To" writings.

OBJECTIVES

Students will write directions for a favorite active, board, or card game. To do this, they will:

- Create a title such as "How to Play _____."
- Capitalize important words in the title.
- Begin the direction paragraph with a topic sentence such as "_____ is an awesome game."
- Include in the directions the objective of the game and how to begin, play, and end the game.
- Write clear, complete directions in chronological order.
- Use at least five transition words such as "first" or "next" to signal the order of the directions.
- List all the objects, materials, and number of players necessary for the game.

MOTIVATORS

1. Have students play a favorite group game at recess. This serves both as a motivator and provides information that will be needed later in the lesson.
2. Instruct students to close their eyes and remember what it's like to be bored. Repeat the following.

   You know (insert a vacation or "the weekend") *is coming up soon. Imagine having nothing fun to do.* (pause) *You are so bored.* (pause) *You wish you had written down how to play some of the neat games we played at school today.* (pause)

If you only knew a few games and all their rules, you would have a great vacation/ weekend. (pause) *If only you could remember how to play, you could teach your friends, cousins, and family.* (pause) *You could have lots of fun.* (pause) *Now open your eyes.*

Share that they are going to write down how to play their favorite games so whenever they get bored, they will know an exciting game to play alone or with friends.

BRAINSTORMING

Favorite Games	Objects/Players Needed to Play	Objectives Special Rules/Penalties
Kickball	large ball	• get other people out
Four Square	driveway	• when the ball doesn't go in
Heads Up	2–5 people	a square that person is out
Magic Window	chalk	• person in square 1 is boss
Lazy Pony		and begins game
Hangman		• beginners get 2 chances
Volleyball		
Old Maid		
Go Fish		
Pictionary		

Key Questions

1. *First, we need to think of lots of terrific games. What is one of your favorite games? What is an easy game to play? What's a game you play outside?* (Allow plenty of time for students to think. As students reply, write their ideas on the chalkboard and respond with specific positive feedback. Continue brainstorming until many ideas are listed.)

2. *Before we go on, we must choose one game. Let's use* (insert game just played) *since we all played that one today at recess.*

3. *What objects (or materials) are needed for this game?* (As students reply, write their ideas on the chalkboard and respond with positive comments such as "A utility ball is a critical object in Four Square.") *How many people are needed to play the game? What have we forgotten?*

4. *What is the goal or objective of the game?*

5. *What rules do people need to know to play this game? What is considered proper and improper behavior? What penalties are necessary for improper behavior in this game? What special privileges do certain players have? How do we make sure the game is fair?*

6. *How do players begin the game? What happens next? After that what do people do? How do you win the game? What determines the end of the game? When is the game over?* (As students contribute ideas, write them on the chalkboard under the heading "Game Directions.")

Game Directions

Boss drops ball and hits it to another square.
That person hits ball into another square.
Don't fall and skin your knees.
Ball can only bounce one time.
If ball touches a line, person is out.
Everyone else moves up a square.
The boss starts the game again.

GROUP COMPOSING

Remind students that they have brainstormed objects, players, special rules, and directions for the game, and they are almost ready to start composing their own game directions. But first, they will write the directions for (the game just played) together so they can see how to use each of their ideas.

1. Explain that the first thing they need to do is write the name of the game. Write the title on the chalkboard.

2. Begin the group directions with the topic sentence "Playing _____ is fun, but you have to think and react quickly." Write the sentence on the board and ask why you indented the first word in the sentence.

   Inform students that when they write their own directions they can use this topic sentence or they can make up their own introductory sentence. Other examples include:

   "Here's an awesome game that will keep you entertained during your vacation."
   "The directions and rules for _____ are listed below."
   "_____ is a terrific game for a boring day."
   "_____ is fun and easy to play."

List of Transition Words	**How to Play Four Square**
First Second Then While After As And then Next Finally	Playing Four Square is fun, but you have to think and react quickly. You will need a driveway, chalk, utility ball, and four to eight players. This is how to play. First the boss drops the ball and hits it . . .

3. Guide students to compose a sentence stating the objects and number of people needed to play the game and another sentence to state the objective.

4. Next ask students to reread the list of directions they wrote and think about in what order to put them. As students make decisions, go back and put a number beside each direction. If you question the order of a particular direction, ask students why they think the direction should go next.

5. As you write the first direction on the chalkboard, point out that you need a transition word to put before it to signal that this is the first direction. You may want to provide a list of transition words such as first, second, then, after, finally for students to choose from.

6. Ask students how you should indicate the beginning and the end of this sentence. (Capital letter; period.)

7. Continue by asking a student to tell which direction comes next. Then before you write the direction, ask another student to choose an appropriate transition word. Continue until all steps are written.

RESPONDING TO STUDENT WRITING

1. As students write their game rules, walk around the room and visit individually with students who need extra help.

   - **Give positive feedback** on clear topic sentences and easy to understand directions.

   - **Ask one or two questions** to clarify a particular direction or to help the student to extend or to order their directions.

   If you want to see how students are meeting the learner outcomes, use a Learner Outcome Chart (Reproducible 28-2) to check off desired outcomes. Put it on a clipboard for easy use as you circulate.

Names	title	topic sentence	indent	objects	players	objective of game	# of directions	begin capital	end period	directions in order	clear concise complete	# of transition words	capitalize	period

2. As students complete their game directions, ask them to self evaluate by reading their directions softly out loud to themselves. As they read out loud have them decide if the directions are clear, concise, and complete. Explain that by reading out loud they are more likely to hear an error than by rereading silently.

3. Provide students with a meaningful reason for revising such as the following.

    When we finish revising our game directions, we are going to post them around the room so everyone can read them and learn some new games for a boring day. If everyone writes the directions to their favorite game, when we are through, we'll have directions for about 30 exciting games to play!

4. As students move into the final stage of their rough drafts, ask them to find a revising partner. Have them trade game directions and read their partner's directions. Then ask them to complete the questions on the Peer Revising Checklist (Reproducible 28-1). Explain that this will help their classmates know what they did well and find out where the game directions can be improved.

5. After students have completed the Peer Revising Checklist, have partners meet and take turns talking through each question and answer on their checklists. They may enjoy getting out of their seats and finding a spot on the floor to work with their revising partner. Finally, have students return to their desks to thoughtfully improve their directions.

PUBLISHING

Explain that now that they've revised their directions for their favorite games, you'll post them around the room so their classmates can learn some new games before they leave for the weekend/vacation.

Alternate Publishing Method

Instruct students to write their directions on 5- by 7-inch lined index cards. Then collect all cards and punch two holes at the top of each card about ½ inch from the top. Put rings through the holes in the cards and snap the rings shut. Place the game directions where students can read them during free time.

MODIFICATIONS TO ENCOURAGE BEGINNING WRITERS

- Pair stronger writers with weaker writers.

MODIFICATIONS TO CHALLENGE ADVANCED WRITERS

- Ask students to focus on making the directions especially clear, concise, and complete.
- Allow students to pick a more complicated game or to write several paragraphs: one paragraph for introducing the game, the objective, the necessary objects and the number of players; one paragraph on how to begin the game, one or more paragraphs on the middle and ending of the game.

• Suggest students write other types of directions. Help students choose a topic that would be really useful to someone. Here are a few examples.

HOW TO CARE FOR A PUMPKIN

Carving a pumpkin is pretty easy.

1. Get a pumpkin.
2. Draw eyes, a nose, and a mouth on it.
3. Cut off the top.
4. Take out the seeds.
5. You can eat the seeds or throw them away.
6. Carve out the face.
7. Put a candle in it and light it.
8. Now it is done. It looks terrific.

HOW TO FLOSS YOUR TEETH

You will need: dental floss, water, towel

What to do:

1. Wash your mouth and hands.
2. Tear off a piece of dental floss.
3. Tie the dental floss in a circle.
4. Slide the dental floss between your teeth.
5. Gently rub it back and forth.
6. Repeat steps 4 and 5 with all teeth.
7. Take the dental floss out and throw it away.
8. Wash your mouth and hands again.
9. Dry your hands with your towel.

HOW TO CHANGE OIL

Changing oil in a car will be simple if you follow my steps. First put an oil pan under the plug. Then loosen the plug and take it off. Next loosen and take off the filter. Let the oil drain for about 30 minutes. Now put a new oil filter on. Put the plug in. Take the oil cap off. Put the amount of oil your car takes in it. Put the cap on. Wipe off the dipstick and measure to see that the oil is full. Start the car up and make sure nothing is dripping.

PEER REVISING CHECKLIST

- What is the name of your partner's game? _____

_____

- What is the topic sentence? _____

_____

- What objects or materials or equipment is needed to play this game? _____

_____

- How many people do you need to play this game? _____

- How does the game begin? _____

_____

- What do the players do next? _____

_____

- List two good transition words the writer uses.

_____   _____

- What is the writer's clearest direction? _____

_____

- What direction could be improved? _____

_____

- What is one good rule that is given for the game? _____

_____

- How do you win the game? _____

_____

- What has the writer left out? _____

_____

Suggestions:

Name of Reader _____

LEARNER OUTCOME CHART

							Names
							title
							topic sentence
							indent
							objects / players
							objective of game
							# of directions
							begin / end
							directions in order
							clear concise complete
							# of transition words
							capitalize
							period

© 1994 Cherlyn Sunflower

Section 5

PERSUASIVE WRITINGS

PERSUASIVE PARAGRAPHS

When a writer wants to persuade, convince, or entice the reader toward a particular point of view, a persuasive paragraph pattern is useful. A persuasive paragraph consists of a topic sentence stating the writer's opinion or feelings and two or more sentences stating reasons, facts, or evidence that supports the opinion.

Reasons are ordered so that they achieve the desired result; often the most powerful or convincing reason is placed last. At the end of a persuasive paragraph, many writers repeat their opinion and/or make a final plea for the reader to do something.

Some Forms of Persuasive Writing

Advertisements
Advice Column
Apology Notes
Book Jackets
Book Reviews
Buyer's Guides
Campaign Speeches
Classified Ads
Commentaries
Commercials (Radio or TV)
Complaint Letters
Congratulations
Consumer Reports

Critiques
Debate Notes
Editorials
Evaluations
Excuses
Letters to the Editor
Letters to Public Officials
Letters of Request
Movie Reviews
Petitions
Political Speeches
Propaganda
Proposals

Protest Letters
Rebuttals
Recommendations
Requests for Forgiveness
Requests for Financial Aid
Restaurant Reviews
Sales Pitches
Solution Letters
Thank-You Letters
Valentines
Warning Labels
Warnings

LESSON 29

UNBELIEVABLE EXCUSES

Your students will enjoy writing unbelievable excuses so much that they won't realize that they are learning to write persuasively. With a slight adjustment this lesson can be used for teaching students to write real, convincing reasons for their actions.

OBJECTIVES

Students will write 5 unbelievable excuses (or one serious convincing excuse). To do this, they will:

- Refer to a real situation or event in each excuse.
- Include one outrageous reason in each excuse (or 3 reasons for a serious excuse).
- Begin each excuse with a capital letter and end it with a period.
- End each excuse by signing their name in cursive.

MOTIVATORS

1. Walk in late to class on purpose. Give a totally unbelievable excuse.
2. Share some real excuses you used when you were young. Tell students that you are going to read them a book that will remind them of excuses they probably used when they were "young children." Read a book such as *Bed Time for Frances* by Russel Hoban, Harper: New York, 1960. Instruct students to pull on one ear or make a thumbs up signal, each time they detect an excuse. Some of the excuses used in this book are about not being able to go to bed until getting another kiss or until the door is left ajar or because there is a tiger in the room.
3. Ask students to share some things they have done lately that have gotten them into trouble. Then ask them for some of the excuses they use frequently.

BRAINSTORMING

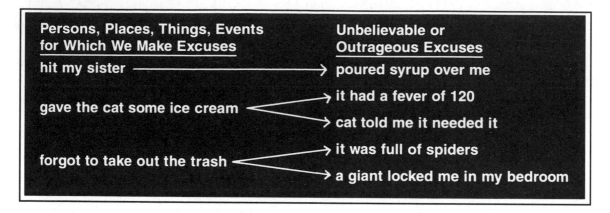

Key Questions

1. *What is something which you need an excuse for? For example, if you didn't do your homework, you would need to tell me why it wasn't done. What is something that you do that needs an excuse? What is something that you don't do, but you should, that needs an excuse?* (As students reply, give positive feedback such as "Hitting your sister would certainly be something *for which you'd need an excuse*" and write their ideas on the chalkboard. Continue brainstorming until many situations are listed.)

2. *What reason could we give for the first event we listed?* (As students respond, make a positive comment such as *"Terrific! Having a fever of 120 degrees is an outrageous reason for feeding your cat all that ice cream."*) *What is an unusual or unbelievable reason we could give for the next event?* (Continue brainstorming until two or more reasons are listed for each situation.)

GROUP COMPOSING

Explain that information from the two brainstorming categories will be used to make some really unbelievable and outrageous excuses (or to explain some real, but unfortunate situations).

Sentence Excuse

1. Remind students that they brainstormed many situations where an excuse is needed. Have them choose one situation for the class to write about.

2. Next ask them to look at the excuses they brainstormed and select the one that sounds the most unbelievable (or the excuse that gives the best true reason for the unfortunate situation).

3. Ask students how they should signal the beginning of their excuse sentence (a capital letter) and how they should end the excuse (a period).

> **Excuse #1:**
>
> I hit my sister because she poured hot syrup all over my head.
>
> **Excuse #2:**
>
> I didn't take out the trash because someone locked me in my bedroom all morning.

Paragraph Excuse

1. Remind students that they brainstormed some situations where a lengthy excuse is needed. Ask them to choose one of those situations for the group to write about.

2. Remind students that they will need a topic sentence to begin their paragraph. Suggest using "I am sorry that (insert situation) ." Ask what they need to do to this first sentence. (Indent.)

3. Point out that next they should choose several reasons to explain the situation. Circle each reason as it is selected.

4. Guide students to decide which of the 3 reasons is the strongest or most unbelievable. Ask where they think this reason should be placed to have the most impact—first or last. As students order the 3 reasons, write them on the chalkboard.

5. Tell students that the ending of an excuse is very important. If necessary, suggest two or three final pleas such as "I won't ever do _____ again" or "Please forgive me. I'll do it right next time." Encourage students to choose a final plea that will make their excuse even more ridiculous (or their excuse accepted).

RESPONDING TO STUDENT WRITING

1. As students begin to write their excuses, circulate around the room. Read back individual students' excuses so that they can hear what they have written.

   • Make positive comments about powerful yet outrageous (and convincing) reasons and about interesting (or special) situations or events that need an excuse. Give positive feedback.

   • Ask questions that help students sharpen their reasons.

2. If you want students to learn to self evaluate, list the following on the chalkboard or on a chart.

   _____ Did you write five unbelievable excuses (or one serious convincing excuse)?

   _____ Does each excuse begin with a situation or event?

   _____ Does each sentence excuse contain one unbelievable reason?

   _____ Does each sentence begin with a capital letter?

   _____ Does each paragraph excuse contain three reasons?

   _____ Is the paragraph excuse indented?

PUBLISHING

Inform students that they are going to share their excuses with another class so that they can see how unbelievable and outrageous some excuses sound. Pass out several "Unbelievable Excuse" sheets (Reproducible 29-2) to each student. Ask students to illustrate each outrageous excuse. Have them compile their excuses in a book titled "Unbelievable Excuses." (Use Reproducible 29-1 for a cover.) If real excuses were written, have students sign their names and personally hand the excuse to the appropriate person.

MODIFICATIONS TO ENCOURAGE BEGINNING WRITERS

- Help students choose a situation and have them write the reason.

- Supply a sheet with a prewritten pattern sentence such as "I didn't _____ because _____" or "I _____ because _____."

- Have students write only one situation and one excuse. Perhaps they would like to make excuse badges instead of a book. (See Reproducible 29-3.)

MODIFICATIONS TO CHALLENGE ADVANCED WRITERS

- Provide additional excuse patterns such as the following.
  1. I was _____(what)_____ because _____(why)_____ .
     _____(signature)_____
  2. I wanted to ___(do what)___ , but I ___(did what)___ when ___(what happened)___ .
     _____(signature)_____
  3. Please excuse __(who)__ from __(doing what)__ because __(why or for what reason)__ .
     _____(signature)_____

- Require students to write excuses in paragraph form. Each paragraph should state the situation, contain the excuse and two or three reasons, and end with a final plea. Example:

    I'm sorry I left my homework at home. (situation) My mom spilled coffee on it. I tried to dry it off but my dog took a big bite out of it and then it accidentally was tossed in the trash. (three reasons) I really worked hard on it and had finished all of it. (final plea)

- Challenge students to write convincing reasons that persuade the reader to feel sorry for the writer.

- Contract with a student whose interest level is high to interview other students at recess and compile a list of convincing excuses for particular situations such as why they didn't do homework, forgot to brush teeth, drank all the pop in the refrigerator, lost their lunch money, and so on.

Unbelievable Excuses

by _____

Unbelievable Excuse Number____

_____

_____

_____

_____

_____

_____

_____

Unbelievable Excuse Number____

I didn't_____

because_____

_____

Unbelievable Excuse Number____

I _____

because_____

_____

LESSON 30

THANK-YOU NOTES

Students can learn important language arts skills, as well as important social skills, by writing thank-you notes. Suggest that they make time to thank the janitor for a clean room or the school principal for a drug free school, or last year's teacher, or the students on the safety patrol for helping students cross the street, or the librarian, the P.E. teacher, or a best friend . . . .

Thank You
Thank You
Thank You
Thank You
Thank You
Thank You
Thank You

OBJECTIVES

Students will compose a real thank-you note and send it to the person thanked. To do this, they will:

- Include the day's date at the top of the thank-you note.
- Begin the note with the salutation "Dear . . ." followed by the person's name and a comma.

- Capitalize and correctly spell the name of the person thanked.
- Begin the body of the note with an opinion sentence telling what the person did that was special. Example: "Thank you for _____." or "Your _____ was _____."
- Indent the opinion sentence.
- Follow the opinion sentence with at least two convincing reasons why the visit was appreciated such as "My favorite thing was _____ because _____," "I'm glad I heard you because _____," or "I learned _____."
- End the note with a closing such as "Sincerely" followed by a comma.
- Use legible handwriting.

MOTIVATORS

1. Invite a speaker to give a presentation on a particular topic. You might invite someone from the community to talk about recycling, a parent to talk about a particular career, or the librarian to speak about some special book found in the library. Afterwards, state that the speaker gave a lot of information. Comment that it would be nice if students let the speaker know how much they appreciated the presentation. Ask students how they might do this without talking to the person.
2. Tell students about a time when you gave or did something and weren't thanked. Explain how you felt. Also bring in a thank-you note that you received. Share how you felt when you received the note and why you felt that way.

BRAINSTORMING

Explain to students that you will help them brainstorm some ideas and compose a group thank-you note to the speaker. Later they will write their own thank-you notes.

Key Questions

1. ***What was your opinion of the speaker's presentation?*** (As students reply, respond positively and write their ideas on the chalkboard. Have the class choose one opinion to use in the class letter.)

> **Your presentation on recycling was _____.**
> exciting
> interesting
> very important
> informative
> powerful

2. *Now let's think of reasons to support your opinion that the presentation was informative. What did you learn from the speaker? What do you want to thank the speaker for? Why did you appreciate the speech? Why was the speech important/educational/thought provoking/needed? What is another reason you liked the speech?* (As volunteers suggest reasons, write them on the chalkboard.)

> ## Reasons
> —learned how to help recycle glass, plastic, cans
> —explained three methods: reduce, reuse, recycle
> —gave us a handout to post on the refrigerator

3. *Now we need to decide how to sum up our thoughts and close the note. How can we tell the speaker how much we enjoyed the presentation? What are some other ways to tell someone thank you without saying the words "thank you"?*

GROUP COMPOSING

> April 25, 19____
>
> Dear Director of Waste Management,
>   Your presentation on recycling was very informative. _____
> _____
> _____
>   _____
>   _____
>   (your name)

1. Tell students that they are now ready to compose their thank-you note. Ask what goes first at the top of a letter, what comes after the date and what greeting many people use.

2. Elicit from students to whom they will address their thank-you note and what punctuation to place after the person's name to signal a pause. Write the information in correct letter form on the chalkboard.

3. Ask students to read the opinion sentence created during brainstorming. Use this to begin their note. Ask what they need to do at the beginning of the paragraph to signal the reader that this is a new thought. (Indent.)

4. Have students review the class list of reasons why the presentation was informative and create sentences telling why they appreciated the presentation.

5. Finally, ask students for a sentence to close the note and say goodbye.

6. Add a closing such as "sincerely" and ask what punctuation should follow this word. Tell students they are now ready to compose their own personal thank-you notes.

RESPONDING TO STUDENT WRITING

1. As students compose their thank-you notes, walk around the room. Visit individually with those who need help. Give positive feedback and ask questions to extend or clarify students' reasons.

   • Opinion

   If a student's opinion is clear and positive, make a comment such as "The speaker will appreciate knowing that the presentation was 'terrific.'"

   If a student's opinion is not positive, make a positive comment and ask a question such as "It sounds like you already knew quite a bit about this topic. Even though you didn't learn much, what is something positive you could say about the presentation or the speaker?"

   • Reasons

   If a student's reasons are powerful, make a comment such as "The speaker will be interested to hear what you learned from the presentation."

   If a student's reasons are not clear or not powerful, ask a question such as "Why did you like _____ coming to our class? What did you learn?"

   • Punctuation

   If a student's punctuation is correct, make a comment such as "Your comma after 'Dear _____' will help the reader know when to pause."

   If a student forgets to put a punctuation mark, make a comment such as "Look at your closing. What do you need to put after the words 'Thank you' to show a reader to pause?"

2. Ask students who have finished their notes to read them out loud to a classmate and consider whether the speaker will understand that they appreciated the visit and why.

PUBLISHING

Tell students that you'll send their thank-you notes to the speaker to show their appreciation. See the note paper (Reproducible 30-1) at the end of this lesson.

MODIFICATIONS TO ENCOURAGE BEGINNING WRITERS

• Have students draw a picture to show what they learned or liked about the presentation.

• Ask students to write a one-sentence note using one of the following patterns.

   "The _____ that you gave was _____."

   "Thank you for _____ because _____."

   "Before hearing your speech, I _____."

   "Your _____ was appreciated. I plan to _____."

Then have students add a hand drawn picture to accompany the sentence.

- During the group brainstorming be sure to call on students who need to see their ideas written on the chalkboard. This will help these students recognize that their ideas are valuable. Later when they write their thank-you notes, they can look back at the chalkboard to see how particular words are spelled.

Modifications to Challenge Advanced Writers

- Require students to add a final summary comment or closing remark such as "I'll remember to take care of my world and to recycle as much as I can."

- Ask students to write two paragraphs. Each paragraph should begin with a different opinion and be followed by two or more reasons which support that opinion.

- Have students write a thank-you note to a real person for an actual gift or act of kindness.

Have them use the following format:
1. Who are you going to thank?
2. What did they give you or do for you? Why are you thanking them?
3. Why did you like/value the gift or act?
4. How have you already used the gift?

   How will you use the gift in the near future?

- Challenge students to write a note of thanks for something they did not like. This is the most difficult personal letter for many people to write. The goal of this type of letter is to focus on the positives. For example, an honest statement might be "I appreciated being remembered on my birthday."

fold

Thank You
Thank You
Thank You
Thank You

cut

fold

Thank You
Thank You
Thank You
Thank You

LESSON 31

THOUGHTS
TO THE PRESIDENT

Persuasive writing can be tied into any current event or issue in the news. Encourage students to send persuasive writings to public officials such as the President, the Vice-President, the spouse of the President, state or national senators and representatives, presidents of large companies, and others.

OBJECTIVES

Students will write a persuasive paragraph to the President stating their opinion on a topic. To do this, they will:

- Start the message with a topic sentence such as "War is _____." The blank will contain a word or phrase expressing the student's opinion about something.
- Follow the topic sentence or opinion sentence with at least two sentences of evidence or reasons that support the opinion sentence.
- Write reasons that are convincing.

- Indent the paragraph.
- Capitalize the main words in the title.

MOTIVATOR

Inquire whether students have been watching the news or reading the newspaper lately. Share several newspaper and magazine articles that you found on current issues or events. Ask students what they have heard recently about the fighting in _____, for example. Accept students' thoughts and ask them to elaborate.

Involve students in deciding to send their thoughts to the President.

BRAINSTORMING

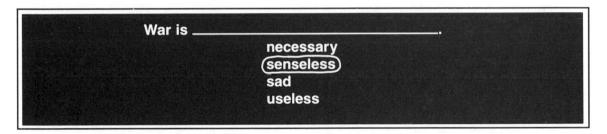

Key Questions

1. *What is your opinion of war or another situation? What are some words that describe your thoughts about war?* (As students reply, respond positively and write their ideas on the chalkboard. Note: You need to recognize students opinions, but you also need to act impartial so that students feel free to be for or against the topic. Here are two examples of positive feedback: "Yes, 'it's necessary' is one view that many people have about war." and "Yes, 'senseless' is another opinion many people have."

2. *Which opinion should we use in our paragraph?* (Use a majority opinion to work with as a class.)

3. *Now let's try to support the opinion that war is senseless (or another chosen opinion). What is some evidence that proves war is senseless?* (Allow plenty of wait time. Coming up with evidence requires higher level thinking than giving one's opinions does. Accept each reason impartially and write it on the chalkboard. Continue until several reasons are listed.)

> **Evidence**
> Families get split up.
> People are killed.
> Buildings are destroyed.

GROUP COMPOSING

Invite students to put their opinion and evidence together in a paragraph to convince other people that war is senseless.

1. *Guide students to compose a sentence stating the chosen opinion. Ask what they need to do to let readers know they are beginning a paragraph.* (Indent the first line.)

2. *Explain that since they have an opinion or topic sentence, they now need to add the reasons to support it. Ask what reason they think is the strongest. Suggest that students might want to put their strongest evidence first or last.*

3. *As students suggest an order for the evidence, number the sentences on the chalkboard. When they are satisfied with the order of their reasons, write the sentences in the paragraph.*

Evidence

1. Buildings are destroyed.
2. Families get split up.
3. People are killed.

---

4. *Tell students that they need one more sentence to conclude or tie their thoughts together. Elicit a sentence that sums up or repeats the topic sentence.*

War

War is senseless. During a war many people are killed. Families are split up. Buildings and homes are destroyed. For these reasons, war is senseless.

Tell students that they are now ready to brainstorm their own opinions and evidence and write their thoughts to the President.

RESPONDING TO STUDENT WRITING

1. As students compose their thoughts to the President, walk around the room. Visit individually with students who are having difficulty coming up with evidence that supports their opinion. Give positive feedback and ask questions to extend or strengthen students' evidence.

   • Opinion sentence

     If a student has stated an opinion (not a fact like "war costs money"), make a comment such as "Your topic sentence, 'War is death' really tells me your opinion of war."

- Evidence in support of the opinion

   If a student's evidence supports the opinion, make a comment such as "Your statement 'Families are split up' is evidence to show that war is useless."

   If a student is stuck, ask a question such as "What is another piece of evidence that you can add to prove that war is awful?"

   If a student needs help ordering the evidence, ask a question such as "Out of all your evidence, which is the strongest?" or "Where in your paragraph do you want to place this evidence?"

2. As students finish, ask them to find a revising partner. Explain that they should read their thoughts to the President aloud to each other to see if their evidence really supports their opinion.

PUBLISHING

Remind students that you are going to send their thoughts about war to the President. Explain that they need to rewrite their paragraphs on the school's special letterhead stationery. Encourage students to use their best handwriting so the President can read their thoughts. Share that their thoughts about war will perhaps influence the decisions the President makes.

President...
White House
Washington, D.C.
                20500

MODIFICATIONS TO ENCOURAGE BEGINNING WRITERS

- Ask students to write one or more opinion sentences about war. A pattern sentence such as "War is _____ because _____," can be provided.
- Show students how to reorder their reasons by numbering the evidence or cutting their paper into strips.

- The day before you teach this lesson give students a homework assignment to 1) listen to the nightly news to see what is happening with a particular current event or 2) find and read an article in the newspaper on the event. This may help the students be more able to contribute (and be positively reinforced) during the motivation discussion and group brainstorming.

- After students have rewritten their paragraphs on the school's letterhead paper, ask a student who needs peer recognition to collect all the paragraphs. Help this student address one large envelope, affix the stamp, and carry it to the office to be mailed.

MODIFICATIONS TO CHALLENGE ADVANCED WRITERS

- Require students to write three persuasive paragraphs. For example, if a student thinks war is cruel, wasteful, and necessary, then this student would write one paragraph with the topic sentence "War is cruel," one with the topic sentence "War is wasteful," and one with the topic sentence "War is necessary." Each topic sentence should be supported with two reasons.

- Contract with students to use one to three transition words to signal a shift to a new piece of logic.

BEGINNING REASONS	FOLLOW-UP REASONS	RESTATING THE MAIN IDEA
One important idea is	Some more evidence is	Therefore
First of all	In addition	Thus
The best proof is	The next piece of evidence is	As a result
The strongest evidence	Finally	In summary
To begin	Lastly	Since
	Similarly	In conclusion
	Besides	Otherwise
	Nevertheless	In view of these
	Also	For these reasons
	Furthermore	It is evident
	Accordingly	Unless
	Another reason	

- Suggest that students include an opposing point of view in their thoughts to the President and give proof that the viewpoint is faulty. Give students a list of transition words to use to help state another point of view.

WORDS SIGNALING AN OPPOSING POINT OF VIEW		
But	However	Unless
While	On the other hand	Yet
Although	In contrast	Conversely

LESSON 32

ADVERTISEMENTS

Advertisements in magazines, newspapers, the yellow pages, and on radio, television, or billboards, are an important way businesses convince readers to buy their product. The product might be an object, a food, a service, a place, or a form of entertainment. The purpose of an advertisement or commercial is always to increase business by selling more of the product.

OBJECTIVES

Students will write an advertisement promoting a product or a place. To do this, they will:

- Begin the advertisement with an attention-getting slogan or title such as "The Ultimate Water Slide."
- State an opinion or belief about the place or product such as "White Water is a great water slide."

275

- Follow the opinion with at least two facts or reasons why potential customers should patronize the place or purchase this product.
- State each reason in a complete sentence and include at least one adjective.
- End the advertisement with a final statement such as "Try White Water this Weekend."
- Capitalize the name of the place or product.
- Illustrate the advertisement with art work or a photograph.

MOTIVATORS

1. Inquire how many students have been to the water slide (or another nearby attraction). Wait for a show of hands. Direct students to sit back, close their eyes, and imagine they are back at the water slide. When students are ready, repeat the following.

   > *You can hear the water flowing down the slide and people splashing in the pool below the slide. Feel the air. It is really hot. Won't that water feel good? You walk over to the lockers and open one. You put your shoes and towel inside and shut the door. You slowly walk over to the staircase and look up, up, way up to the top of the slide. You think about how much fun it will be. You and your best friend start climbing the stairs. Soon you are high above all the people and cars. You can see a long way off. Now you reach the lifeguard and hand her your ticket. Carefully you sit in the water and quickly push off. Down, down and around you slide. Water splashes in your face. You see your friend behind you and you wave. Suddenly you see the pool ahead. Splash! And you swim to the steps and get out. Wow! What fun! What a great way to cool off!*

   Instruct students to open their eyes. Tell students that many of them have told you about the water slide (or other attraction) in town. Explain that they are going to create some advertisements to persuade more people to go to the water slide.

   Share that when they are finished, you'll take their advertisements to the manager or the owner so they should try to make their ads really sound convincing.

2. Review the definitions of opinions and facts. Then ask students to look for examples of convincing facts in various magazine advertisements.

3. Ask students why a company advertises a product. Explain that an advertiser's main purpose is to encourage, convince, persuade, or entice people to buy a product.

BRAINSTORMING

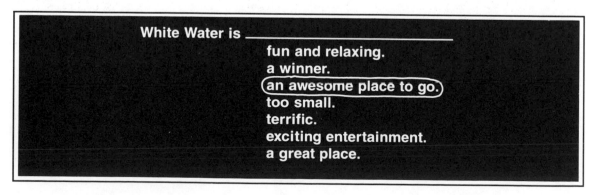

Key Questions

1. *What is your opinion of White Water? What was your reaction to the water slide?* (Continue brainstorming opinions, reactions, and evaluations until six or seven opinions are listed. Note that at this point in the lesson you are not asking for "facts." If a student suggests a fact, respond by accepting the idea and saying that this is some information "we may want to use later." Or write the fact under a fact column but not in the opinion column.)

2. *We have listed lots of opinions. Now we need to choose one positive opinion for our class ad.* (Point out that advertisements focus on the positive aspects of a product. Explain that other opinions are fine to have, but that they just wouldn't end up in an ad. Instead a negative opinion could end up in an editorial. Circle the opinion the class selects. Comment that when they create their own ads, they can choose any of these positive opinions or new opinions for their topic sentence.)

3. *Next we need to think of some facts or reasons to convince people to agree with our opinion. What do people need to know about the water slide to convince them to visit it? What kinds of things could we say about White Water that would convince people it is great entertainment? What could we say about the slide itself? Guide students to supply some objectives and write their suggestions under an appropriate heading on the chalkboard.*

4. *Why else do people like to go to a water slide? What other things do we need to tell people about besides the slide?* (Elicit responses such as food and video games. Add these two information categories to the chalkboard.)

   What other things do we need to put into an ad to convince people to go to the White Water for entertainment? (Accept any other information categories that are suggested and add these to the chalkboard.)

5. *Now we need to go back to each of the categories and think about some specific facts and reasons that will entice other people to visit. What else could we say about the slide itself?* (Encourage students to state what they specifically like about the slide—for example that it's fast.)

Slide	Food	Videogames	Other
fast	fresh hot	new games	cool music
long	popcorn	only 25¢	clean bathrooms
the water	cokes	air conditioned	lockers
was not cold	candy	at least 8	no lines
you could seat	gum	up-to-date games	only $7.50 for all
2 on the mat	lemonade		day
they let you go			shade for parents
down backwards			tables
wet and slippery			

6. *Next we need to think of some specific facts about the food. What did you like about the food? How could we describe the popcorn? What else could we say about the food to entice people to go to the water slide?* (Continue brainstorming this and the other information categories.)

7. *To begin our advertisement, we need a title that catches the readers' attention and makes them want to read the rest of the ad.* (Show several attention getting slogans or titles you found in various advertisements.) *How could we draw attention to our ad for the water slide? What other short phrases could we use to get people to read our ad?* (Point out that a question is often a good attention getter. Respond positively to students suggestions and continue brainstorming attention getters.)

Attention Getters

Fargo's Answer to Boredom
Want to Slide All Day?
For a Cool Day Go With White Water
Slide All Day for Only $7.50
Fastest Ride in North Dakota
Slide Over to White Water

GROUP COMPOSING

Point out that since they have an opinion, convincing reasons, and attention getters, they are now ready to create an ad together.

1. Tell students that the opinion goes first, and write the previously selected opinion on the chalkboard.

2. Remind students that next they need to give facts and reasons to convince people that White Water is a terrific place to go for entertainment. Ask what they would like to tell people about first—the slide, the food, the video games? Here you are asking the students to organize and order their thoughts. Guide them to see that telling about the slide first seems logical because that is the main reason why people would go.

3. Ask students to look at the slide list. Have a volunteer reread the facts and reasons on the list out loud. Comment that ads need to be as concise as possible. Suggest that they combine several of the ideas about the slide into one sentence. Add this sentence to the chalkboard.

4. Have students choose other categories of reasons they want in their ad and compose a sentence for each one. Add the sentences to the ad.

5. Inform students that next they need to add a snappy final plea or concluding sentence such as "Try it," "Don't pass us by," or "You won't get a better deal in a million years" to complete the ad. Write the sentence on the board.

6. Finally have students select one attention getter or eye catcher as a heading or title for their ad.

Slide Over to White Water

White Water is an awesome place to go. The slide is really long and fast and they let you go down backwards.

Invite students to study the sample ads that you showed them earlier before they begin composing. Explain that looking at other ads may help them think of more ideas for their own ad.

RESPONDING TO STUDENT WRITING

1. As students write their advertisements, walk around the room assisting those who need special attention. Comment positively and ask questions to help students "re-see" the effectiveness of their attention getting title, opinion, reasons with adjectives, and final plea.

   - **attention getting title**

     If a student has written a strong attention getter, make a comment such as "Your attention getter 'The Best in Minnesota' really caught my attention." If a student is stuck, ask a question such as "What phrase or sentence could you add to draw people's attention to your advertisement?"

   - **opinion**

     If a student has stated an opinion, make a comment such as "'White Water is an awesome place to go' starts off your advertisement with a very positive opinion."

     If a student has trouble coming up with a positive opinion, ask "What is one opinion you have about this product that is positive?"

   - **reasons with adjectives**

     If a student has included reasons with objects, make a comment such as "Your three reasons 'convenient location,' 'long hours,' and 'friendly lifeguards' clearly support your opinion that White Water is the place to go."

     If a student has not included any adjectives, ask a question such as "What word could you use to tell what kind of slide?"

   - **final plea**

     If a student has failed to include a final plea, ask a question such as "What could you say at the end of your ad to summarize your reasons and your opinion of White Water?"

2. When students have finished writing their advertisements, instruct them to find a classmate who is also finished and read their ad to that person. Ask if their slogan catches the partner's attention. Then ask which of their reasons are the most convincing and why.

PUBLISHING

Tell students that their ads are so good that you are going to take them to the owner of the water slide. Suggest that maybe the owner will display or use their advertisements to convince people in the community to go to the water slide.

MODIFICATIONS TO ENCOURAGE BEGINNING WRITERS

- Suggest students use an attention getting title and some art work or photographs instead of developing a paragraph advertisement.

- Have students use the opinion statement as a title. Do not require an attention getting slogan or a final plea. Also allow students to use words and short phrases instead of requiring the reasons in sentence form. Bring in some less complicated ads as models for how to create a simpler advertisement.

> **White Water
> is
> terrific!**
>
> - two long, fast slides
> - eight videogames

- As you choose what your students will write their ads about, select topics that will interest even your hard to motivate students. Design the visual imagery to stimulate recall of *that* place or product. You can even get your students to help you choose the place or product. But remember, students must have had the necessary background experiences or they will experience failure.

Request students who are unfamiliar with a particular place or product to write an advertisement for something they own and would like to sell.

- Prepare students by having them collect advertisements for several kinds of products such as toys, cars, clothing, snacks. Help students identify facts or reasons given to convince people to buy the product (such as enriched taste, functions of the product, quality, cost, and so on) but which ignore the unhealthy aspects of it.

- Require students to collect slogans from many advertisements to help them design an effective slogan.

- Give students large pieces of paper to lay out their ideas on as they compose. As you circulate around the room, encourage students to write in large bold letters, cross out words and sentences that they don't like, draw arrows, and abbreviate words or leave blanks as they come up with ways to visually display their ideas on large paper. These suggestions make mistakes less threatening and give the best ideas freedom to develop.

MODIFICATIONS TO CHALLENGE ADVANCED WRITERS

- Focus students' attention on creating a really powerful ad that convinces the reader to purchase a product in as few words as possible.

- Have students add to the ad, information on name of service provider, the establishment's hours of operation, cost, where to find the product, or who to contact if the potential buyer has questions. Ask students how they can combine two ideas such as where to find the product and who to contact if the potential buyer has questions. Explain that extra words or time is costly. Good advertisements are brief and to the point. Challenge students to delete unnecessary words. During revising, stress leaving out words or changing them into more powerful ones.

- Require students to include their own persuasive statement about cost. Point out that when advertisers talk about cost, they use words like the following.

    Too good to pass up

    On sale today only

    You only pay

    For only

    A bargain at

    We'll let you steal it at our rock bottom price

    Today only you can get it at

    It is yours for the very low price of

    You'll find a deal like this only once in a million years

    Act now before the price goes up

- Provide a list of transition words used in logical thinking. Encourage students to use these or other words to signal a change to a new point or a shift in an argument.

First	Also	And then	Some more evidence
Second	Next	In addition to	In other words
Third	Lastly	Another good reason	Best of all

- Encourage students to consider the psychological needs of the audience such as prestige or glamour, security, a sense of well-being, or control over one's life. Raise the ethical question of using the language of persuasion verses using straightforward facts and accurate reasoning.

- Suggest students write a product advertisement instead of a place advertisement. To help students get started, ask what product they would like to promote.

Then ask students to come up with at least three brainstorming categories such as taste, characteristics of product, how product makes life easier, fair price/cost, quality, and so on before proceeding.

- Invite students to turn their written advertisement into a one or two minute radio or a television commercial designed to convince potential customers to buy their product or service. Have them include two speakers and visual aids that add to the commercial. Point out that in the commercial the product's name should be repeated several times.

Record a radio commercial on a cassette tape or a television commercial on video tape. When students are ready to revise the commercial, play it back to get audience reactions. Have students interview the audience to see if they were persuaded and whether they acquired the necessary information. Their reactions will help the writers know which parts of the commercial are effective and which parts need to be revised.

LESSON 33

CAMPAIGN SPEECHES

This lesson may be taught at the time of any local, state, or national election, with campaign speeches written for the actual candidates who are running for election. Or students may write speeches for themselves as they run for various offices at the class or school level such as class president or student council member, line leader, hall monitor, or keeper of the class gerbil.

OBJECTIVES

Students will write and deliver a campaign speech of at least one paragraph. To do this, they will:

- Title the speech to catch the voters' attention.
- Begin the speech with an opinion/topic sentence such as "_____ is the best candidate for _____ position."
- Capitalize names of candidates and official titles.
- Give three or more reasons why the person is the best candidate for the particular office. Reasons may include qualifications of the candidate, promises, ideas on how to improve the country/state/town/school.
- Use reasons that influence/convince/persuade voters to vote for the candidate.
- End the speech with a final plea such as "Vote for _____" or "Remember to Vote."
- Indent each paragraph.

MOTIVATORS

1. Point out that Election Day is coming up in November. Ask students if they have been following the presidential (or other) election. Inquire whether they know who the candidates are and for what office or position they are running.
2. Share current campaign posters, flyers, and advertisements from magazines and newspapers. Ask students to look for each candidate's qualifications, position on issues, and campaign promises.

3. Play a videotape of one or more campaign speeches. Ask students to listen and take notes on the points the candidate makes in the speech.

4. Give students an interview form with two parts: best candidate and reasons the candidate should be elected. See the Election 199___ Interview Form (Reproducible 33-1) at the end of this lesson. Have students interview their parents and other adults in the community. Discuss the results. Show students a sample ballot with candidates' names on it. Ask why it is important to vote in an election.

5. Act silly and wave a sign that says "Vote for Me" on one side and on the other side says "Don't vote for him/her. Vote for Me." Give a funny campaign speech like the following.

"Vote for me. I'm the best! Please elect me. I'm great. I sure will do a good job! Remember when you vote, vote for me!"

Ask students why they would or would not vote for this candidate. Ask how a campaign speech helps influence voters.

BRAINSTORMING

Explain that the election process is the same whether the office is a local, state, or national one. First, candidates have to be nominated for each office that needs to be filled. After that, campaign speeches must be written and presented. Then voters consider the issues and finally they vote.

Explain that students are going to write a campaign speech to persuade other students to vote for them or their candidate on Election Day. Later they will give their speech on television. After everyone has had time to think about the candidates, the class will get to vote.

Key Questions

1. ***What offices do we need to have filled in our classroom? What jobs do we have right here in our classroom? In our school?*** (List ideas on the chalkboard.) ***Which job should we think about first?*** (Circle the office or job selected.)

Position or Job	Reasons/Evidence
Class President	likes animals—plays with gerbils
(Gerbil Keeper)	dependable—comes to school every day
Hall Monitor	—always turns in homework
Playground Equipment	has experience—feeds his own dog
	parents have agreed to help

Candidates

Ramona

Tony

(Simon)

Carla

2. **Who might make a good candidate for this job?** (Elicit several names and write them on the board.) **Which of these candidates would you like to support?** (Have the class decide on one candidate. Circle the candidate's name. Explain that later everyone will get to choose their own candidate to support.)

3. **Now we need to come up with ways to convince, persuade, or influence voters to vote for our candidate. Caution students that their reasons, promises, and qualities must be true.** (Use one to three of the following questions to elicit qualifications, promises, or ideas of the candidate.)

   What kind of experience does candidate have?

   What are the candidate's qualifications?

   What characteristics does someone need to be elected to this office?

   Why should this candidate be elected?

   What does the candidate's past record show?

   What is the candidate's position on the issue of _____?

   What does the candidate promise or pledge to do if elected?

   What problems will the candidate solve? How?

   What changes are necessary for a better nation/state/town/school?

GROUP COMPOSING

Inform students that now they must put their ideas together in a convincing speech.

1. Tell students that first they need to write a title for their speech. Write "Vote for ____" on the chalkboard, filling in the chosen candidate's name. Ask what they need to do to the candidate's first and last name? (Capitalize.)

2. Explain that next they need to write a topic sentence such as "_____ is the best candidate for _____." Ask what they need to do to show that they are beginning a paragraph? (Indent.)

> ## Vote for Simon
> <u>Simon</u> is the best candidate for <u>Gerbil Keeper</u>. Simon has had experience nursing and taking care of his dog. He comes to school everyday and always turns in his homework on time. Simon likes animals and his parents have agreed to help. For these reasons you should vote for Simon on Tuesday!

3. Remind students that to persuade others to vote for their candidate, they need to give serious reasons. Encourage individual students to compose sentences stating important qualities, reasons, or promises. Remind them to use the information they brainstormed. Point out that they may want to place the strongest reason first (to gain the voters' attention) or last (so they will remember it). As students choose reasons add them to the speech.

4. Suggest that students compose a concluding sentence which restates their opinion and then add a final plea to vote for the candidate such as "Make your vote count, Vote for _____." Add these sentences to the paragraph.

5. Ask students to read the paragraph out loud to see if it sounds convincing and to see if they want to make any changes.

Tell students they are now ready to write their own powerful campaign speech.

RESPONDING TO STUDENT WRITING

1. As students write their campaign speeches, walk around the room. Hold mini-conferences with those who need assistance coming up with reasons or evidence to support their reasons. Good questions to ask are "How convincing is your speech? What could you do to it to make it even more powerful?"

2. If you want students to think critically about particular learner outcomes, give each student the Peer Evaluation Checklist (Reproducible 33-2) provided at the end of this lesson.

3. When students have finished writing their speeches, ask them to practice their speech by reading the speech in front of a mirror.

PUBLISHING

Tell students that before they listen to the campaign speeches, they need to construct the ballots that they'll use when they vote.

1. Ahead of time run off copies of the blank ballots (Reproducible 33-3) for students to use.

2. Have students write the office/position/job that needs to be filled.

3. Next have them write in the names of the persons running for the office/job.

4. Allow time to complete this task. Then collect all the ballots to keep them safe. You may want to assign a committee of students to check over the ballots to make sure each one is correct and complete.

5. Clear off a table or set up a podium so speakers will have a place for their notes.

6. Explain that before students vote, they'll listen to each other's campaign speeches so that they can decide how to vote. Instruct students to listen carefully to the points made in each speech so that they can be an informed voter. Remind students that they will vote tomorrow!

7. (Optional) Videotape the speeches to play back later. After each speech is made, post the speeches on a bulletin board so students can review the campaign promises before they vote.

   Note: You may wish to have two students who finish their speeches early set up a private area (for example, at the end of a hallway) for the voting booth.

   You may also wish to have two different students who finish their speeches construct a television screen.

a. To make the television screen, cut a large hole in one side of a large box. This will represent the television screen.

b. Next have the students cut off the back and top of the box. Keep the bottom of the box attached. Use masking tape if necessary to keep the box together.

c. Place the television screen on a table. Put a chair behind the table so the speaker can sit during his/her speech.

d. Videotape the speeches.

THE NEXT DAY

1. Remind students that their vote can make a big difference in deciding who is elected for each position or office. (You may want to ask students to listen to the videotaped speeches one more time and write down the keypoints of each speaker.)

2. Have students complete a ballot for each position and fold it and deposit it in a special ballot box you have prepared.

3. Appoint a committee to count the ballots after school.

MODIFICATIONS TO ENCOURAGE BEGINNING WRITERS

- Allow students to write their speeches for themselves. This will be easier because we usually know more about ourselves than others.

- Give students a pattern to follow such as:

  _____ is the best choice for _____. One important reason to vote for _____ is _____. He/she has had experience _____. _____ believes _____ is important and promises to _____. _____ is _____. He/she will _____. Another reason for electing _____ is _____. Vote for _____ today.

- Request that students list 3-6 reasons to vote for the candidate, instead of writing a persuasive paragraph, which requires a higher level of mental organization. Use the "Vote for _____" (Reproducible 33-4) provided at the end of this lesson.

- Ask students to create flyers based on what they composed. Have them bring in a photo to glue at the top of their flyers to make them more exciting and attention-getting.

- Suggest that students brainstorm their reasons on strips of paper that you provide. When it comes time to compose the campaign speech, they can arrange and rearrange the strips of paper until a satisfactory order is achieved. Then the student can tape the strips down and add a topic sentence that you supply.

> *I have a plan for feeding the homeless.*

> *I'll build shelters for the homeless.*

> *I'll keep Fargo clean.*

MODIFICATIONS TO CHALLENGE ADVANCED WRITERS

- Have students collect examples of candidates' flyers that contain slogans and then create a catchy attention-getting slogan for their candidate.
- Challenge students to brainstorm the issues in a current election. Ask "What are the issues that are important to voters in this election?" Issues in a national election might be social issues such as education, health care, the environment, or other policies such as national defense, budget, the economy or taxes.
- Suggest that students write a three, four, or five paragraph speech that contains at least two facts or examples to back up their reasons. A format to guide them could be:

   1. Begin the first paragraph with a topic sentence introducing the candidate, followed by at least three reasons why the person is the best candidate for the particular office.

   2. Begin the second paragraph with a topic sentence restating reason #1, followed by two sentences containing two or more facts that prove it. For example:

      Topic sentence—Amy is a proven leader.

      Proof—She has been a Girl Scout Leader for 10 years.

      Proof—Amy organized the PTA carnival.

      Proof—She is Treasurer of the F/M Kennel Club.

   3. Follow the same format for the third and fourth paragraphs.

   4. In the fifth paragraph, summarize the reasons why the candidate should be elected and makes a final plea to vote.

Election 199_

Interview Form

Best Candidate	Reasons
For	
For	
For	
For	
For	
For	
For	
For	
For	

Information Collected By _____

Name: _____ Date: _____ (33-2)

PEER EVALUATION CHECKLIST

Reread and rethink your partner's campaign speech.

1. What is the title of this speech? Does it catch your attention?

_____ Yes   No

2. Did the writer capitalize the name of the candidate and the office?   Yes   No

   Did the writer indent the paragraph?   Yes   No

3. What are the two strongest reasons the writer gives to elect this candidate? How strong is each reason? Remember you do not need to like this candidate. You are only rating how effective the speech sounds.

   OK   Good   Excellent

   _____   _____

   _____   _____

4. What final plea is given at the end of the speech? How effective is it?

   OK   Good   Very effective

   _____   _____

5. Does this speech make sense?   Yes   No

6. What can be done to improve the speech?

   _____

   _____

I have carefully evaluated my partner's campaign speech.

_____

Signature

I have carefully read what my partner found out about my speech, and I have tried to improve at least one thing to make it more interesting.

_____

Signature of Author

293

ELECTION
BALLOT

Instructions: Vote for <u>only</u> <u>one</u> candidate for each office.
Make an "X" in the box next to their name.
Voting for more than one candidate in a box is illegal and will
disqualify your ballot.

Candidates For _____

☐ _____

☐ _____

☐ _____

Candidates For _____

☐ _____

☐ _____

☐ _____

VOTE for _____

Glue candidate's
photo here.

☑ _____

☑ _____

☑ _____

☑ _____

☑ _____

☑ _____

☑ _____

It's time for a change!

Elect _____ for _____.

Section 6

INFORMATIVE
(REPORT)
WRITING

REPORTS

There are two types of reports: the "all about" report and the research report. The "all about" report is based on knowledge that students have already acquired. The students must recall their knowledge on a particular subject and then organize that knowledge and put it into written form.

In a research report, students ideally decide what they want to learn and then search for information on the subject before they organize their knowledge and put it into written form. This search often includes interviews, observations, experiments, and/or library research and may include note-taking and the citing of knowledge sources.

SOME FORMS OF REPORTS

"All about . . . ." Reports

Fact Books

Research Reports

LESSON 34

FORMULATING FIELD TRIP QUESTIONS

When students hear a speaker or go on a field trip and are encouraged to ask questions, teachers are usually disappointed in the quantity and quality of questions asked. That is easy to change with a little preparation.

OBJECTIVES

Students will write five important questions to investigate/research during an upcoming field trip (or during the visit of a guest speaker). To do this, they will:

- Start each question with who, what, where, when, why, or how.
- Complete each question with a verb phrase.
- Capitalize the first word of each question.
- Put a question mark at the end of each question.

MOTIVATORS

1. Inform students that asking questions is an important way to acquire information and learn more about topics they're interested in. Encourage volunteers to suggest places where they might ask questions to learn something new. Discuss places such as the playground, a toy store, a library, a movie theater, a shopping center, or a record store, and ask what kinds of questions they might ask in each of these places.

   Remind students that good open-ended questions usually start with one of these words or phrases: who, what, when, where, what kind of, why, and how. Write these question words on the chalkboard.

2. Plan and announce that the class will be going on a field trip in the near future. For example, if they have been studying the dairy industry, you might want to plan a trip to a local creamery. Explain that if they think of questions now, they'll know what they want to find out during the visit.

BRAINSTORMING/GROUP COMPOSING

Involve students in brainstorming a list of questions they have about the place you will visit. Remind them that they should start each question with one of these six question words: who, what, when, where, why, and how. Write the question words on the chalk-board.

Who   What   When   Where   Why   How
Questions We Want to Ask

Getting Milk to the Creamery
   How does the milk get from the farm to here?
   Where is the milk stored when it gets to the creamery?

Cleanliness of Milk
   When are the tanks cleaned?
   Why is keeping the milk so clean that important?

Dairy Products that are Made
   What is done to turn the milk into ice cream?
   Why is the cottage cheese put in such big vats?

Jobs at the Creamery
   Who's in charge of paying the farmers?
   What does the person who makes the butter have to do?

Key Questions

(For the purposes of this lesson, a creamery has been used as an example. Adapt the questions to the place your class will visit.)

1. ***What would you like to know about milk getting to the creamery?*** (Allow plenty of time for students to think. Creating good questions requires a lot of thought. Give positive feedback such as "'How does the milk get from the farm to here?' is a great HOW question that we'd like to know the answer to.") ***What else might we want to know about milk arriving at the creamery?*** (Respond with a positive comment such as "'Where is the milk stored when it gets to the creamery?' is a WHERE question we'd all like to hear answered." Continue brainstorming questions about getting milk to the creamery.)

2. ***What questions might we have about the cleanliness of the milk?***

3. ***What questions do you have about the dairy products made there?***

4. ***What are some questions we might have about jobs at the creamery?***

(Ask students what other areas they might want to learn about and have them compose additional questions. Comment that they have brainstormed a lot of good questions and that you can hardly wait to get the answers. Tell students that now they should think of ten individual questions that they would like answered and write them on index cards so they can remember their questions during the field trip. Explain that they can follow the same steps used to create the group questions.)

Remind students of the six words used to create questions (who, what, when, where, why, and how) and the categories of questions they asked about the creamery. Tell them that their questions can come from any of the categories discussed earlier and *other areas as well*

RESPONDING TO STUDENT WRITING

1. As students write their questions, walk around the room. Visit individually with students. Give **positive feedback** on thoughtful and useful questions such as, "'Why does milk have to be so clean?' is a great question about cleanliness."

   Ask questions to clarify or extend their thinking such as "What do you want to know about people who work at the creamery?"

2. Since only the student will see and read his/her own cards, there is no need to work on mechanics such as spelling, capitalization, and punctuation.

3. Place students in cooperative groups of three to five students. In each group include at least one student who is a leader and stays on task. Do not include more than one student who gets off task. Be sure each group has one academically strong student and one student who is less skilled in reading and/or writing.

   Instruct students to take turns slowly reading their questions out loud to the group. Point out that since time will be limited on the field trip, they need to consider which questions are most important to ask. Tell students they may get a chance to ask only a few. Explain that when they hear a good question, they should tell that person why they like the particular question. If they don't understand the question, instruct students to politely ask that person what he or she means.

4. After students have listened to their classmates' comments, ask them to do the following:
   - Silently reread each of their own questions.
   - Reword weak or confusing questions. Change yes/no questions to who, what, when, where, why, and how questions.
   - Put a star by the five most important questions.

PUBLISHING

Have students put a rubberband or paper clip on their index cards for easy carrying. Once a day until the field trip, have students reread their questions and review what they want to find out.

```
              My Questions
 * How does the milk get from the farm to here?
 * Why is keeping the milk clean so important?
 * Who pays the dairy farmers?
 * When do you make butter?
 * What kinds of jobs can I get at your creamery?
```

MODIFICATIONS TO ENCOURAGE BEGINNING WRITERS

• Require students to brainstorm only five questions. Then ask them to select their best two to write on one index card.

• Have students who are less articulate interview the school nurse, librarian, cafeteria cook, principal, special education teacher, music teacher, or others to get ideas and words for questions.

• Provide a special sheet of question patterns like the following for students.

```
┌─────────────────────────────────────────────────────────────────────────┐
│           What questions would you ask if you went to the creamery?       │
│  What _____ ?         │
│  How _____ ?         │
│  Why _____ ?         │
│  Where _____ ?         │
│  When _____ ?         │
└─────────────────────────────────────────────────────────────────────────┘
```

MODIFICATIONS TO CHALLENGE ADVANCED WRITERS

• Expect students to write questions about topics other than those on the chalkboard (for example, packaging the dairy products, transporting dairy products to the stores, development of new milk products, or costs and profit in dairy products).

• Have students also write "what kind of," "which one," and "how many" questions.

LESSON 35

CHOOSING A TOPIC

Choosing the topic is the first step in writing an "All I Know About . . . " report or a research report. For a research report the next three steps are collecting information, drafting an outline, and writing the report. The "All I Know About . . . " report follows the same steps but skips collecting information since students choose a topic about which they are more knowledgeable than their intended audience.

Students should start out writing "All I Know About . . . " reports until they are comfortable choosing the topic, drafting an outline, and writing the report. Once comfortable with the process, they can be gradually challenged to seek out knowledge that is new to them. Students as young as first and second graders will enjoy writing reports if they are guided through each of these steps.

OBJECTIVES

"All I Know About . . . " Report

Students will choose a topic on which they are knowledgeable.

Research Report

Students will choose a topic and write five to twenty questions about it to guide their search for knowledge. To do this, they will:

- Begin the majority of questions with who, what, where, when, why, or how.
- Write questions that cover a wide range of areas within the research topic.
- Brainstorm at least one place to visit, one person to talk to, and one magazine, book, or movie to see to search for needed information.

MOTIVATORS

"All I Know About . . . " Report

1. Talk about a topic that you know a lot about. Ask students to share something that they just learned from you. Explain that everyone knows some things that other people don't. A report is a way to share what we know with other people.

Research Report

1. Tell students about something you are interested in learning more about. Share three to five questions that you really would like the answer for. Ask students where you could find this information. (Talk to people, go to library, visit a particular place, and so on.)
2. Remind students that all of us have something we want to know more about, but often we don't have time to find the answers. Inform students that this week they will have an exciting opportunity to explore one of their interests.

BRAINSTORMING/GROUP COMPOSING

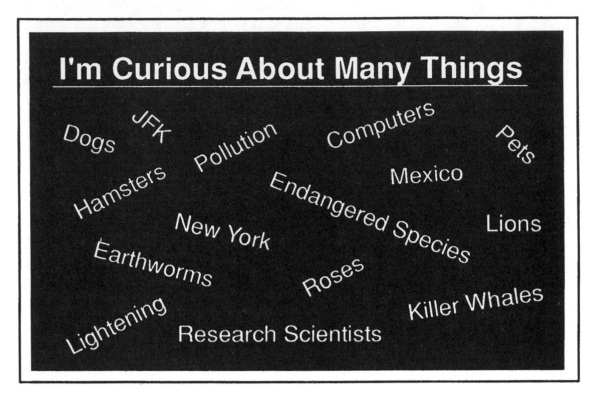

Key Questions for "All I Know About . . . " Report

1. *What is something you know a lot about? What do you know that other people might like to learn? What is something exciting you want to teach other people?*
   (Help students brainstorm a list of 15 to 20 topics. Write the topics on the chalkboard.)
   (If students aren't in touch with their own interests, ask more specific questions such as the following.)

   What object or machine do you know a lot about?

   What place do you really like?

   Who is someone you know about that other people might like to learn more about?

2. *Out of all the topics we brainstormed, which is a topic the whole class knows a lot about? Out of all these interesting topics, which one shall we explore as a class?*

   Stop the "All I Know About . . . " report lesson here.

Key Questions for Research Report

1. *What are you curious about? What do you want to find out? What is something exciting you'd like to learn more about?* (If students find these questions too open-ended, choose a broad topic such as reptiles, weather forecasting, South America, or something that students have just studied. Then brainstorm what subtopics within the broad topic they want to learn more about. For example, if they have just studied reptiles, subtopics to investigate could be snakes, lizards, crocodiles, or turtles.)

    Which reptiles would you like to learn more about?

    When we studied weather forecasting, what was something that interested you that you'd like to gather more information about?

    We studied a lot about South America. What else would you like to know? (List the topics students suggest on the chalkboard.)

2. *Out of all these interesting topics, which one shall we explore as a class?* (For the purposes of this lesson, we'll assume "pets" was chosen for the class topic.)

3. *In order to learn more about pets, we need to think of some questions we want answered. Questions are important tools that help us find answers. What are some good words to start a question with?* (Elicit the words **who**, **what**, **when**, **where**, **why**, and **how**. Write these question words on the board.)

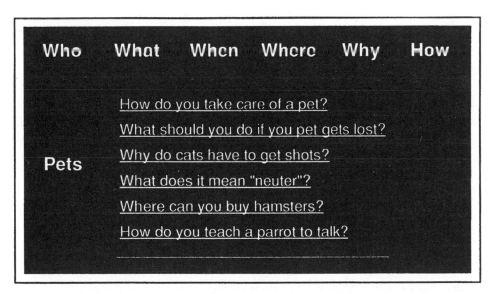

Who	What	When	Where	Why	How

Pets

How do you take care of a pet?

What should you do if you pet gets lost?

Why do cats have to get shots?

What does it mean "neuter"?

Where can you buy hamsters?

How do you teach a parrot to talk?

4. *What is one question you or your friend might have about pets? What would you like to know about pets?* (If students give you a phrase instead of a question, ask a follow up question such as "How could we phrase 'lost pets' as a question?" Continue

brainstorming questions until ten to twenty questions covering many different areas have been generated.)

Tell students that they are now ready to compose their own questions about a topic that they want to learn more about.

RESPONDING TO STUDENT WRITING

1. As students compose questions to guide their own research, walk around the room. Each time you find an exciting who, what, when, where, or why question read it out loud to the group and comment positively. Note: A few yes/no questions are fine.

2. If you want students to work towards particular learner outcomes, focus your positive comments and questions to help each student self-evaluate the following outcomes:

   - choose a topic
   - write five to twenty questions to investigate on that topic
   - begin questions with who, what, where, when, why, or how

3. Have students meet in revising teams: cooperative groups of three to five students pre-selected by you. Provide the following guidelines.

   - Students should take turns reading their questions out loud.
   - If they don't understand a question, they should politely ask what the person means.
   - When a person is finished reading his or her questions, the revising team should share new questions that they thought of after listening to the list.
   - The researcher can add any interesting questions that he or she or the team thought of.
   - When the whole group has finished, students should put a star by their ten best questions.

PUBLISHING

Remind students that they will use the questions they composed today when they begin the next part of their research reports. Explain that all they need to do now is to find the answer to each question. The questions will be their guide as they search for answers.

To help prepare students for this next step, ask the following questions.

Where can you find answers to your questions?

What things can you read, listen to, or watch?

What people can help you?

Who can you call, write, or go see?

What places can you visit?

Accept all ideas about where to find answers and write them on the blackboard. Call attention to innovative resources such as calling the local bike shop for information on types of bikes, talking to a grandparent to learn about old school cheers, interviewing a vet to learn about responsibilities of being a pet owner, or visiting an airport to learn about changing the responsibilities of a pilot.

MODIFICATIONS TO ENCOURAGE BEGINNING WRITERS

- Guide students to select topics that they are already familiar with and do an "All I Know About . . . " Report. Ask them to find out (research) one or two new pieces of information and add these to their report.

- Have an aide or another student write each question on a separate lined index card as the student dictates. Then when students go hunting for answers, they can write a short word or phrase (take notes) directly on the card.

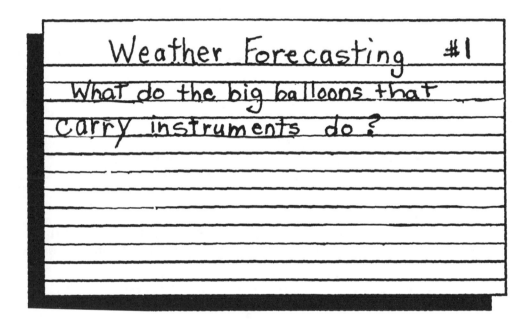

- Require students to generate only two to five questions to research.
- Put a group of students together at a small table to guide their brainstorming. Give students six index cards each.

Next select a key question word such as "when." Ask students to think and share a "when" question about their topic. When a student comes up with a good question have him/her write the question on one index card. Supply more cards as students think of additional questions. If students are having trouble coming up with enough questions, ask them to tell friends and parents their topic and ask for more questions about their topic.

MODIFICATIONS TO CHALLENGE ADVANCED WRITERS

• Challenge students to formally interview several knowledgeable people about their topic. To learn how valuable interviewing can be as a prewriting activity, read the article: "Interviewing: A Means of Encouraging the Drive to Communicate" by Shirley Haley-James and Charles Hobson. It can be found in *Language Arts* 57, Number 5 (May 1980) pages 497–502.

A useful tool for getting students started is "Interview Notes on _____." (See Reproducible 35-1 at the end of this lesson.) Before your students interview, have them write their questions on this sheet. Explain that as questions are answered, the answers should be written down. Give students clip boards with pencils attached before they leave.

Interview Notes on _____

(person interviewed)

Question	Answer
Question	Answer
Question	Answer

• Expect students to choose a more difficult topic, formulate more thoughtful questions, and eventually use multiple sources including interviewing and nontraditional sources.

Name: _____ Date: _____ (35-1)

Interview Notes on _____

(person interviewed)

Question	Answer
Question	Answer
Question	Answer
Question	Answer
Question	Answer
Question	Answer
Question	Answer

LESSON 36

CREATING AN OUTLINE

Creating an outline is the second step in writing an "All I Know About . . . " report and the third step (after collecting the information) in writing a research report. The final step in both types of reports is writing the report. Students of all ages will learn to enjoy creating outlines and come to see their value, if they are guided through the following steps many times.

OBJECTIVES

Students will write an outline based on the information they know or learned while researching a topic. To do this, they will:

- Title the outline "All About _____" and fill in the blank with the subject of the report.
- Include an introduction, at least three subtopics, and a conclusion.
- Have a heading for each subtopic in the outline that tells how the ideas in that group are related.
- Place the Roman numeral I in front of the heading labeled "Introduction."
- Place the Roman numerals II, III, IV in front of each subtopic heading in the body of the outline. Order the subtopics logically.
- Place at least two facts, details, or supporting pieces of information under each subtopic heading.
- Indent each subcategories under its heading and begin each subcategory with a capital letter of the alphabet, starting with the letter "A."
- Use facts, details, or supporting information from at least two sources.
- Place the Roman numeral V in front of the final heading labeled "Conclusion."

DAY 1
MOTIVATORS

1. Ask students how many of them have owned a pet. Lead a discussion on pets (or another subject with which all your students are familiar). Inquire what kinds of pets

312

they have had and how long they owned the pet. Also ask what they especially liked about the pet. For those students who have never owned a pet or who don't presently own one, ask what kind of pet they would like to have.

2. Tell students about a pet you have had. If possible, bring in pictures of your pet or the actual pet.

Share something special your pet does or a problem you had with your pet. Comment that there are a lot of things to know about having a pet. Pets can be a lot of fun; but when people make a decision to get a pet, they often don't realize what the responsibilities will be.

Explain that today the class is going to make a list of everything they know about owning a pet. From this list they will develop an outline. Tell students that after they've finished, each of them will write their own outline from the notes they've made on their topic. Explain that their outlines will help them organize the information so that later they can write their report more easily.

BRAINSTORMING

All About Pets	
1. feeding your pet	11. train it
2. play with it	12. buy food
3. name your pet	13. vacations
4. large or small pets	14. sick pets
5. tricks	15. needs water
6. pet stores	16. vets
7. shots	17. newspaper ads
8. clean aquarium	18. brush it
9. change kitty litter	19. cost $
10. lost pets	20. mean or friendly pets

Key Questions

1. *What is something other children need to know about owning a pet?* (Use a black magic marker to write students' ideas on a large piece of lined and pre-numbered chart paper instead of on the chalkboard, since you'll use this list again later.)

2. *What is something you think of when you think of getting a pet?*

3. *What else should you consider before you get a pet?* (Continue brainstorming until students have generated at least twenty ideas. Accept all ideas that relate to pets. If you are not getting a variety of ideas on the list, be more specific in the questions that you ask. For example, ask "What are some things people need to know about taking care of a pet?", "What kinds of things do you need to teach a pet?", "Where do you look if you want to get a pet?", "What should you know about choosing a pet?")

GROUP COMPOSING

Tell students that they have brainstormed many kinds of information that a person should consider before getting a pet. State that next they need to read through all of the ideas and think about which ones go together. Read through the entire list in unison.

Group Ideas for Headings

1. Ask students which of the ideas can be grouped together. Allow plenty of time for students to think before you expect responses. Respond with a positive comment such as "Super, grouping 'feeding your pet' and 'needs watering' is a good idea." Circle these two ideas with a red marker so that students can remember which ideas go together.

2. Encourage volunteers to suggest other ideas that can be grouped together. Respond with positive comments and circle the ideas with a different colored magic marker. Continue grouping until you have at least three or four different groups. These groups will coincide with the number of paragraphs in the final report.

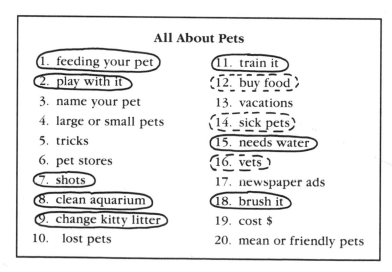

3. Choose an idea that hasn't been placed into a group. What group can we fit "name your pet" into?

What ideas do we have left over that we haven't put in a group yet? Will these fit into one of our established groups or do we need to create a new group?

Day 2

Create the Outline Headings

1. Ahead of time, tape chart paper to the chalkboard to use in this part of the lesson. Use chart paper because you will need to save this group outline for the next lesson.

2. Tell students that since they have listed all their ideas and have grouped them, they are ready to name each group. Elicit a name for each group by asking what all of the ideas circled in red (blue, green, and so on) have in common. Allow plenty of wait-time for students to think. This task requires students to analyze each piece of information and then to generalize a name for the group. Respond with a positive comment such as "Yes, all these ideas are about taking care of pets."

Explain that since Roman numeral I will be the introduction, you'll put the heading "Taking Care of a Pet" next to the Roman numeral II on the outline. Fill in the headings in the outline for each group of ideas.

All About _____

   I. Introduction
  II. Taking Care of a Pet
     A.
     B.
     C.
     D.
 III. Things to Do With Your Pet
     A.
     B.
     C.
     D.
 IV. Choosing a Pet
     A.
     B.
     C.
  V. Where to Buy a Pet
     A.
     B.
 VI. Conclusion

Create Subcategories Under Each Heading

1. Point to the ideas circled in red on the chart. State that next they need to decide which of the ideas they want listed first, second, third, and so on.

   Ask students which responsibility they think is most important. Write a capital letter "A" and then list this responsibility under the heading "Taking Care of a Pet." Also cross out this idea on the brainstormed list.

   Guide students to group similar ideas together and list them in order of importance. Write the ideas after the letters B, C, D, and so on in the outline.

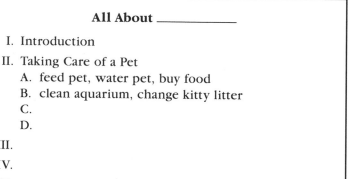

2. Tell students that now they are ready for the next part of the outline. Ask how all the ideas circled in blue are related. Remember to allow students time to think. If a student's response makes sense, write this heading by Roman numeral III on the outline and make a positive comment such as "'Things to Do With Your Pet' would make a fine name for the ideas circled in blue." If a student's name for a heading doesn't make sense, accept it as possible, but don't list it. Then ask for another way the blue circled ideas are related. Guide students to select and arrange the ideas in this category in a logical order. Write the ideas after capital letters in the outline.

3. Continue brainstorming headings and ordering ideas under headings until the body of the outline is complete.

All About _____

   I. Introduction
  II. Taking Care of a Pet
      A. feed pet, water pet, buy food
      B. clean aquarium, change kitty litter
      C.
      D.

```
III. Things to Do With Your Pet
     A. name it
     B. play with it
     C. train it
     D. teach it tricks
 IV. Choosing a Pet
     A.
     B.
     C.
  V. Where to Buy a Pet
     A.
     B.
 VI. Conclusion
```

Introduction and Conclusion

1. Point out that they now need to plan an introduction and conclusion for the report. Comment that the introduction is an important part of a report because it tells people what the report is about. Ask students to look back at Roman numerals II, III, IV, and V on the outline. Have them read the headings with you:

   "Taking Care of a Pet,"

   "Things to do With a Pet,"

   "Choosing a Pet," and

   "Where to Buy a Pet."

   Explain that for now, they will list these subtopics in the outline under the introduction, after the letters A, B, C, and D. That way when they are ready to write the report, they will know that they need to include these ideas in their introductory paragraph.

2. Tell students that they are ready to plan the conclusion of their report. Explain that a conclusion should review what the reader has learned from the report; a conclusion is a summary at the end of a report. Write the capital letters A, B, C, and D under the conclusion and write the headings from the body of the outline.

Title

Inform students that the outline is complete except for one thing—the title. Point to the partial title at the top of the outline. Ask students what this report is about. (Pets.) State that in a title all important words are capitalized. Add the word "pets" to the title and elicit whether it should be capitalized.

Note: SAVE this outline that your students have just generated. You will need to use this outline in the next lesson.

RESPONDING TO STUDENT WRITING

1. As students are listing their information, organizing it into groups, and writing their outlines, walk around the room and visit individually with students. Give positive reinforcement and ask questions to help them generate long lists, find and title groups, and order their ideas.

   • Find groups and create headings

   If a student has an effective heading, make a comment such as "Your heading 'Qualities of a Friend' really catches the main idea of your green group."

   If a student is having trouble coming up with a good title, ask a question such as "How are all of your blue ideas—handle bars, banana seat, brakes, and chain—related?"

   • Order ideas logically

   If a student has ordered some information logically, make a comment such as "The way you ordered your subtopics makes a lot of sense to me. 'Sorting your rocks into similar piles' would be an important step to do before 'Classifying the Rocks,'"

   If a student is having trouble ordering thoughts, ask a question such as "Which of your 'Handling an Emergency' ideas do you think should go first?" or "What Roman numeral will you put by this heading to show it will be the third paragraph in your outline?"

   *** Remember that the students' outlines are only a means to an end. The purpose of the outline is to help students' get their ideas organized. The Roman numerals, capital letters, lower case letters, and so on have little value in themselves. **The important thing is get students to start organizing and ordering their ideas.** Another thing to remember is that it doesn't matter how messy the outline is as long as the student can read it. The student is his/her own audience for the outline not the teacher.

2. When students have finished writing their outline, have them reread it and ask themselves these questions:

- Does my introduction tell what will be covered in the report?
- Do all of the headings make sense?
- Are the categories under each heading in a logical order?
- Have I left out any important ideas?
- Is all the information correct?
- How many resources did I use?
- What idea(s) should I eliminate?
- Does my conclusion wrap things up?

PUBLISHING

Tell students that later this week they will begin writing their reports. Explain that they will use their outlines to help them write their reports. Writing the reports will be really easy now that they have all of their information grouped and ordered in their outlines.

MODIFICATIONS TO ENCOURAGE BEGINNING WRITERS

- With younger children or students who are seriously limited academically, stop the lesson after writing the group outline (i.e. after Group Composing). This is similar to a "language experience" approach.
- Create an all-class report outline. In an all-class outline, the title, introduction, all headings for the body of the report, and the conclusion are developed as a group. Particular headings are then assigned to individuals or pairs of students. Each individual or pair organizes the information under that heading only and writes only that section of the outline (e.g., III A, B, C, and D). When students have completed their part of the outline, the group is reassembled to finish creating the group outline.
- Ask students to create a shortened outline—for example, an outline that includes only an introduction and two subtopics.
- Have students write an outline for a one paragraph report instead of an outline for a five paragraph report. Such an outline would consist of a title and headings for introduction, body, and conclusion but would not include subtopics (A, B, C) under each heading.

MODIFICATIONS TO CHALLENGE ADVANCED WRITERS

- Encourage students to consider various ways to group their information *before* deciding on headings.
- Also help these students to order headings and subtopics under headings in a logical way. For example, if the student's report is on trees and the headings are Roots, Leaves, Trunks, and Branches, you might guide students to order the categories in the order the parts appear on the tree, or in another order that makes sense.

LESSON 37

WRITING THE REPORT

Rarely do teachers actually show students how to use an outline for writing a report. This lesson takes students through this important last step. Students need to see that once they have chosen a topic, collected their information, and created an outline, they have done most of the work necessary for writing a report. All they have to do now is use the information to draft their report. Students need many experiences to see that it is really easy to write the report once their outlines are composed.

OBJECTIVES

Students will write a five paragraph report based on their outline. To do this, they will:

- Write a short introductory paragraph, the body (at least three paragraphs), and a concluding paragraph.

- Begin the introductory paragraph with a topic sentence (such as "This report is on _____.") that states the topic of the report, followed by two or more sentences describing the subtopics that will be covered in the body of the report.

- Write three or more paragraphs that make up the body of the report. Each of these paragraphs will cover one subtopic (such as "tricks this pet can learn") generated by the students during the development of their report outlines.

- Begin each of the subtopic paragraphs with a topic sentence (such as "There are many places in Moorhead that sell pets.").

- Summarize the topics covered in the report in the concluding paragraph and also express their opinions about the subject of the report.

- Indent each paragraph.
- Title the report "All About _____" or "My Research on _____," completing the title with the subject of the report.
- Capitalize important words in the report's title.

GROUP COMPOSING

State that you are impressed with all the work students have done on their reports. Review what they have done already:

1. They brainstormed questions they had about their subjects.
2. Then they tracked down the answers to their questions. (for a research report)
3. Later, they created an outline from the information they knew or learned during their search.

All About _____ Pets _____

I. Introduction
   A. taking Care of a Pet
   B. things to Do With Your Pet
   C. choosing a Pet
   D. where to Buy a Pet

II. Taking Care of a Pet
   A. feed pet, water pet, buy food
   B. clean aquarium, change kitty litter
   C.
   D.

III. Things to Do With Your Pet
   A. name it
   B. play with it
   C. train it
   D. teach it tricks

IV. Choosing a Pet
   A. mean and friendly pets
   B. small or large pets
   C. healthy pets

V. Where to Buy a Pet
   A. pet store
   B. newspaper

VI. Conclusion
   A. taking Care of a Pet
   B. things to Do With Your Pet
   C. choosing a Pet
   D. where to Buy a Pet

Tell students they have already done most of the work. Point out that now all they need to do is write their reports. Share that before they begin, you will show them how to use their outline to make writing the report easy.

Display the outline generated by your students in the previous lesson where everyone can see it.

Report's Title

Comment that the first thing to do when writing a report from an outline is to write the report's title. Tell students the title will tell everyone the main idea of the entire report. Remind them they already wrote the report's title in their outline. Copy the title of the class report on chart paper.

Introductory Paragraph

1. Inform students that the first paragraph of a report is called the introduction. Point to Roman numeral I on the outline. Explain that the introductory paragraph introduces the various topics that will be covered in the body of the report. When writing an introductory paragraph, they should state the subject of the report first.

2. Write the pattern sentence "This is a report on _____" and have students fill in the subject. Ask what you did to the topic sentence to show you were starting a new paragraph. (Indented it.)

3. Explain that the next thing is to state the kind of information that will be found in the report.

Have students refer to Roman numeral I in the outline and the list of subtopics that they wrote there. Guide students to use the list to complete the pattern sentence "In it you will find information about _____, _____, _____, and _____."

> **All About Pets**
>
> This is a report on _pets_. In my report you will find information about _taking care of a pet_, _things to do with a pet_, _where to buy a pet_, and _choosing a pet_.

Body of Report (Three Information Paragraphs)

1. State that now that they've written the introduction, they are ready to start writing the body of the report. Each part of the outline (Roman numerals II, III, IV, and V) will

become one paragraph in the report. Draw students attention to these sections of the outline constructed in the previous lesson.

2. Tell students they will use the ideas they listed under Roman numeral II to write the second paragraph of the report. Read the heading beside Roman numeral II. Explain that the heading "Taking Care of a Pet" will become the topic sentence in this paragraph of the report.

3. Ask students to express the idea "Taking Care of a Pet" in a sentence. Give one or two examples of topic sentences such as "Taking care of a pet is time consuming," if students have difficulty. If your students are not comfortable generating topic sentences, you may want to give them a pattern topic sentence to complete such as "The next thing you need to know about _____(insert topic)_____ is _____(insert the heading)_____."

   As students create topic sentences, respond in a positive manner. Before writing a topic sentence on the chart paper, ask students how you should show you are starting a new paragraph. (Indent.)

4. Inform students that next they need to put the ideas under Roman numeral II into sentences. Elicit a sentence or two incorporating the ideas in letter A. Write the suggested sentence and respond in a positive manner.

All About Pets

This is a report on _pets_. In my report you will find information about _taking care of a pet_, _things to do with a pet_, _where to buy a pet_, and _choosing a pet_.

You will have many responsibilities if you get a pet. Every day you will have to feed and water your pet. You will also have to buy food for your pet.

---

5. Elicit sentences for each remaining subtopic under Roman numeral II.
6. Repeat steps 2–5 for Roman numerals III through V.

Concluding Paragraph

1. Tell students that all they have left to write is the conclusion. Explain that a concluding paragraph summarizes all the information that has been presented in the report. Direct students' attention to Roman numeral VI in the outline. Have them use the ideas they listed there to complete the pattern sentence "In this report you have learned about _____, _____, _____, and _____."

2. State that they need to write just one more sentence to complete the report. Write the final sentence, "We hope you will consider these ideas _____," and have students offer suggestions to complete it.

> In this report you have learned about _____, _____,
> _____, and _____. We hope you consider these ideas
> _____
> _____.

Tell students now that they know how easy it is to write a report from an outline, they are ready to write their own reports. Ask them to get out the outline that they wrote earlier and begin using it to write their report.

RESPONDING TO STUDENT WRITING

1. Walk around the room as students use their outlines to write their reports. Visit with students who need guidance or encouragement. Give students positive feedback and ask one or two questions to help students create effective topic sentences and smooth introductory, body, and concluding paragraphs.

   - **topic sentences**

     If the student's topic sentence "works," make a comment such as "Your topic sentence 'Rocks are formed in many ways' gives me a good indication of what your fourth paragraph will contain."

     If a student is having difficulty coming up with a topic sentence for one of the information paragraphs, ask a question such as "What topic sentence could you write based upon the heading the Moon's Surface?"

   - **introductory, information, and concluding paragraphs**

     If the introductory paragraph clearly tells what the report will contain, make a comment such as "I am glad you told me in your introduction what three subtopics you'd be discussing in your report. This lets me know what ideas I will find in the body of your report."

     If a student has left out of the concluding paragraph one or more pieces of information, ask a question such as "What could you add to your concluding paragraph to help readers remember all the main topics you covered in the body of your report?"

   - **title**

     If a student's title is effective, make a comment such as "Your title 'Everything You Wanted to Know About Baseball' is terrific because it catches my interest and it lets me know what your report will cover."

   - **conventions of writing**

     If a student has remembered to indent every paragraph, make a comment such as "Terrific! You indented the first word in each paragraph of your report. This will let people who read your report know when you are starting a new idea."

If a student has remembered to indent some paragraphs but not all, ask a question such as "What could you do to this group of sentences about clouds to let us know you are presenting another new idea?"

If a student has forgotten to capitalize the words in the title, ask a question such as "What should you do with your title 'all about bugs' to signal which words are important?"

2. Instruct students to read their finished report aloud to a classmate and consider the following questions.

   • Are my ideas clear?

   • Have I eliminated unnecessary words or thoughts?

   • Does each paragraph begin with a topic sentence?

PUBLISHING

Tell students that you are proud of how hard they worked on their reports and all that they learned as they researched their subjects. Explain that now they have come to another exciting part of report writing. They will now share their reports with each other so that everyone can learn from them.

Publishing Method 1

Choose two students per day to present their reports to the class. Let students know ahead of time what day they will present their report. Explain that they will want to practice reading this report out loud before they read it to the class.

Publishing Method 2

Tell students you are going to put their reports together to make a class encyclopedia. Explain that you will put the final drafts of their reports in alphabetical order and copy a whole set for each student to keep and use. Tell students that you will also put one copy in the class library.

MODIFICATIONS TO ENCOURAGE BEGINNING WRITERS

- Allow students to put together a photo or picture essay instead of a written and oral report.

- Use a "language experience" approach. Stop your lesson after writing the group report (after Group Composing). Publish the group's composition. Students can add drawings to the final copy.

- Write a class report. In an all-class report, the title, introduction, and conclusion are written as a group. Each sentence or paragraph in the body of the report is assigned to a particular student who researches and writes that part of the report. Once the pieces are written, the report is compiled by the teacher, who gives each student a copy of the whole report.

- Suggest students make tape recordings or video tapes instead of giving an oral report in front of the class.

- Require students to write a one-paragraph report. Such a report could be built from a topic sentence "This is a report on _____" plus three or four sentences of information about the subject.

- Require students to write a three-paragraph report. This shorter report should include an introductory paragraph and two or three information paragraphs in the body of the report. Don't require a concluding paragraph.

MODIFICATIONS TO CHALLENGE ADVANCED WRITERS

- Allow more flexibility when writing the title, introduction, and conclusion. For example, instead of limiting a title to "All About _____," ask students to create their own title as long as the title states the main idea or subject of the report.

- Request students to brainstorm their own beginning sentence to tell readers the subject of the report, instead of limiting them to the provided pattern. For example, a student could write "Raising fish is an exciting hobby" instead of "This is a report on pets."

  Next, instead of asking students to complete the pattern "In my report you will find information about _____, _____, _____, and _____," ask them to brainstorm ways to tell readers what subtopics will be covered in the report.

- Allow more flexibility in the concluding paragraph. Instead of requiring students to complete the pattern, "In this report you have learned about _____, _____, _____, and _____," ask them to brainstorm ways to summarize the information covered in the report.

Section 7

EXPRESSIVE WRITINGS

POEMS AND CHEERS

There are four basic kinds of poems that children can create: rhythm poems, pattern poems, rhyming poems, and free verse poems. In rhythm poems, new words of the same part of speech and the same number of syllables can be substituted for words in the original poem to recreate the beat. In pattern poems, specified types of words, phrases, and sentences must go into each line of the poem. In rhyming poems, the end words in particular lines must rhyme. Finally, in free verse, there is no particular form or pattern in which thoughts and feelings must be placed. While writing poems can be an exciting and powerful way to put thoughts into words, many people are frightened by the idea. The poems in this section have been selected because they will allow every student to end up feeling successful.

Working with poetry is important because students learn a lot about language. The knowledge they learn can be transferred to narrative, persuasive, descriptive, and informative writings. While writing poetry, students can learn rhythm, structure, imagery, and figurative language:

- Rhythm is created by the careful selection of words. Sometimes writers use a rhyming pattern and/or a set pattern of syllables to create rhythm.

- The structure of poetry differs from descriptive, narrative, persuasive, and informative writings because it is written in lines instead of sentences and paragraphs. Some poems have a set form; others have no fixed pattern.

- Imagery or mental pictures are created by using words or short phrases that appeal to one or more of the senses: sight, hearing, touch, smell, and taste.

- Figurative language such as similes and metaphors creates powerful images by comparing one thing to another.

Poetry is also important because it helps students to express deep feelings about something.

SOME FORMS OF POETRY

Acrostic Poems
Bio Poems
Cheers
Cinquain Poems
Color Poems
Concrete Poems
Couplets
Diamante Poems
Drawn Poems
Five Word Poems
Free Verse Poems

Haiku Poems
Jump Rope Rhymes
Limericks
Nursery Rhymes
Rhymed Poems
Rhythm Poems
Sensory Poems
Shape Poems
Tanka Poems
Three Line Poems

SONGS

Songs are really poems put to music. Sometimes a songwriter writes the words or lyrics first, and other times the music or melody comes first. Almost any song from "Mary Had a Little Lamb" to a popular current song can be used as a pattern for students' ideas. When lyrics are rewritten for an old melody, the desired rhythm has already been established. The writer need only choose words and phrases that fit the rhythm to communicate his or her thoughts or feelings.

SOME FORMS OF SONGS

Anthems	Jingles
Ballads	Lullabies
Chants	Nursery Rhymes
Folk Songs	Raps
Hymns	Popular Song Lyrics

LESSON 38

SHAPE POEMS

Beginning writers through advanced writers can have success with shape poems. In a shape poem, the writer uses shapes and spaces in addition to words to create a mental picture of a particular topic.

OBJECTIVES

Students will write a shape poem about a particular topic. To do this, they will:

- Draw a large shape of the topic.
- Write at least ten words that describe the topic on the outline of the shape.
- Place commas between words in a series.

MOTIVATORS

1. Show students several shape poems. See Reproducibles 38-1 through 38-3 or share a shape poem that you have written. Ask students what is special about these poems. Ask them how the shape poems are alike. (They are made up of a group of words arranged in the shape of the poem's topic. The words do not rhyme.)

2. Ask students to think of some favorite animals (such as cats, fishes, or worms) and things (such as a football, a tree house, or an apple) that are simple to draw and to write about.

FOOTBALL by Becky

tackle, kick, win, game, touchdown, field goal, throw, cheerleaders, referee, fans, goals, hot dogs

If you want to integrate this language arts lesson with another subject, review what your students have recently learned in science, health, or social studies before they choose a topic. Here's a shape poem written by a third grader after a unit on birds.

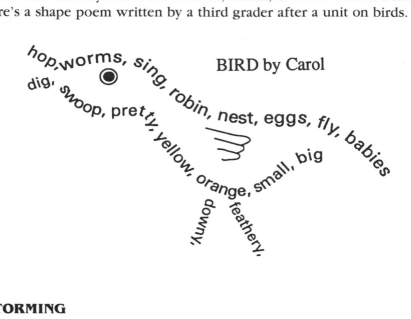

BIRD by Carol

BRAINSTORMING

For the purposes of this lesson, key questions related to the science topic "body parts" have been used. Develop similar questions for a topic of your choice.

Body Parts	Describing Words	Action Words	Other Words
eyes	muscle	pumping	blood
bones	hollow	beating	arteries
teeth	two parts	loving	veins
(heart)	red	circulating	oxygen
kidney			heart attack
			heart beat
			transplant

Key Questions

1. What are some parts of the body that we have studied so far? (Or if you want the topic to be open, ask "What would be a good topic for a poem? List the ideas on the chalkboard.)

2. From this long list of ideas, which should we choose as the topic of our group poem? What would you like to write about? Which body part should we choose? (Circle the selected word.)

3. What are some words that describe a heart? What does a heart look like?

4. What action words do you think of when you think about a heart?

5. What other words do you think of when you hear the word "heart"?

GROUP COMPOSING

1. Explain that first, you are going to draw a simple shape in the center of a sheet of paper. Tape a sheet of paper to the chalkboard. Draw a large shape, in this case a heart, with a wide black marker. Caution students to draw the shape they choose so it fills at least one half a page. Then they will have room to write all their describing words.

2. Point out that next you will cover the picture with another sheet of paper. Paper clip or tape the blank sheet of paper over the picture so that it won't move. Call students' attention to the outline of the shape that shows through this sheet. Explain that the outline shows where to write the describing words.

3. Have students select the describing word they wish to start with and ask where you should place the word. Write it on the outline. Have students select and decide how to arrange the other describing words. Continue until the heart outline is filled. Be sure you call attention to the commas you placed between words in a series.

Remind students that they will need enough words to go around their shape, but they don't have to use all their describing words, only the best ones.

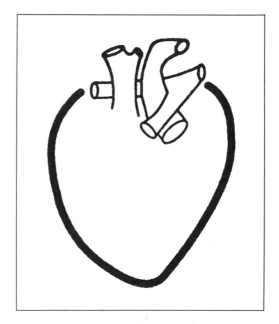

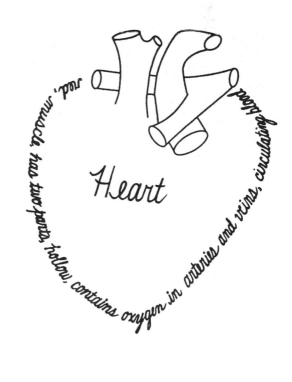

RESPONDING TO STUDENT WRITING

1. As students draw an outline of their topic, walk around the room. Make sure that the shapes being drawn are large enough to hold at least five words.

2. As students brainstorm words for their topic, hold mini-conferences with those who need assistance or attention. Individually read back the students' words so that they can check to see if all the words describe the topic.

3. As students move into the final stages of their drafts, ask them to find a revising partner. Write these steps on the chalkboard or on a chart for them to follow.

   • Guess what your revising partner's shape is.

   • Listen as your partner reads his/her shape poem out loud to you.

   • Tell your partner which words you think are the most powerful for describing the topic.

   • Look at each other's poem to see if commas have been placed between words in a series around the poem's shape.

PUBLISHING

Invite students to display their shape poems in the hallway so that other students can learn more about their bodies.

MODIFICATIONS TO ENCOURAGE BEGINNING WRITERS

• Limit topics to objects that can be seen.

• Provide predrawn simple shapes for students who would find it difficult to draw one.

• Suggest students draw an outline of their topic with a light pencil so they won't have to deal with a second sheet of paper.

MODIFICATIONS TO CHALLENGE ADVANCED WRITERS

• Direct students to evaluate each word carefully to see if it clearly adds to the mental picture before adding it to the perimeter of the poem. Explain that unnecessary words will weaken their poems. Suggest students eliminate unnecessary words by drawing a line through the weaker words on their list.

• Encourage students to circle words that create vivid or interesting images.

• Have students consider how to arrange or order their words before placing them on the shape.

• Suggest students make up sentences from their brainstormed words and place these sentences around their shape.

FOOTBALL by Becky

field goal, throw, cheerleaders, referee, fans, goals, hot dogs, tackle, kick, win, game, touchdown,

BIRD by Carol

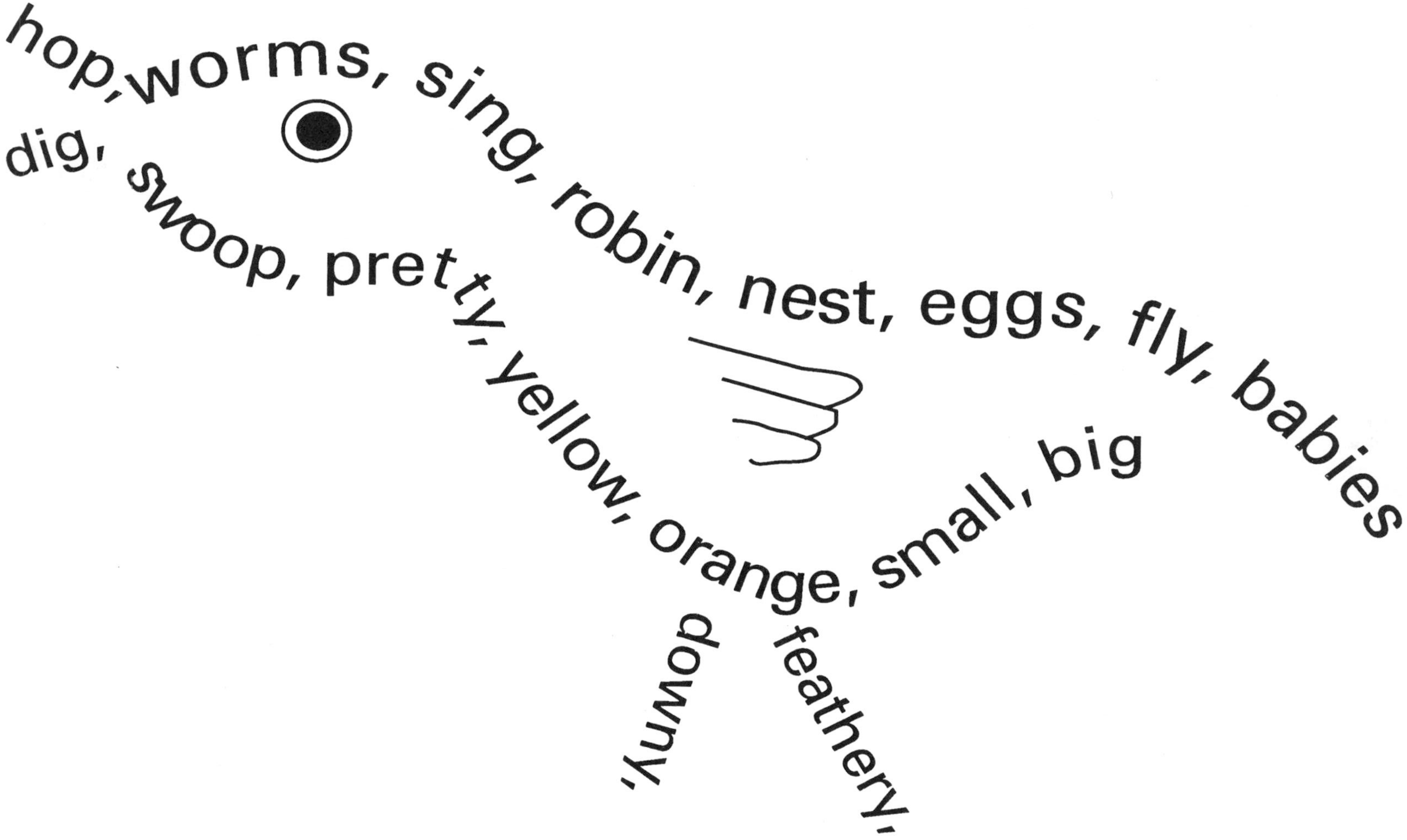

hop, worms, sing, robin, nest, eggs, fly, babies, big, small, orange, yellow, pretty, swoop, dig, feathery, downy,

338

DINOSAUR by Eric

animals, extinct, meat eaters, cold blooded, dinosaurs, huge, skin, wrinkles, fat, huge, cool, magnificeant, like elephants but bigger, some are plant eaters walked the earth they long ago they dangerous, strong, large, eat

LESSON 39

RHYTHM POEMS

Many people consider writing poetry a frightening or an impossible task. This lesson on rhythm poems is easy to teach and produces an exciting poem in just a few minutes. Rhythm poems are great for describing an idea just studied in social studies or science or for describing current events. These poems are fun to read and write and then read again. And while your students are having fun, they will be learning quite a bit about using adjectives to describe a topic.

OBJECTIVES

Students will write rhythm poems that follows the pattern of the "Friends, Friends, Friends" poem. (This rhythm poem is an adaptation of the poem "Beans, Beans, Beans" by Lucia and James Hymes. It can be found in the book *Hooray for Chocolate and Other Easy to Read Jingles,* Katonah, N.Y.: Scholarship Books, 1965.) To do this, they will:

- Select a one-word topic.
- Fit 21 different descriptive words (adjectives) about the topic in the appropriate places.
- Capitalize each word in the poem's title.
- Insert commas between the words in the title.
- Capitalize the first word in each line of the poem.
- End lines 5, 10, 13, and 16 with exclamation marks.

MOTIVATORS

1. Share a picture of your best friend. Tell why you like this person. Ask students who their best friend is and why this person is so special.

Friends, Friends, Friends

Girl friends
Boy friends
Neat, smart, handsome friends
Short, fat, cool friends
Those are just a few!

Happy friends
Gloomy friends
Tall, awesome, preppie friends
Poor, lonely, sad friends
Weird friends, too!

Thoughtful friends
Mean friends
And don't forget teacher friends!

Last of all
Best of all
I like best friends!

Snakes, Snakes, Snakes

Skinny snakes
Slithery snakes
Ugly, slimy, scary snakes
Awesome, green, useful snakes
Those are just a few!

Old snakes
Deadly snakes
Teeny, tiny, red snakes
Yellow striped, garden snakes
Rattle snakes, too!

Strangling snakes
Poisonous snakes
And don't forget long snakes!

Last of all
Best of all
I like helpful snakes!

2. Post a copy of the "Friends, Friends, Friends" poem. Say the poem for your students. Next chant and clap the poem as your students silently read the words. When students are familiar with the words, ask them to chant and clap with you. See the "Friends, Friends, Friends" rhythm poem at the end of this lesson. It will show you when to clap your hands and when to slap your legs.

3. Read a poem with the same rhythm, but on another subject such as "Snakes, Snakes, Snakes" or "Books, Books, Books." At the end of this lesson are several rhythm poems (Reproducible 39-1) with guidelines so you will know when to clap your hands and when to slap your legs.

BRAINSTORMING

Topic Ideas	Descriptors	
(Books, Books, Books)	small	short
Shoes, Shoes, Shoes	big	tall
Cars, Cars, Cars	funny	friendly
Dogs, Dogs, Dogs	sad	fun
	scary	tattered
	old	torn
	new	silly

Key Questions

1. *What other topics besides friends and snakes could we write about? What else would make a good topic for a poem?* (As students reply, respond positively and write their ideas on the chalkboard.)

2. *Which one of these topics should we pick to write about?* (Circle the chosen topic. For the purposes of this lesson, the topic "books" will be used.)

3. *What kind of books do you like? What are some powerful words we can use to describe books?* (While you could ask for adjectives, a more helpful method of eliciting this type of word is to ask for descriptors or "what kind of." Elicit a long list of words.)

GROUP COMPOSING

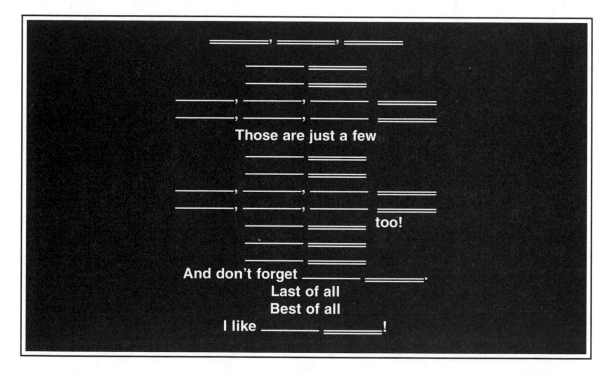

1. Post a "skeleton" of the poem on a wall or draw one on the chalkboard. Explain that first the word "books" needs to be written in all the blanks where the word "friends" originally appeared. These places are shown by a double underscore. Ask students to help you find those blanks.

2. Next ask students to help you fill in the other blanks with some of the describing words that were brainstormed.

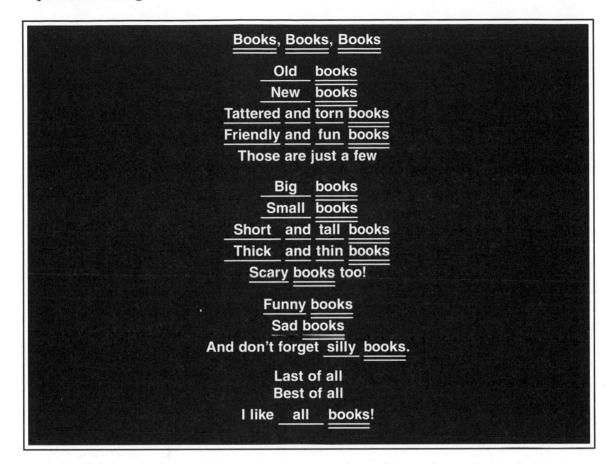

Books, Books, Books

Old books
New books
Tattered and torn books
Friendly and fun books
Those are just a few

Big books
Small books
Short and tall books
Thick and thin books
Scary books too!

Funny books
Sad books
And don't forget silly books.

Last of all
Best of all
I like all books!

3. After each new line is created, clap out the rhythm together to see if the new words "sound right."

4. Review these steps with students before they begin composing their own poems.

   a. What is the first step you have to do? (Choose a topic.)

   b. Where does your topic word go? (Where the double lines are.)

   c. Then what do you need to brainstorm? (Describing words for the topic.)

   d. What words will go on the single lines? (The describing words.)

   e. After you finish writing each new line, what do you do? (Clap out the rhythm to see if it "sounds right.")

5. Tell students that when they have chosen their topic and brainstormed their describing words they are ready to compose their poem.

RESPONDING TO STUDENT WRITING

1. As the students write their rhythm poems, walk around the room. Visit individually with students who need assistance.

- Read back portions of students' rhythm poems so that they can hear how they sound.

- Make one or two **positive comments** about especially powerful words and vivid images that effectively describe their topic such as "'Dry and burning' are super words to describe summer winds."

- **Ask a question** about over-used words such as "What is a more powerful word than 'nice' that you could use to describe birds?"

- Ask students to read and clap the words of their poem with you to see if it fits the rhythm. If there is a problem, ask, "How can you change your poem so that it has the same rhythm as the 'Friends, Friends, Friends' poem?"

2. Ask students who have finished the rough draft of their poems to find a revising partner and follow these directions or use the Self Evaluation Checklist (Reproducible 39-2) at the end of this lesson.

- Read your poem out loud to a friend as you clap it.

- Decide whether the rhythm of your poem sounds right.

- Decide whether any words could be replaced with more descriptive and interesting words.

- Decide whether any words should be added or deleted to make the poem better fit the rhythm?

PUBLISHING

Tell students that they will invite another class to their room and that they will read and share their poems with the other class. This will be an opportunity for everyone to relax and enjoy listening to each other's poems.

Students can attractively display their poems by drawing a large shape of their topic on a piece of construction paper. The shape should be big enough for their poem to fit on it. Once they've cut the shape out, they should glue their rhythm poem onto it.

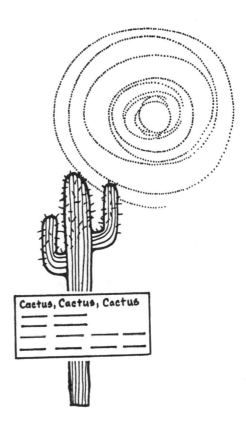

MODIFICATIONS TO ENCOURAGE BEGINNING WRITERS

- Write a rhythm poem as a whole class. End the lesson after writing the group poem. Do not require individual writing.
- Shorten the number of lines in the poem. One way to do this is to use only lines 1, 2, 3, 4, 14, 15, and 16. Thus the poem would become:

Bikes, Bikes, Bikes

Red bikes (line 1)
Blue bikes (line 2)
Fast, slick, 10-speed bikes (line 3)
Sad, old, squeaky bikes (line 4)

Last of all (line 14)
Best of all (line 15)
I like my bike! (linc 16)

Another way to shorten this poem is to use lines 1, a new line with two blanks, 3, 5, a new line with two blanks, 13, 14, 15, and 16. Thus the poem would become:

Bikes, Bikes, Bikes

Red bikes (line 1)
Short, blue bikes (new line)
Fast, slick, 10-speed bikes (line 3)
Those are just a few! (line 5)

Fast, green bikes (new line)
Slow, tiny, kids' bikes (line 8)
And don't forget birthday bikes! (line 13)

Last of all (line 14)
Best of all (line 15)
I like my bike! (line 16)

- Provide special form (Reproducible 39-3) that cues students where to put the topic word or noun (on double lines) and where to put the describing words or adjectives (on the single lines).
- Guide students to choose concrete nouns (such as cars, bikes, lakes) as the topic of their poem.

MODIFICATIONS TO CHALLENGE ADVANCED WRITERS

- Have students write opposite descriptors for particular lines in their poem such as "girl friends, boy friends" or "fast bikes, slow bikes."
- Guide students to select abstract nouns (such as parents, winter, vacations, or energy) as the topic of their poem.
- Suggest that students create their own version of the "Friends, Friends, Friends" poem with its own structure in this example.

WEATHER, WEATHER, WEATHER

Calm weather
Stormy weather
Hot sticky, tornado weather

Cool weather
Rainy weather
Those are just a few!

Dangerous weather
Safe weather
And don't forget fickle weather!

Snowy, freezing weather
Warm, sunny weather
Can be fun for you!

- Ask advanced writers to assist students who are having difficulty with the rhythm of their poems.

Planets (slap legs), Planets (slap), Planets (slap)

Large (slap legs) **planets** (clap hands)
Small (slap legs) **planets** (clap hands)
Red (slap), **hot** (clap), **steaming** (slap) **planets** (clap)
Blue (slap), **rocky** (clap), **freezing** (slap) **planets** (clap)
Those are (slap) **just a** (clap) **few** (snap fingers)!

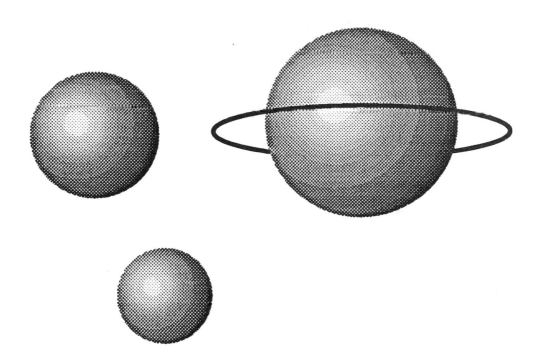

Old (slap legs) **planets** (clap hands)
New (slap legs) **planets** (clap hands)
Dark (slap), **windy** (clap), **cold** (slap) **planets** (clap)
Bright (slap), **spinning** (clap), **fiery** (slap) **planets** (clap)
Twinkling (slap) **planets** (clap), **too** (snap fingers)!

Close (slap legs) **planets** (clap hands)
Far (slap legs) **planets** (clap hands)
And don't (slap) **forget** (clap) **ringed** (slap) **planets** (clap)!
Last of all (slap legs)
Best of all (clap hands)
I (slap) **like** (clap) **alien** (slap) **planets** (clap)!

347

Moms (slap legs), Moms (slap), Moms (slap)

Happy (slap legs) moms (clap hands)
Teasing (slap legs) moms (clap hands)
Gorgeous (slap), skinny (clap), loving (slap) moms (clap)
Serious (slap), protective (clap), fat (slap) moms (clap)
Those are (slap) just a (clap) few (snap fingers)!
Proud (slap legs) moms (clap hands)
Athletic (slap legs) moms (clap hands)
Kissing (slap), hugging (clap), sweet (slap) moms (clap)
Mad (slap), picky (clap), mean (slap) moms (clap)
Step (slap) moms (clap), too (snap fingers)!

Funny (slap legs) moms (clap hands)
Thoughtful (slap legs) moms (clap hands)
And don't (slap) forget (clap) busy (slap) moms (clap)!

Last of all (slap legs)
Best of all (clap hands)
I (slap) love (clap) my (slap) mom (clap)!

Candy (slap legs), Candy (slap), Candy (slap)

Sweet (slap legs) candy (clap hands)
Sour (slap legs) candy (clap hands)
Big (slap), pink (clap), cotton (slap) candy (clap)
Tiny (slap), red (clap), hot (slap) candy (clap)
Those are (slap) just a (clap) few (snap fingers)!

Hard (slap legs) candy (clap hands)
Chewy (slap legs) candy (clap hands)
Black (slap), sticky (clap), gooey (slap) candy (clap)
Minty (slap), brown (clap), chocolate (slap) candy (clap)
Candy (slap) bars (clap), too (snap fingers)!

Fruity (slap legs) candy (clap hands)
Caramel (slap legs) candy (clap hands)
And don't (slap) forget (clap) licorice (slap) candy (clap)!

Last of all (slap legs)
Best of all (clap hands)
I (slap) like (clap) peppermint (slap) candy (clap)!

Bikes (slap legs), Bikes (slap), Bikes (slap)

Red (slap legs) bikes (clap hands)
Blue (slap legs) bikes (clap hands)
Fast (slap), slick (clap), 10-speed (slap) bikes (clap)
Sad (slap), old (clap), squeaky (slap) bikes (clap)
Those are (slap) just a (clap) few (snap fingers)!

Fast (slap legs) bikes (clap hands)
Slow (slap legs) bikes (clap hands)
Teeny (slap), tiny (clap), kids' (slap) bikes (clap)
Sleek (slap), speedy (clap), motor (slap) bikes (clap)
Grown-up (slap) bikes (clap), too (snap fingers)!

Rusty (slap legs) bikes (clap hands)
Shiny (slap legs) bikes (clap hands)
And don't (slap) forget (clap) birthday (slap) bikcs (clap)!

Last of all (slap legs)
Best of all (clap hands)
I (slap) like (clap) my (slap) bike (clap)!

Friends (slap legs), Friends (slap), Friends (slap)

Girl (slap legs) friends (clap hands)
Boy (slap legs) friends (clap hands)
Neat (slap), smart (clap), handsome (slap) friends (clap)
Short (slap), fat (clap), cool (slap) friends (clap)
Those are (slap) just a (clap) few (snap fingers)!

Happy (slap legs) friends (clap hands)
Gloomy (slap legs) friends (clap hands)
Tall (slap), awesome (clap), preppie (slap) friends (clap)
Poor (slap), lonely (clap), sad (slap) friends (clap)
Weird (slap) friends (clap), too (snap fingers)!

Thoughtful (slap legs) friends (clap hands)
Mean (slap legs) friends (clap hands)
And don't (slap) forget (clap) teacher (slap) friends (clap)!

Last of all (slap legs)
Best of all (clap hands)
I (slap) like (clap) my (slap) friend (clap)!

Name: _____ **Date:** _____ (39-2)

SELF EVALUATION CHECKLIST

Reread and rethink your Rhythm Poem.

1. What is your topic? _____

2. What are your most powerful describing words?

   _____   _____   _____

3. Have you used any describing words more than once?   Yes   No

   If yes, what are two other words that you could use to describe your topic?

   _____   _____

4. How does your rhythm poem sound when you read and clap it? Circle one.

   Some lines sound good.   All the lines sound good except line _____.

   What word or words can you add, change, or remove to make this line sound better?

   _____

5. Did you capitalize the three words in the title?   Yes   No

   Did you put commas between each word in the title?   Yes   No

6. Did you capitalize the first word in each line of your poem?   Yes   No

I have carefully read and evaluated my poem. _____
                                                                    Signature

_____ , _____ , _____

_____ _____

_____ _____

_____ , _____ , _____ _____

_____ , _____ , _____ _____

Those are just a few.

_____ _____

_____ _____

_____ , _____ , _____ _____

_____ , _____ , _____ _____

_____ _____ too!

_____ _____

_____ _____

And don't forget _____ _____ .

Last of all
Best of all
I like _____ _____ !

LESSON 40

CINQUAIN POEMS

A cinquain is a short poem, five lines in length, whose form can be based on words or syllables. The word form is easy enough for second graders to write, yet it yields a result that can make sixth graders through adults proud.

While this lesson on cinquain poetry is designed around Father's Day, the lesson may be integrated with any area of the elementary curriculum. Cinquain poems are simple but powerful tools for communicating to others what has been learned in science, health, and social studies, particularly when these subjects are taught via a "hands on—minds on" approach.

OBJECTIVES

Students will write a cinquain poem about their real father, stepfather, or other "father" figure. To do this, they will:

- State the subject "father" on the first line and spell this word correctly.
- Write two words that describe their father in the second line, separating the two describing words by a comma.
- Write three action words about what their father does in the third line. The action words will end in "ing" and will be separated by commas.
- Make a statement about how their father makes them feel in the fourth line. End the statement with a period.
- State another name for their father in the fifth line.
- Start each line with a capital letter.

MOTIVATORS

1. Involve students in a discussion about the significance of Father's Day. Ask students questions about a father's role. Discuss what makes fathers special and what dads do for us. Ask students why we have this special day every year. Be sensitive to students who may not have a father in residence. Maybe these students can think about a grandfather, an uncle, a stepfather, or a significant other in their mother's life.

Relate that today they will do something special for their fathers for Father's Day.

2. Share a cinquain poem written by you or by a student. This is a poem written by a fifth grade girl.

Mother
Gorgeous, pretty
Cooking, exercising, reading
She makes me feel proud.
Miss America.

3. Post two cinquain poems. Write your own or use the ones that follow. (Note: Concrete topics/nouns work best.) Have students read the poems together.

Spider Furry, black Climbing, spinning, weaving They make an intricate web. Tarantula	Polar bear White, large Hunting, eating, roaming You are an excellent fisher. Carnivore

Now show students these cinquain poems written by children their age. Request they read these two poems together with you.

Birthdays Fun, happy Eating, playing, opening Birthdays are happy. Party	Baseball Great, exciting Pitching, catching, running Baseball is fun. Sport

3. State that cinquain poems are easy poems to write. Then inquire how all four poems they read are alike. Ask the following questions to establish an understanding of cinquain poems.

   a. ***What do you notice about all four cinquain poems? How many lines does each poem have?*** (As you ask students to describe the cinquain pattern, draw an illustration of it on the chalkboard.)

   b. ***How many words are in the first line?*** (One; two if a compound noun.) ***What did the first line of the poems do?*** (Name the subject of each poem.) (Write "subject" under line one.)

   c. ***How many words are in the second line?*** (Two.) ***What kinds of words are they?*** (Descriptive words about the subject.) (Insert this information under line two.)

   d. ***What is special about the third line?*** (Three words that describe what the subject does.) ***How do the words end?*** (In -ing.) (Insert this information under line three.)

e. **What is different about the fourth line?** (Complete sentence about the subject.) (Insert this information under line four.)

f. **What does the fifth line contain?** (Another name for the subject.) (Insert this information under line five.)

g. **What did each line of the poem start with?** (Capital letter.)

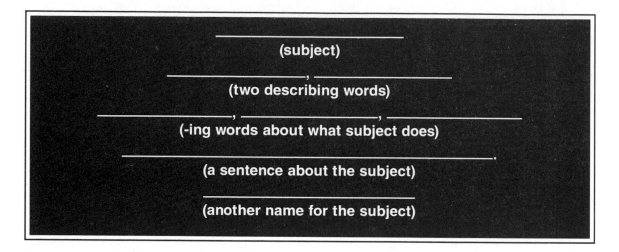

(subject)

(two describing words)

(-ing words about what subject does)

(a sentence about the subject)

(another name for the subject)

BRAINSTORMING

Point out that since they are going to write poems for their fathers, you will write Father, Grandpa, Uncle, or Stepfather on the first line of the class poem.

Father			
Words to describe	Things fathers do	How he makes you feel	Another name
dependable	cooking	He makes me happy	Dad
happy	laughing		Hero
trusting	loving	He makes me feel	Friend
angry	playing	loved	Parent
playful	supporting		Pop
	chasing		
	scolding		
	helping		

1. **What are some words that describe a father? What is a father like? What does a dad look like?** (As students reply, respond positively and write their ideas on the chalkboard.)

2. What does a dad do? How does he act? (Guide students to use words that end in "ing.")

3. How does your father make you feel? What is another feeling you have when you think of your dad? (As students reply, respond positively and write a complete sentence on the chalkboard.)

4. What is another name for a father? What do you call your dad?

GROUP COMPOSING

Comment that students have brainstormed many good ideas about fathers. Tell them that first they create a group poem about fathers in general, then they will get to write one especially for their own father.

1. Ask what goes in the first line. Write the word "father" in the first line on the chalkboard.

2. Remind students that the second line needs two words to describe a father. Have them choose two describing words from the list to use in the poem.

3. Cue students that the third line needs three words that describes what a father does. Write the words that students choose in the poem.

4. Remind students that the fourth line should have a statement of their feelings toward their father. Have them select a statement and write it on the board.

5. Point out that the fifth line needs one word giving another name for a father. Ask which idea they want to include in the poem.

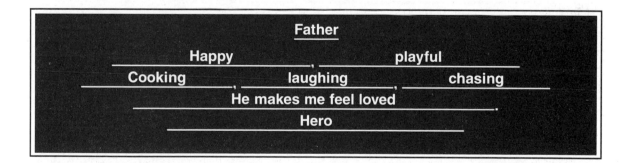

Impress on students that they will write a poem especially for their own father, so they should use words that describe their dad. Remind students again that they don't have to limit themselves to the words on the board. Explain that their job is to make sure that their poem is especially appropriate for their father and that they tell how he is special.

Take down or erase the poem the group composed together so that a less confident student doesn't copy it, but leave up the brainstorming list so everyone can look back at it if necessary for ideas.

RESPONDING TO STUDENT WRITING

1. As students begin to write the rough drafts of their cinquain poems, move around the room looking for especially thoughtful or meaningful ideas that are unique to a particular student's father.

   • Make **positive comments** about word choice such as "Dependable is a word that really describes your father" and "Teacher is a special name to call your father."

   • If a student seems stuck, **ask a question** for the student to ponder such as "What action word can you use to tell what your father does?" or "What is something special your father does with you?"

2. Direct students who have finished their rough draft to read it out loud to a classmate and do the following.

   • Listen to see if they've really described their dad.

   • Decide which parts of the poem their Dad will like.

3. Since the Father's Day poem will be a very special gift, it may be kept for a long time. Because of this you may want to have a formal conference with each student before the final draft is written to see if each line of the poem sounds appropriate.

PUBLISHING

Ask for volunteers who are willing to share their poems with the class. Explain that you'll put the poems up on the bulletin board so that others can read them. Inform students that at the end of school you'll take their poems down so that they can take this very special gift home for their dad.

MODIFICATIONS TO ENCOURAGE BEGINNING WRITERS

- Simplify the poem's pattern. Have students write only four lines (1, 2, 3, and 5) for their poem.
- During individual composing provide students who need more support, with a special piece of paper on which you've drawn the cinquain pattern and inserted the commas and the period.

_____

_____, _____

_____, _____, _____

_____.

_____

MODIFICATIONS TO CHALLENGE ADVANCED WRITERS

- Direct students to capture personality traits of their dads such "thinking," "powerful," and "carefree" verses physically observable traits such as "playful," "cooking," and "chasing."
- Suggest that students consider whether the overall picture or central idea of their poem will be meaningful to their dads. If necessary they should replace certain words or concepts with ones that better fit their poem's central idea.

LESSON 41

"IF ONLY" POEMS

This exciting, yet easy to use, poem pattern lets students play with the English language while sharing wishes in a meaningful way. The "If Only" poem pattern was created by an elementary teacher named Joy Lindner.

OBJECTIVES

Students will write a poem about a special person, animal, place, or thing using the "If Only" poem pattern. To do this, they will:

- Give (in line 1) the name of a special person/animal/place/thing.
- Write (in line 2) two adjectives describing the special person. Connect the descriptive words with the word "and" or "but."
- Write (in line 3) a typical action the special person does (verb) and how the person typically does the action (adverb).
- Write (in line 4) a comparison using the words "As _____ as a/an _____" to show a special quality the person has.
- Write (in line 5) an "If only" wish for the special person.
- Begin each line with a capital letter.
- End the last line with a period.

MOTIVATORS

1. Share a real story about a person who is or was very special to you. Here is a true story about me and a poem to give you some ideas.

   Today I want to tell you about a person who was very special to me. Her name was Mrs. Murphy. I don't know if she is alive now, but she had a lot of influence on my life. She was my sixth grade teacher.

   When I started sixth grade, I couldn't read except for about ten words. In fact I couldn't read any of our sixth grade science, social studies, math, or music books. I didn't even

fit into a reading group. I felt really miserable. No one wanted to work with me even though I had lots of good ideas. When Mrs. Murphy found out how miserable I felt, she talked to me. She was great! She told me I wasn't stupid even though I didn't read.

One day Mrs. Murphy took me to the school library and we picked out a lot of neat picture books that didn't have many words. Then she told my class, "Every time you read a book you will get a sticker to put up on a chart next to your name." I thought I wouldn't get any stickers because I couldn't read. But no! Mrs. Murphy told me to pick out one of the books that we found in the library. Then she sat beside me as we looked at the pictures. When we finished she said, "Cherlyn, you are the first person to get a sticker." She held a box of the most wonderful stickers. I found a beautiful butterfly sticker, and Mrs. Murphy helped me put the sticker by my name on our chart.

Before I knew it, I had ten different butterfly stickers and four bird stickers beside my name. By the end of sixth grade, I had more stickers than anyone else in my class! And I could read almost as well as all my friends. I wrote this poem about her.

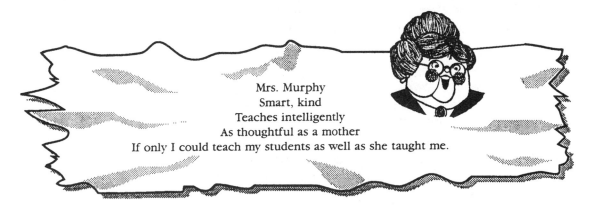

Mrs. Murphy
Smart, kind
Teaches intelligently
As thoughtful as a mother
If only I could teach my students as well as she taught me.

2. Ask students to raise their hands if they have a special person in their life. Allow a brief sharing period. Then explain that they're going to think about some favorite or special people.

BRAINSTORMING

Who	What kind of	Does what	As tiny as a _____
Grandpa	tall	laughs	butterfly
Cheryl	beautiful	sings	Volkswagon
(Ms. Martin)	helpful	dances	chair
Mom	talented	(listens)	
Mr. Kirt	funny		If only _____
Lacy	(tiny)	**How**	I were as funny.
	clever	carefully	I could sing as well.
		quickly	she was my mom.
		softly	

Key Questions

1. *Who are some of your favorite people?* (Note: You could change this to animals, places, or things.) *Who is one of your favorite people at school? Which person in your family is special to you?* (Continue brainstorming until many ideas are listed. Then have students choose a person from the list that everyone knows. Circle students' choice. For the purposes of this lesson, we will use Ms. Martin.)

2. *What kind of person is Ms. Martin? What is it about her personality that makes her so special?* (Elicit several describing words and write them on the chalkboard.)

3. *What does Ms. Martin do? What is something special Ms. Martin does for you?* (As students suggest action words, write them on the board. Then have them choose one of the action words to use in the poem.)

4. *How does Ms. Martin* (<u>Insert the doing word students just chose</u>.)*?* (Elicit a list of adverbs.)

5. *Now we need to choose a word from the list of describing words that we brainstormed earlier. Which descriptor do you want to use for Ms. Martin?* (Circle the word and write it in the first blank of the sentence "As <u>tiny</u> as a _____.")

6. *What is Ms. Martin as tiny as? To what small animal, person, place or thing can we compare her?* (Ask students to try out the words in the sentence to see how they sound. Make a positive comment for appropriate suggestions such as "As tiny as a butterfly" is a wonderful comparison and it fits Ms. Martin.)

7. *Now let's think about the last line of the poem: "If only _____."* If only what? In what ways would you like to be like Ms. Martin?* (Guide students to express what they admire about Ms. Martin or what they wish for her.)

GROUP COMPOSING

1. Tell students that they'll use the brainstorming categories to help write a powerful poem for Ms. Martin. Point out that they have already completed the first line: the person's name. Remind students that later they will write their own poem and will get to choose their own favorite person.

2. For the second line of the poem, have students choose two describing words from the "what kind of" category. Write the words in the poem pattern.

3. Remind students that they have already chosen the action word "listens" for line 3. Now have them choose a word from the "how" list to tell how Ms. Martin listens.

4. Ask students to read what they have written so far to see how it sounds and to see if it describes Ms. Martin. If students like the poem, proceed. If a student is unhappy, ask for suggestions for what word or words to change to improve the poem.

5. Remind students that for line 4 they already chose the describing word "tiny" from the "what kind of" category. Then they compared Ms. Martin to many things. Have them choose the one comparison they want to use in the poem.

6. Finally, ask which one of the "If only" wishes they want to use. Write the sentence, calling attention to the fact that you ended it with a period.

	Ms. Martin	
Beautiful	and	funny
	Listens	carefully
As	tiny	as a butterfly
If only		.

Tell students that they are ready to write their own "If Only" poems.

RESPONDING TO STUDENT WRITING

1. As students write their "If Only" poems, walk around the room.

   - Read back students' poems so that they can hear how they sound. Evaluate parts that sound awkward.

   - Make positive comments about adjectives, verbs, adverbs, nouns, and statements that characterize or create a powerful picture of the special person.

   - Ask questions that help students clarify their thoughts about the person.

2. If you want students to work towards particular learner outcomes, focus your positive comments and questions so they guide each student to self evaluate one or two of these outcomes.

- Line one names a special person.
- Line two contains two descriptive words separated by "and" or "but."
- Line three tells what the person does and how.
- Line four contains a comparison (simile) using "as."
- Line five contains a wish.
- Each line begins with a capital letter.
- The last line ends with a period.

3. Once students have completed the rough draft of their poems, have them do the following.

- Exchange with a partner.
- Read their partner's poem out loud.
- Listen for the imagery that creates a picture in their mind.
- Consider what new words might be used to create a stronger and more emotionally powerful picture.

PUBLISHING

Encourage students to give their poems to their special person so that person will know how important he or she is to them.

MODIFICATIONS TO ENCOURAGE BEGINNING WRITERS

- Supply a sheet with a predrawn poem pattern and have students insert their ideas in the blanks.

```
          _____
     _____ and _____
     _____   _____
  As _____ as a _____
I wish _____.
```

- Replace the "how" category with a "when" category. Also, the "If only" line can be changed to "I wish," which is an easier linguistic response. Be sure to help students brainstorm for these categories.

MODIFICATIONS TO CHALLENGE ADVANCED WRITERS

- Instruct students to focus on choosing precise describing words that tell about personal characteristics instead of physical ones.

- In line 2 ask students to use the word "but" instead of the word "and." This will require that students choose contrasting qualities.

- In line 4 ask students to capture the special person's characteristics in a "_____ than a/an _____" comparison instead of a "_____ as a _____" simile. Example: "Smarter than a computer."

- Ask students to close the poem with a promise instead of a wish. Instead of using "If only," have them make an "I will always _____" or "I will never _____" statement.

- Encourage students to write a poem about an occupation of their choice after completing their poem about their special person. Example:

Nurse
Busy but caring
Holds you strongly
As friendly as a police officer
Someday I will give the shots.

LESSON 42

DIAMANTE POEMS

Diamante poems are another type of pattern poem that compares opposites. While the diamante pattern is more complex than the cinquain pattern, once students have discovered the poem's pattern, they can create new poems about any contrasting ideas quite easily. The diamante poem structure was devised by Iris Tiedt.

OBJECTIVES

Students will write a diamante poem about two contrasting ideas. To do this, they will:

- Write (in line 1) a noun.
- Write (in line 7) another noun that is the opposite of the noun in line 1.
- Write (in line 2) two words that describe the noun in line 1.
- Write (in line 3) three participles ("ing" or "ed" words) that refer to the noun in line 1.
- Write (in line 4) four words that refer to both the noun in line 1 and the noun in line 7.
- Write (in line 5) three participles that refer to the noun in line 7.
- Write (in line 6) two words that describe the noun in line 7.
- Begin each line with a capital letter.
- Insert commas between the words in lines 2, 3, 4, 5, and 6.

MOTIVATORS

1. Dress in summer clothes from the waist down and in winter clothes from the waist up. Encourage students to guess why you're dressed this way. Accept all students' ideas as a possibility; do not reveal the reason yet.
2. Display these two poems or two other diamante poems on the overhead or on a chart. Ask students to read the poems out loud along with you.

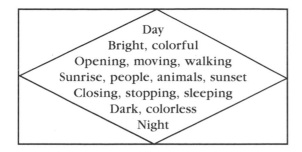

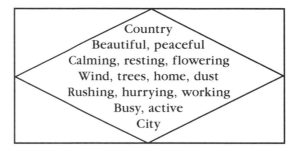

Inform students that these poems are called diamante poems and that diamante poems are special because they can help organize thoughts about two different things.

Have students help you number the lines of each poem. Then use the following questions to guide them to discover the pattern of these poems. As students reinvent the diamante pattern, write information on the chalkboard and comment positively on their observations.

1. What can you tell me about the shape of this poem? (Shaped like a diamond.)

2. What do you notice about lines 1 and 7? (The words are nouns; they are opposites.)

3. How are lines 2 and 6 alike? (2 adjectives that describe the nouns that they're close to.)

4. How are lines 3 and 5 alike? (3 doing words.)

5. What is in line 4? (4 nouns that relate to both nouns.)

6. How many lines does each poem have? (Seven lines.)

7. What do you notice about each line? (Begins with a capital letter.)

8. What punctuation is common in both poems? (Commas between words in lines 2–6.)

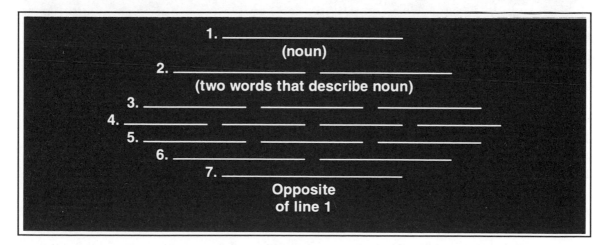

1. Explain that they have just discovered the basic pattern of a diamante poem.

2. Ask your students if they now know why you dressed this way today. (Because summer and winter are opposites.)

3. Invite students to listen to this poem written by two sixth graders.

Pollution

Ugly, grotesque

Lying, sitting, floating

Cans, paper, sewage, smog

Recycling, saving, collecting

Pretty, tidy

Cleanliness

Please note: Although line 4 in this child's poem doesn't exactly match the diamante pattern, it is still a very powerful poem.

BRAINSTORMING

Tell students that first they are going to write a diamante poem together about summer and winter. Explain that later they will write their own diamante poem about something they've studied this year.

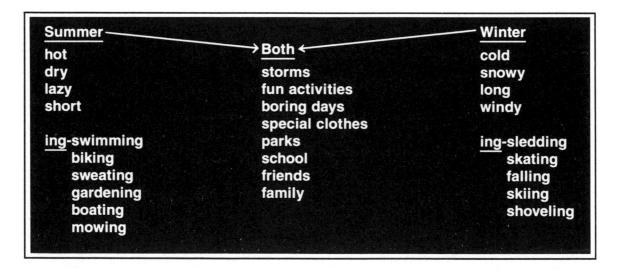

Key Questions

*Line 2. **What are some words that describe summer?*** (As students reply, respond positively and write their ideas on the chalkboard.)

*Line 3. **What are some words that end in "ing" that you think of when you think about summer? What are people or animals doing during the summer?*** (Give a positive response such as "'Swimming' is a good doing word for summer.")

(Note: Brainstorm lines 7 and 6 next. Hold off brainstorming line 4 until later.)

*Line 7. **What is winter like? What are some words that describe winter?***

Line 6. **What are some words that end in "ing" that you think of when you think about winter? During the winter what are people doing?**

Line 4. **Now what are some things or objects that relate to both summer and winter?** (This cognitive task is quite difficult so allow plenty of time for thinking. Give positive feedback such as "Terrific, 'fun activities' do occur during both the summer and winter.") **What places do you think about when you think of summer and winter? What people do you think about during both seasons?**

GROUP COMPOSING

1. Relate that next students will use the ideas that they brainstormed to create a class diamante poem. This next step is very important to help students see how to put their ideas together.

2. Guide students to use the ideas to fill in the pattern they created earlier. Encourage volunteers to offer suggestions to complete each line. Write the information in the appropriate place.

3. As you write words in a series ask students what you should put between the words. (Commas.)

4. Ask how you should start each line. (Capital letter.)

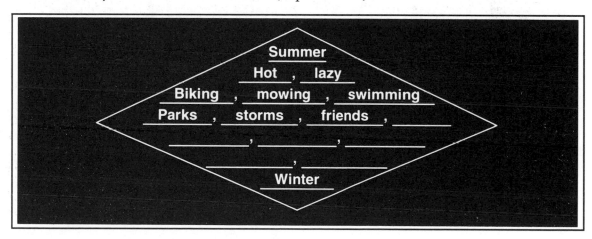

Before students create their own diamante poems, you can get them thinking of some possible topics by asking these questions:

1. **What are some things we've studied in science, health, or social studies so far this year? What else have we studied?** (Continue brainstorming until a long list of ideas has been generated.)

2. **Now let's try to think of some opposites related to these topics. What different kinds of rocks did we study?** (Respond positively and write the contrasting nouns— for example, volcanic and sedimentary—across from the word "rocks." Comment that the nouns would work for lines 1 and 7 of a diamante poem on rocks.)

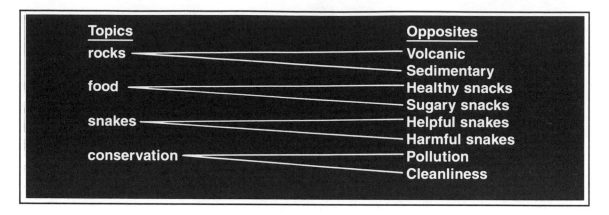

a. *What about our unit on food and nutrition? What opposites can we come up with for food?* (Respond positively such as "Health snacks would work for line 1 or line 7.") Then probe for an opposite. *If someone used healthy snacks in their poem, what could be used for its opposite?* (Respond positively such as Wonderful! Sugary snacks are definitely something we want to avoid for a healthy diet. In a similar manner continue brainstorming pairs of opposites for each topic in your list.)

RESPONDING TO STUDENT WRITING

1. While students write their diamante poems, circulate around the room and hold mini-conferences with those who need special attention. Focus mainly on students' idea for their poems.

- **lines 1 and 7 are opposites related to the chosen topic**

  If a student has chosen two words that are about the topic and the words are clear opposites, make a positive comment such as "Minnesota and Texas are two states that are very different."

  If a student has chosen two words that are about the topic, but the words won't work as opposites, ask a question to redirect the writer such as "What kind of rock is very different from volcanic rock?"

- **line 2 contains two words that describe the noun in line 1**

  If a student has two words that clearly describe the noun in line 1, make a comment such as "'Ugly' and 'grotesque' are vivid descriptors for pollution."

  If a student has vague descriptors such as "good" or "pretty," ask a question to help the writer be more precise such as "What is a stronger word for 'pretty'?" or "What do you mean by the word 'good'?"

- **line 3 contains three doing words that describe the noun in line 1**

  If a student has chosen three "ing" words that describe the noun in line 1, make a comment such as "'Recycling,' 'saving,' and 'collecting' really help me picture what people do to make our world clean."

If a student has chosen an adjective or a noun instead of a doing word, ask a question to redirect the writer such as "What doing word could you use in line 3 in place of 'float'?"

- **line 4 contains four words that go with the nouns in lines 1 and 7**

    If a student has come up with four words that go with the nouns in lines 1 and 7, make a positive comment such as "All four of your words in line 4 fit with summer and winter."

    If a student is stuck and can't think of another word for line 4, ask questions such as "What's another word that goes with both healthy and sugary snacks?"

2. As students finish writing their poems, direct them to find a peer who is also finished. Tell the two students to find a quiet spot in the room and softly read their poems out loud to each other.

    When they are finished, instruct them to go to their desks and revise any parts of their poems that need to be improved so that they will make more sense, flow more smoothly, and/or better convey the message.

PUBLISHING

1. Instruct students to rewrite their final poem neatly on a special diamond-shaped paper. Remind them to space the poem carefully so that everyone will see the poem's special diamond shape.

2. Next have students glue the poem to two contrasting pieces of construction paper. (See example.) They may want to choose colors that go with each part of their poem.

Publishing Option 1

Explain that the diamante poems will be posted in the hall so that other students in their grade level will learn about the exciting things they have learned this year.

Publishing Option 2

Inform students that you'll send their poems to the local paper to publish so other people in town can enjoy the poems and learn about what they've studied this year. You will find that small town papers are particularly receptive to publishing children's writings.

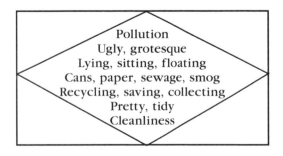

Pollution
Ugly, grotesque
Lying, sitting, floating
Cans, paper, sewage, smog
Recycling, saving, collecting
Pretty, tidy
Cleanliness

MODIFICATIONS TO ENCOURAGE BEGINNING WRITERS

- Guide students to choose manageable opposites. Concrete (observable) nouns such as "helpful snakes/harmful snakes" are much easier for students to handle than abstract nouns such as "pollution/cleanliness" or "summer/winter."

- Line number 4 is usually the most difficult part of a diamante poem to write. Line 4 is composed of four words that refer to both nouns. One way to assist low achievers is to individually help students brainstorm line four. Ask questions such as "What are some things that go with both (noun in student's line #1) and (noun in student's line #2)?"

If students can't think of anything, offer one or two of your own ideas or ask an easier question. For example, if a student was writing about the "opposites" shells and rocks, you could ask questions such as "Where is a place you find both shells and rocks?" or "How are shells and rocks alike?"

MODIFICATIONS TO CHALLENGE ADVANCED WRITERS

- Encourage students to choose more abstract topics such as "pollution/cleanliness" or topics that require a background of knowledge such as "volcanic/sedimentary rocks."

- Expect students to reevaluate each word in the poem to see if it is specific and adds to the central idea of the poem.

LESSON 43

GROUP CHEERS

Cheers are one way to show encouragement, approval, or happiness. Cheers also help people become excited and happy. Writing and shouting cheers are excellent ways to promote mental health.

Cheers need not only be connected with a physical activity; they also can be created for individuals to read and enjoy—for example, to celebrate a birthday or to cheer someone who is sick. Your class can compose cheers to celebrate a special book or author or to tell others about learnings in math, science, social studies, health.

OBJECTIVES

Students will write a group cheer that follows the pattern and rhythm of "Open the Barn Door." To do this, they will:

- Write what they hope a person or group will do (lines 1 and 2).
- Write who the cheer is for and where they come from (line 3).
- Write what will be turned on so that the cheer will be heard (line 4).
- Repeat the pattern "Who do you hear?" (line 5).
- Write who will be singing the cheer (line 6).
- Spell out the encouraging word that will be cheered (lines 7 and 8).
- Repeat the encouraging word three times and then tell when it will occur (line 9).

MOTIVATORS

1. Put on a baseball cap or bring in a football or basketball or something else that students will recognize from their favorite team. Ask them why fans yell loudly and cheer at games. Inquire why we have cheerleaders at sporting events.

2. Teach students the words and actions to a cheer such as "Open the Barn Door" or another cheer that you know. Words are provided on Reproducible 43-1 at the end of this lesson. Be dramatic and students will get caught up in your excitement. If you know someone who has pom poms, ask to borrow them. Perhaps one of your students owns a set.

371

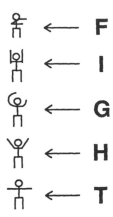

OPEN THE BARN DOOR	

Open the barn door.
Kick out the hay.
We are the kids from the U.S.A.

Turn on the radio.
Who do you hear?
Whitney Houston singing a cheer!

F-I-G-H-T
F-I-G-H-T
Fight! Fight! Fight tonight!

3. Demonstrate how to "body spell" the word fight, using the body and arm movements given earlier or your own motions.

THE GIRL SCOUT CHEER

Raise the flag.
Lay a trail.
We are the Scouts from Bixby.

Gather wood.
Build a fire.
Who do you see having a ball?
The Girl Scouts from Bixby.

(Roll over and spell Girl Scouts.)
G-I-R-L S-C-O-U-T-S
Girl Scouts, Girl Scouts
The Girl Scouts are here!

4. Read a cheer made up by a student. Here's a Girl Scout cheer created by a fourth grader. It differs slightly from the "Open the Barn Door" pattern.

BRAINSTORMING

For What Group	Where	Do What	Who/What
Wildcats	Minnesota	Save . . . . can
6th graders	Edison Elementary	Reuse . . . . sack
Edison Moms	Halley	Turn off . . . . . light
		Recycle . . . . . . paper

Who Cheers	"ing" Word	Encouraging Word	When
President Clinton	yelling	Recycle	Now
Olivia Newton John	whispering	Save	Today
our parents	shouting	Don't Waste	Soon
	echoing	Think	

Key Questions

1. ***What group could we cheer for?*** (As students reply, respond positively and write their ideas on the chalkboard. Continue brainstorming until several ideas are listed.)

2. ***Where is/are*** _____(chosen group's name)_____ ***from?***

3. ***What could the*** _(chosen group's name)_ ***do?*** (If you want to influence the topic of the cheer, you could vary question three. For example, you might ask "What could the 6th graders from Halley do to save the world's resources?") ***What can the group*** _(save, for example)_ ***?*** (Repeat this sequence of questions, eliciting several verbs and direct objects.)

4. ***What special or famous person could cheer for our group? Who might say our cheer?*** (Explain that someone could be shouting or singing the cheer. Point out these are "ing" words. Elicit other "ing" words that tell how someone might be saying the cheer?)

5. ***What short encouraging word can we spell out in our cheer? What powerful word can we cheer instead of "Fight"?***

6. ***When should the group be doing this?*** (Elicit "time" words to complete the cheer.)

GROUP COMPOSING

Invite students to help write a class cheer. Comment that after they write a cheer together, they will create their own cheers.

1. Call students' attention to the fact that first they need to decide on line 3. Have students decide on whom they want to cheer for and where the group is from. Insert these ideas in the blanks then have the students clap the line together to check if the new words fit.

2. For the first two lines of the cheer, have students choose two actions from the "Do What" category and two direct objects from the "Who/What" category. Insert the words in the blanks. Then have students read and clap the lines together to see how they sound. Make any necessary changes.

Save the can .
Turn off the light .
We are the 6th graders from Halley .
Turn on the stereo .
Who do you hear?
Pres. Clinton shouting a cheer!
T-H-I-N-K
T-H-I-N-K
Think, think, think, now !

3. Guide students to select words from the brainstorming list to complete the remaining lines of the cheer.

Tell students that they are now ready to compose their own cheers.

RESPONDING TO STUDENT WRITING

1. As students write their cheers, circulate around the classroom. Spot students who need assistance. As you circulate, make positive comments on strong parts of their cheers and ask questions to help students self evaluate weaker parts.

2. If you want students to self evaluate, direct them to use Reproducible 43-2.

3. As students finish, ask them to say their cheer to see if the words fit and the rhythm matches.

PUBLISHING

If possible, invite students from another school to visit your school. If this is not possible, invite another class to visit. Tell students that the other students will be excited to hear and see their cheers. Maybe they can teach them some cheers.

1. Divide students into small groups to practice their cheers. Direct each group to select one cheer to work on first. (They can do the other cheers later.)

2. Instruct students to *quietly* practice reading the cheer for ten minutes until everyone in the group can say it clearly. Explain that they must keep their voices down now; they will get to yell and shout later. Encourage them to help each other remember to whisper; otherwise they won't get to practice the cheers.

3. Allow each group to perform their cheer in class just before recess or before going home.

4. Allow time for students to practice their other cheers also. You may want to have the groups tape record all or one of their cheers.

MODIFICATIONS TO ENCOURAGE BEGINNING WRITERS

• Pair less able students with a more able partner.

• Provide a blank pattern that shows were to put particular words. See Reproducible 43-3 at the end of this lesson.

• Ask students with social or emotional problems to tape or videotape the cheers.

MODIFICATIONS TO CHALLENGE ADVANCED WRITERS

• Contract students to find and rewrite another cheer such as one of the following.

We have the spirit.   We have the brains.
We have the might.   We have the power.
We are the Tulsa Panthers.   We are the mighty third graders
Fight team fight!   Ready to study now!

• Encourage students to create motions for their cheers.

OPEN THE BARN DOOR

Open the barn door.
Kick out the hay.
We are the kids from the U.S.A.

Turn on the radio.
Who do you hear?
Whitney Houston singing a cheer!

F-I-G-H-T
F-I-G-H-T
Fight! Fight! Fight tonight!

OPEN THE BARN DOOR

Open the barn door.
Kick out the hay.
We are the kids from the U.S.A.

Turn on the radio.
Who do you hear?
Whitney Houston singing a cheer!

F-I-G-H-T
F-I-G-H-T
Fight! Fight! Fight tonight!

SELF EVALUATION CHECKLIST

Reread and rethink your cheer.

1. In the first line did you tell what you hope someone will do?   Yes   No

2. In the second line did you tell another thing that you hope the person or group will do?
   Yes   No

3. In the third line did you tell who the group is?   Yes   No

   Where they are from?   Yes   No

4. In the fourth line did you tell what will be turned on so that the cheer can be heard?
   Yes   No

5. Did you write "Who do you hear?" in the fifth line?   Yes   No

6. In the sixth line did you tell who will be singing the cheer?   Yes   No

7. What encouraging word did you spell out in lines seven and eight?

   _____

8. In line nine did you repeat the encouraging word three times?   Yes   No

   Did you tell when everything will occur?   Yes   No

9. Whisper your cheer out loud. Does it follow the rhythm and beat of the cheer "Open the Barn Door"?   Yes   No

I have carefully read and evaluated my cheer. _____
                                                                              Signature

_____ the _____

_____ the _____.

_____ the _____.

We are the _____ from _____.

Turn on the _____.

Who do you hear?

_____ _____ a cheer!

____-____-____-____-____

____-____-____-____-____

____! ____! ____ ____!

LESSON 44

FOLK SONGS

Students find rewriting familiar songs easy and fun to do. In the process they will gain a lot of useful knowledge about grammar.

OBJECTIVES

Students will compose a new song that follows the pattern and rhythm of the song "The Bear Went Over the Mountain." To do this, they will:

- Substitute a new one-word subject for the word "bear."
- Substitute a new one-syllable adjective and a one-syllable noun (or just a two syllable noun) for the word "mountain."
- Use the correct pronoun in the line "To see what (he/she/it) could see."
- Begin each line with a capital letter.
- Place a comma after the word "oh" to show a pause.
- Capitalize the important words in the title.

MOTIVATORS

1. Use a stuffed animal or make a bear finger puppet. Put the puppet on one hand. Drape a green or brown piece of material over your other hand to simulate a mountain. Hum the tune of the song "The Bear Went Over The Mountain" and add actions to the song with the finger puppet.

   Inquire how many students recognize this tune. Then ask what the song's name is. Share with students that "The Bear Went Over The Mountain" was a favorite song of yours when you were a child.

2. Show students the words for "The Bear Went Over the Mountain" on a chart and ask them to read the words of the song together. Then have them sing the song together while doing the actions.

379

> **The Bear Went Over the Mountain**
>
> Oh, the bear went over the mountain,
> The bear went over the mountain,
> The bear went over the mountain,
>   To see what she could see,
>   To see what she could see,
>   To see what she could see.
> Oh, the bear went over the mountain,
> The bear went over the mountain,
> The bear went over the mountain,
>   To see what she could see.

3. If you work with older students, ask them what songs they know that have new words in place of old lyrics. Or sing them an old familiar of yours that has new words. Students will enjoy hearing you sing whether you are a good singer or not.

BRAINSTORMING/GROUP COMPOSING

Invite students to become songwriters. Inform them that they will use the pattern of "The Bear Went Over the Mountain" to make up their very own songs.

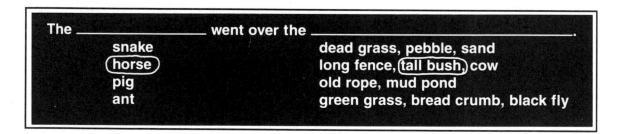

Key Questions

1. ***Who could move over something? What else could go over something?*** (Write students' ideas under the first blank.)

2. ***Which person or animal would you like us to write this song about? What word should we select to replace "bear"?*** (Circle it.)

3. (Point to the next blank in the song.) ***What is something a/an*** (horse) ***could go over? What else might a/an*** (horse) ***go over?*** (Continue to brainstorm ideas for the second blank.)

4. ***What do you want*** (the horse) ***to go over?*** (Circle it.)

5. (Direct students' attention to the fourth line of the song. Ask what pronoun they want to use to go with the subject they chose. Guide them to choose a pronoun that agrees.)

6. *Now let's sing the first verse to make sure it fits the pattern and rhythm.* (As students sing, run your hand under the words.) *How does it sound?*

```
The   Horse   Went Over the   Tall Bush

Oh, the   horse   went over the   tall bush   ,
The   horse   went over the   tall bush   ,
The   horse   went over the   tall bush   ,
      To see what   it   could see,
      To see what   it   could see,
      To see what   it   could see.
Oh, the   horse   went over the   tall bush   ,
The   horse   went over the   tall bush   ,
The   horse   went over the   tall bush   ,
      To see what   it   could see.
```

7. (Involve students in helping you write another verse. Continue until 3–4 verses are written. Have students sing each verse after it is finished to see how it sounds.)

Tell students that they can now write their own verses to "The Bear Went Over The Mountain." Inform them that they may use some of the ideas on the board or come up with their own.

RESPONDING TO STUDENT WRITING

1. As students write their own "Over the Mountain" songs, walk around the room. Visit individually with those who need special attention.

   • **Make positive comments** about students' strong ideas such as "A snake will make an interesting subject for a song" or "Your line 'slithered across the water' makes a vivid picture."

   • **Ask specific questions** to get students thinking about improving ideas such as "What small word could you add to 'lake' so that the rhythm matches the 'Bear' song?" or "Which pronoun (he, she, it) should you use if you are singing about a truck?"

2. After students have revised their song, ask them to find a partner and quietly sing their song to the partner to see if the words fit the song's rhythm and sound right. Instruct them to make changes as needed.

PUBLISHING

Explain that later, as a group, they will entertain another class by singing their new songs. Point out that before they can entertain students in the other class, everyone in this class will need copies of each other's songs. Suggest that they need to rewrite their song neatly on a new sheet of paper so that everyone can read their handwriting and learn their song. Show the song book cover (Reproducible 44-1) to your students and tell them you will put their songs together in a class book.

MODIFICATIONS TO ENCOURAGE BEGINNING WRITERS

- Provide students with the song partially written out and blanks for the words to be added. See Reproducible 44-2.

MODIFICATIONS TO CHALLENGE ADVANCED WRITERS

- Request students to change the song even more. For example, experienced writers could brainstorm other verbs and prepositions such as "galloped by," "slithered over," or "crawled up" to replace the words "went over."
- Prompt students to brainstorm new words such as "To _find_ what she could _find_" or "To _buy_ what he could _catch_" for "To _catch_ what (he/she/it) could _see_."

The _____ Went Over the _____

Oh, the _____ went over the _____,

The _____ went over the _____,

The _____ went over the _____,

    To see what _____ could see,

    To see what _____ could see,

    To see what _____ could see.

Oh, the _____ went over the _____,

The _____ went over the _____,

The _____ went over the _____,

    To see what _____ could see.

Songwriter _____

LESSON 45

LULLABIES

Many of your students will know the song used as a model in this lesson from childhood. If they don't, you or the music teacher can teach them the lyrics. Once students have experienced rewriting "The Bear Went Over the Mountain," they will find this more complicated song easy to rewrite. After that you can teach your students to rewrite the lyrics of almost any song.

OBJECTIVES

Students will compose a new song that follows the pattern and rhythm of the song "Hush, Little Baby." To do this, they will:

- Complete the line "Hush little _____, don't say a word" and the line "You'll be the sweetest little _____ in town" with an original noun.
- Complete the second line with a person and what that person is going to buy (an adjective and a noun that adds up to 3 syllables).
- Complete the line "If that (purchased object) _____ _____," with a verb phrase telling what could go wrong with the purchased object.
- Complete the next line with what the person will buy instead.
- Capitalize each word in the title.
- Place a period at the end of each sentence.

MOTIVATORS

1. Ask students if they have ever sung a lullaby and if their parents ever sang lullabies to them when they were young. Then inquire how many of the students remember the song "Hush, Little Baby."

    Share a lullaby that your mom, dad, grandma, or another person sang to you when you were little.

2. Post the words to "Hush, Little Baby." Have students read the words first and then sing the song together. (Explain to the class that the song has some grammatically incorrect forms: "don't" in stanzas 2, 5, and 7 and "broke" in stanza 4.)

385

Hush Little Baby

Hush little baby don't say a word.
Mama's going to buy you a mocking bird.

If that mocking bird don't sing,
Mama's going to buy you a diamond ring.

If that diamond ring turns brass,
Mama's going to buy you a looking glass.

If that looking glass gets broke,
Mama's going to buy you a billy goat.

If that billy goat don't pull,
Mama's going to buy you a cart'n'bull.

If that cart'n'bull turn over,
Mama's going to buy you a dog named Rover.

If that dog named Rover don't bark,
Mama's going to buy you a horse'n'cart.

If that horse'n'cart fall down,
You'll be the sweetest little baby in town.

3. Read students this new version of the lullaby written by a sixth grader. While this student has used some rhyming do not expect rhyming until grades 7–12.

Hush Little Puppy

Hush little puppy don't say a word.
Terri is going to buy you a new chain.

If that chain busts in two,
Terri is going to buy you a rubber shoe.

If that rubber shoe tastes awful,
Terri is going to buy you a telephone.

If that telephone doesn't ring,
Terri is going to buy you a diamond ring.

If that diamond ring is fake,
Terri is going to buy you a steak.

If that steak is raw,
Terri is going to get you a new mother-in-law.

If that mother-in-law is mean,
You'll still be the sweetest puppy in town.

BRAINSTORMING

Explain that students will use the pattern of "Hush Little Baby" to make a new song. Now model out loud how a writer thinks:

Let's see, when we write we need to think about what kind of information we need and then set up our brainstorming categories. First, we need to know who or what the song will be about. We'll call that category "who receives gift." (Write that category on the chalkboard.) *Next we need to know who buys.* (Write "who buys" on the chalkboard.)

Key Questions

1. *What person or animal could we write our song about? What else could we write about besides a baby? Who or what else could receive a gift?* (Continue brainstorming possible topics until many ideas are listed on the chalkboard.)

2. *Which one of these people or animals should we choose for our song?* (Circle students' choice.)

3. *Who could buy something for a/an (puppy)? Who else might buy something for a/an (puppy)?* (Continue brainstorming until you have 6–8 ideas.) *Which one of these people should we choose for our group song?*

Who buys	Who receives gift
Dad	(puppy)
(Grandma)	a frog
Larry	sister
lady	

4. *What other types of information do we need for our song?* (What the person's going to buy and what might go wrong with it. Add these two brainstorming categories to the chalkboard.)

5. *What could (Grandma) buy for (the puppy)? What might go wrong with it? Elicit a variety of responses. Respond positively and list students suggestions on the chalkboard. Insert the various responses in the pattern and have students sing the line to see if it sounds right and matches the rhythm of the song.* (Guide students to develop combinations of adjectives and nouns that add up to three syllables.)

What is bought	What goes wrong
big red ball	.goes flat
meaty bone	.gets eaten
clean soft bed	.gets dirty

GROUP COMPOSING

1. Remind students that they have already decided who is going to buy something and who will receive the gift. Write those words in the blanks of the song. Tell students that now they'll get to choose what other information to use.

2. Have students select what is bought first and what goes wrong with it. Insert their choices in the proper blanks.

3. Then ask what they think the person should buy next and what could go wrong with it. Continue this pattern until all of the lines are filled in. At regular points, sing the song together to see if it sounds right or if it fits the song's rhythm.

4. Comment that only the last line of the song needs to be completed. Ask what word goes in the blank. Elicit the name of the person or animal the song is about.

Hush Little __Puppy__

Hush little __puppy__ don't say a word,
Grandma's going to buy you a __big meaty bone__.
If that __meaty bone gets eaten__,
Grandma's going to buy you a _____.
If that _____,
_____ going to buy you a _____.
If that _____,
You'll be the sweetest little _____ in town.

written by _____

Tell students that they are now ready to write their own songs using the rhythm of "Hush Little Baby." Explain that they will follow the same writing steps used in the group brainstorming and composing.

RESPONDING TO STUDENT WRITING

1. As students write their own "Hush Little Baby" bedtime songs, walk around the room. Visit individually with those who need special attention. Give positive feedback and ask questions to extend or clarify their thoughts and check the song's rhythm.

2. As students finish their drafts, tell them to find a classmate who is also finished and sing each other's songs to see how they sound. Instruct them to make any changes that will make their song sound better.

3. When students have done this, ask them to pair up with a different partner and evaluate each other's songs using the evaluation checklist. See Reproducible 45-1 at the end of the lesson.

PUBLISHING

Inform students that they will publish their songs in a large song book so that the whole class will be able to enjoy them. See Reproducible 45-2. Tell them that they will have the opportunity to sing their songs to the class throughout the week.

Provide the following instructions for preparing their individual songs.

1. Choose a piece of colored construction paper on which to mount your song.

2. Put glue on the back of your song and press it down hard on the construction paper.

3. Make sure your song is titled and that your name is on it.

MODIFICATIONS TO ENCOURAGE BEGINNING WRITERS

- Have students write only the title, the first two lines, one verse, and the last two lines.

- Put students into cooperative groups or teams for the brainstorming and composing. Prearrange these groups so that each group has at least one strong student and only one special needs student. Ask each group to choose a group recorder to write down the group's ideas.

- Provide special paper with pattern sentences and blanks for students to complete. See Reproducible 45-3.

MODIFICATIONS TO CHALLENGE ADVANCED WRITERS

- Lead students to brainstorm new words for "sweetest" and "little" in the last line of the song.

- Suggest students write eight or more verses.

Name: _____ **Date:** _____ (45-1)

PEER EVALUATION CHECKLIST

Quietly sing your friend's song to yourself.

What person or animal is the lullaby about? _____

Who buys the person or animal something? _____

Verse I

1. What was bought first? _____

2. Would the person or animal like this gift?   Yes   No

3. What happened to it? _____

4. Does what happened make sense?   Yes   No

5. Why or why not? _____

Verse II

1. What was bought next? _____

2. Would the person or animal like this gift?   Yes   No

3. What happened to it? _____

4. Does what happened make sense?   Yes   No

5. Why or why not? _____

I have carefully thought about your song. _____

Signature

391

OUR SONGS

Hush Little _____

Hush little _____ don't say a word.

_____ going to buy you a _____.

If that _____,

_____ going to buy you a _____.

If that _____,

_____ going to buy you a _____.

If that _____,

You'll be the sweetest little _____ in town.

Songwriter's Name _____